The Social Dimension of Higher Education in Europe

Studies in Inclusive Education

Series Editor

Roger Slee (*University of Leeds, UK*)

Editorial Board

Mel Ainscow (*University of Manchester, UK*)
Felicity Armstrong (*Institute of Education, University of London, UK*)
Len Barton (*Institute of Education, University of London, UK*)
Suzanne Carrington (*Queensland University of Technology, Australia*)
Joanne Deppeler (*Monash University, Australia*)
Linda Graham (*Queensland University of Technology, Australia*)
Levan Lim (*National Institute of Education, Singapore*)
Missy Morton (*University of Auckland, New Zealand*)

VOLUME 48

The titles published in this series are listed at *brill.com/stie*

The Social Dimension of Higher Education in Europe

Issues, Strategies and Good Practices for Inclusion

Edited by

Joaquín Gairín, David Rodríguez-Gómez and Fabio Dovigo

BRILL
SENSE

LEIDEN | BOSTON

All chapters in this book have undergone peer review.

The Library of Congress Cataloging-in-Publication Data is available online at http://catalog.loc.gov

Typeface for the Latin, Greek, and Cyrillic scripts: "Brill". See and download: brill.com/brill-typeface.

ISSN 2542-9825
ISBN 978-90-04-44631-1 (paperback)
ISBN 978-90-04-44629-8 (hardback)
ISBN 978-90-04-44630-4 (e-book)

Copyright 2021 by Koninklijke Brill NV, Leiden, The Netherlands.
Koninklijke Brill NV incorporates the imprints Brill, Brill Hes & De Graaf, Brill Nijhoff, Brill Rodopi, Brill Sense, Hotei Publishing, mentis Verlag, Verlag Ferdinand Schöningh and Wilhelm Fink Verlag.
All rights reserved. No part of this publication may be reproduced, translated, stored in a retrieval system, or transmitted in any form or by any means, electronic, mechanical, photocopying, recording or otherwise, without prior written permission from the publisher. Requests for re-use and/or translations must be addressed to Koninklijke Brill NV via brill.com or copyright.com.

This book is printed on acid-free paper and produced in a sustainable manner.

Contents

List of Figures and Tables   VII
Notes on Contributors   VIII

Introduction   1
   Joaquín Gairín, David Rodríguez-Gómez and Fabio Dovigo

PART 1
Conceptual Framework

1   Quality and Equity in Higher Education   9
      Joaquín Gairín

2   Diversity, Access, and Success in Higher Education: A Transnational Overview   29
      Fabio Dovigo

PART 2
Fostering Good Practices for Inclusion

3   Good Practices and Experiences for Inclusion in Finland   63
      Saana Mehtälä, Kati Clements and Tiina Mäkelä

4   Fostering Good Practices for Vulnerable Students in Higher Education: Suggestions from Italy   81
      Fabio Dovigo

5   Good Practices and Experiences for Inclusion in Portugal   104
      Miguel Jerónimo and Fernanda Paula Pinheiro

6   Good Practices and Experiences for Inclusion in Higher Education in Romania   116
      Elena Marin, Miaela Stîngu and Romiță Iucu

7   Good Practices and Experiences for Inclusion in Spain   139
      Cecilia Inés Suárez

8   Policies and Strategies on Widening Access and Experiences of Inclusive
    Practices in Higher Education in England   160
        Lisa Lucas and Sue Timmis

PART 3
*Promoting Strategic Change for Inclusion in
Higher Education*

9   Developing Strategic Change Moving towards Inclusion of
    Underrepresented Students in Higher Education   183
        Fabio Dovigo

10 The ACCESS4ALL Toolkit for Promoting Inclusion in Higher
    Education   213
        David Rodríguez-Gómez

    Index   231

Figures and Tables

Figures

3.1   Student Life Support for Inclusion in Finnish HEI (Source: https://www.jyu.fi/studentlife).   65
3.2   Results of A4A self-assessment in Finnish HEI.   76
5.1   Organisational values, strategic plan Polytechnic of Leiria 2020 (Source: Polytechnic of Leiria).   106
5.2   Results of self-assessment at the Polytechnic of Leiria, A4A, 2017.   110
5.3   Ecosystem of inclusion at the Polytechnic of Leiria (Source: Polytechnic of Leiria).   112
5.4   Academic community engagement matrix (Source: Polytechnic of Leiria).   113
6.1   Romania's higher education system.   117
6.2   Main aspects presented in the National Strategy on Social Inclusion and Poverty Reduction 2015–2020.   120
6.3   A4A profile of the University of Bucharest.   128
8.1   Inclusion as a nested process (adapted from Wray, 2013).   171
10.1 A4A Bank of Good Practices (Source: https://access4allproject.eu/bestpractices).   219
10.2 Example of the organisational profile output.   223
10.3 Building the Pyramid Inclusion Model.   226

Tables

1.1   The Multidimensional Equity Model (from Espinoza, 2013, p. 28).   19
6.1   A4A self-assessment tool diagnosis and suggestions at the University of Bucharest.   129
6.2   A4A strategic plan at the University of Bucharest.   132
7.1   Inequality axes used in the analysis model.   143
7.2   Good practices in inclusion analysed in Spain.   144
7.3   Gender equality units in Spanish universities.   147
7.4   Universities participating in the Refugees Welcome Map.   151
10.1 Criteria for selecting good practices.   218
10.2 A4A self-assessment tool: dimensions and factors.   220
10.3 A4A Pyramid for Inclusion Model: key questions guiding the process.   227

Notes on Contributors

Kati Clements
(PhD) is a post-doctoral researcher at the Faculty of Information Technology at the University of Jyväskylä and visiting professor of Xi'an Jiaotong University, China. She works in the field of Learning Technologies and Open Education.

Fabio Dovigo
(PhD, University of Padua) is Professor for Psychology of Education at Aarhus University, Denmark. He edited *Special Educational Needs and Inclusive Practices* (Sense Publishers, 2016) and *Challenges and Opportunities in Education for Refugees in Europe* (Brill | Sense, 2018).

Joaquín Gairín
is Professor of Didactics and school organisation at the Universitat Autònoma de Barcelona. He is leading projects on social and educational development, educational change processes, leadership, evaluation of programmes and institutions, ICT in training and impact evaluation. He is the leader of EDO Research Group (http://edo.uab.cat/en).

Romiță Iucu
is the President of the Board of Trustees, of the renowned higher education institution in Romania's Capital City, the University of Bucharest and professor at the Department of Educational Sciences. He has been appointed as Steering Committee Member of the EUA – European University Association, Teaching and Learning Initiative.

Miguel Jerónimo
is Pro-President of the Polytechnic of Leiria for the area of Students, Citizenship and Social Responsibility. He received a PhD in Educational Sciences – Didactics and School Organisation, from the University of Extremadura in 2011. Researcher at Ci&DEI – Center for Education and Innovation Studies.

Lisa Lucas
(PhD, Warwick) is Associate Professor in Higher Education at the University of Bristol and Co-Director of the Centre for Higher Education Transformation. Her research involves an international perspective on social justice and equity in higher education.

NOTES ON CONTRIBUTORS

Tiina Mäkelä

has a PhD in Education, University of Jyväskylä. She is currently Postdoctoral Researcher and her latest publication is a contribution to the *Proceedings of EdMedia + Innovate Learning 2020* (AACE, 2020).

Elena Marin

is lecturer at the Faculty of Psychology and Educational Sciences, University of Bucharest. She received her PhD in Education in 2015. Her latest publication has been published in the *Journal of Pedagogy*.

Saana Mehtälä

works as a doctoral student at the University of Jyväskylä, Faculty of Information Technology. In her doctoral studies, she aims to further understanding of information technology use in youth wellbeing promotion.

Fernanda Paula Pinheiro

is a graduate in Sociology and has a master's degree in Education Sciences at the University of Coimbra. Her research interests have centered on the education policies and higher education. She has professional experience as team coordinator for social and educational research and projects.

David Rodríguez-Gómez

(PhD, Universitat Autònoma de Barcelona, 2009) is an Associate Professor in the Department of Applied Pedagogy (UAB). His research interests include innovation, change management, organisational learning and university dropout.

Mihaela Stîngu

is a Lecturer at the Department of Educational Sciences, University of Bucharest. His latest article has been published in *Research Papers in Education* (2018).

Cecilia Inés Suárez

(PhD, Universitat Autònoma de Barcelona, 2017) is a Postdoctoral Researcher in the Department of Applied Pedagogy (UAB). Her research interests include equity and diversity, minority students in higher education and college retention.

Sue Timmis

(PhD, Bristol) is Associate Professor in Education at the University of Bristol and her research interests include the lived experience of students in higher education, particularly those from under-represented or marginalised groups.

Introduction

Joaquín Gairín, David Rodríguez-Gómez and Fabio Dovigo

Higher education is an important educational stage for all societies, both because it is an engine of personal, social and territorial development and transformation, and because it has the capacity to be a key instrument in promoting equity and social justice.

The university is, without a doubt, a space for personal and social development. Furthermore, the relationship between education and development is undeniable. In fact, the countries with the highest school enrolment rates are the countries with the higher levels of well-being. We cannot demonstrate to what extent education contributes to development, nor whether higher levels of development have resulted in higher quality education, but the fact is that a causal relationship exists.

Strengthening educational institutions will be, in this regard, a key factor in increasing the competitiveness of the social, economic and productive structure of a society and in promoting the development of a competent and committed citizenry. Currently, one of the indicators of a community's degree of development is the measurement of its tertiary education systems. In doing so, we measure not only the highest level of education and training, but also rates of R&D, the possibilities of transfer and development in collaboration with the productive sector and the processes of creating new scientific–technical knowledge.

But a university education is not only desired for its utilitarian benefits, but instead, and fundamentally, because it is a personal and social need. Education facilitates the development of personal capacities and enables active participation in democratic societies. It is not surprising, therefore, that societies call for education – and specifically education for all – because it is necessary, though not solely sufficient, for development.

Educational development can contribute to social development and the reduction of social inequalities and injustices, if we understand that a part of its origin is in the inequality of educational opportunities for various reasons (ethnicity, gender, culture and socioeconomic level, among others) that perpetuate and accentuate social exclusion. Its promotion must allow people to establish a responsible, open and critical relationship with their environment, which allows them to move towards fairer societies.

National education systems are not, in essence, the sole or primary cause of social inequality; however, they occupy a privileged place from which to develop compensatory actions that contribute to reducing inequalities among young people of all classes and conditions. The development of policies, including educational policies, that expand access to opportunities is essential to combat the permanent nature of exclusion.

One of the most important challenges for today's universities is to redefine their current role. No one questions their research and teaching functions or their ability to connect students to their environment, but there is debate about the meaning these functions must have in the 21st century. In relation to teaching, there are ongoing discussions about student-centred training based on competencies, the incorporation of technologies and new social values, as well as the role of teachers. Regarding research, the emphasis is on applied research and the formation and development of large research groups. Concerns about connecting students with their environment drive calls to transcend the university's traditional actions of university extension activities and knowledge transfer, instead emphasising a more collaborative relationship and teaching and research that respond to the social challenges of today's reality.

But universities and institutions of higher education, as organisations created by and for society, also have responsibilities of citizen formation and strengthening the democracies where they are located. From this point of view, they are required to continue to be spaces for the development of the citizenry and prevailing social values, adapting their systems of organisation and operation to these new realities.

In some way it is understood that the future depends not only on the evolution of the productive and educational systems, but also on the vitality of the citizen and institutional values and attitudes that direct and feed it. This is where education makes sense as a conscious and intentional collective project, as an expression of the utopia that we want to achieve, and as a methodology to achieve it.

Analysing the connections that university centres maintain with their environment acquires, in this context, a capital importance. It is not only about knowing the social reality and responding to its demands, but also about working together on the construction of a new reality. In this sense, universities' social responsibility is a call to replace the inbred and knowledge-centred operation with one that's more linked to the needs of the surrounding environment and more focused on collaboration.

This new orientation, presented as both a challenge and a goal for the future, obliges us to reread university functions, redefine existing tasks and incorporate new ones. Thus, it seems essential to update the training systems and modernise the programmes, along with their methodologies and evaluation systems. For example, it has become commonplace to talk about active methodologies based on case studies or on solving real problems, at the same time as new work systems such as the flipped classroom or new ways of working with the environment (service learning) are introduced. Also, the need for training spaces to adapt to a world of lifelong learning is often pointed out, developing flexible and interrelated educational tracks and accepting work experience as learning. Thus, education is shaped as a factor of both personal and professional development, as well as social cohesion.

The social dimension of higher education, in the framework of the Bologna process, has been present since the 2001 Prague Declaration, which emphasised the need to work for student inclusion and the need to promote the possibility of mobility for all. Successive declarations and communiqués have continued to insist on the need to promote the social dimension to build and consolidate the European Higher Education Area (EHEA) and, specifically, on the need to create more flexible learning pathways within higher education, as well as the provision of adequate services for all students and, above all, for those who have more difficulties due to their background or personal, social or economic situation.

It is true that, in recent years, projects have been developed and research groups created that have allowed considerable progress in the identification of vulnerable groups and in the promotion and monitoring of more inclusive policies in higher education. But large deficits still persist. Programmes providing attention to vulnerable people and groups at the university thus remain a challenge for European universities. Although there have been advances in these students' access, their representation at the university is lower than what would correspond to them demographically, and their dropout rates and difficulty in accessing the job market are higher. Geographical, economic, social, gender and other factors continue to set people apart in ways that society and non-university education have not been able to compensate for.

The social dimension of higher education, as well as the institutions responsible for it, has always been an element of interest and concern for politicians and other stakeholders. Recent reports underscore this when they indicate that, despite the great progress made in European education systems, there are still some challenges that must be met, like promoting measurable and socially established goals and establishing systems to monitor the participation of underrepresented groups in higher education, among others.

The EHEA thus faces the challenge of incorporating traditionally excluded groups without forgetting that it must also aspire to convert universities into an appropriate framework to develop a set of skills that allows for active, critical and transformative citizen participation in their economic and social systems.

Currently, it is not a privilege but a right that must be scrupulously respected in all countries and regions, and that provides its graduates with a series of very important personal and social benefits in terms of development. No society can allow particular individuals and groups to be excluded from higher education; exclusion leads to failure as a country, as a university system and as individuals. Identifying the causes that generate exclusion from the tertiary education system, identifying the most vulnerable groups, designing prevention and treatment actions and raising awareness of the importance of the effective universalisation of higher education through specific policies and programmes are actions that each government must attend to.

The university, through inclusion, tries to respond to all individuals, as students, and rebuilds the curriculum to reach all of them individually or through the common characteristics they share. Inclusion highlights the importance of promoting active and committed participation – and we add criticism and collaboration – in education, where diversity is recognised as a value and opportunity. It is also linked to social justice in that it recognises those who are excluded as human beings with rights, and society as an institution with obligations of justice towards them.

The defence of social justice as a principle translates, then and in the field of higher education, into the debate on how to bridge the gap for those who are in intermediate situations on the inclusion–exclusion continuum. And moving in that direction means being proactive in understanding the social difficulties that exist and in contributing efforts aimed at reducing them. It also means being proactive in forming alliances between organisations, in promoting principals committed to equity and in maintaining a permanent protest against all kinds of manifestations of discrimination and social exclusion. United in the desire for this end goal, we will be able to achieve, over time, a society in which everyone feels included.

The challenge of equity and inclusion does not only imply opening higher education (HE) institutions to those groups traditionally excluded from this educational space, but also and mainly guaranteeing all citizens the full development of the virtuous circle of access–retention–achievement. The main challenge then is to promote a university career understood not only as a formal or administrative procedure, which is reflected in a numerical expansion, but rather as a process that guarantees all students the learning, skills and competencies they need to function as citizens in different social areas (economic, productive, political, health, cultural, among others).

The commitment to equity is not at odds with the quality and excellence that is required of university education; instead, it is considered complementary and should without a doubt be demanded. If we understand that quality is linked to the principle of relevance, we have to relate it to social responsibility and to the contexts in which institutions of higher education operate and develop. In a way, only inclusive institutions can aspire to be of quality.

The inexcusable challenge of quality education thus becomes one of the strategic factors to guarantee equity, lessen the effects of inequalities and promote social justice, consolidating democracy and social cohesion. We are no longer speaking only of formative quality, but we are also integrating equity into this construct – we can even speak of the quality of that equity.

The university can be more inclusive if it takes into consideration – and takes on as a responsibility – the diversity of its students, ensuring all students' learning regardless of their individual characteristics. Surely, different entry conditions require differentiated actions; however, this does not need to mean that the levels of rigour and exit rates won't guarantee the same professional competencies required from everyone upon graduating from university. With this perspective in mind, quality is linked to the principle of relevance, social responsibility, cultural diversity and the contexts in which HE institutions are situated and develop. In fact, quality universities can only be so if they are also inclusive.

Making progress within this outlook requires a commitment from everyone (faculty, managers, students and administrative and service staff) and demands maximum collaboration and coordination between university system management teams and the different institutions themselves. This progress will also depend on the development of studies and innovations that allow for the creation of new knowledge about reality and that guide the processes of change and improvement that are detected as necessary.

Again, it bears repeating that any progress in achieving university inclusion is linked to the cross-sectional nature and coordination of actions both external and internal to the institutions. Carrying out this kind of action involves not only having students in situations of vulnerability as recipients of change, but also incorporating strategies and programmes that have an impact on the university's structures, dynamics and professionals. It also involves a systematic and planned process that includes gathering information on the reality of inclusion, preparing and managing intervention plans, and incorporating good practices that are gleaned along the way. All of the above must take place in a university context whose mission and objectives are aimed at fomenting conditions that promote the inclusion of all students – especially those who are in vulnerable situations – understanding that all of them are subjects of the law with equal possibilities.

This approach is about guaranteeing a rights-based approach in which all people are subjects of the law, not only those with greater or lesser capacities or deficits. It is also about training that must be high quality and the result of the involvement of different personal, social and institutional agencies. In this way, the relationship between society, university and responsibility must be configured, in a way that is possible and real, making it possible for the university to return to society a large part of the heritage it has received and to give meaning to its own existence. Ultimately, it is about considering inclusion as a global project that affects the institution as a whole and that it shares with the rest of society.

This publication includes the most significant contributions of the 'Laboratorio de políticas y prácticas para el desarrollo social en la Educación Superior' ['Laboratory of policies and practices for social development in Higher Education'] Project.[1] Specifically, it presents conceptual aspects related to the inclusive university, such as the quality and transitions linked to the treatment of diversity, good inclusion practices in six European countries, and a set of tools to identify dysfunctions and promote inclusion in higher education. The countries' different contributions seek to reflect their reality. Their purpose is not so much to identify all existing achievements as it is to familiarise readers with the significant contributions and to have a qualified assessment of the reality and outlook of the topic addressed.

The ultimate goal is to provide elements to improve the actions of an inclusive university and to contribute to bringing about a balance between quality and equity in university systems. This publication can and should also be seen, therefore, as a general approach to the improvements that can be made in organisational processes to improve equity: inviting readers to delve deeper into aspects they find relevant, using the documentation generated and referenced in the texts themselves.

Note

1 See ACCESS4ALL, https://access4allproject.eu

PART 1

Conceptual Framework

CHAPTER 1

Quality and Equity in Higher Education

Joaquín Gairín

Abstract

The desirable link between the university and society justifies its inclusive approach and its social orientation. However, in practice not everyone accesses it, not everyone wants to access it and not everyone should complete their studies if they do not develop the skills of the degree that they attend. Combining equity and quality is possible and desirable, although is not achievable if the processes involved are not properly organised. In this regard, we analyse curricular, organisational and social demands of an inclusive university, focusing the attention on vulnerable groups, including the attention to personal characteristics. We also highlight normative, institutional and operational advances and challenges related to the diagnosis, the intervention and the evaluation of the results. We conclude that: (a) promoting and drive inclusive processes could be the most effective way to tackle discriminatory and exclusionary attitudes; (b) is necessary to restructuring the training institutions to guarantee the properly attention to all students and (c) occasionally, school and university exclusion is the prelude to some social exclusion trajectories.

Keywords

higher education – equity – inclusion – quality – social justice – vulnerable groups – inclusive practices – institutional challenges

1   Introduction

Most universities and countries have been implementing and increasing various actions aimed at achieving equality and equity in education. We can identify progress and achievements at universities in terms of access, retention and completion of studies. For example, we must recognise the attention given, in terms of legislation, to certain collectives (people with disabilities or indigenous populations) or to specific institutional strategies (development of scholarship and financial aid programmes, academic support and advising for students in situations of vulnerability, to mention but a few). However, it is also important to recognise that challenges remain for the achievement of inclusive universities.

The issues to be resolved are as much conceptual as methodological and operational. At a conceptual level, progress needs to be made in clarifying the intrinsic relationships between quality, equity and excellence; at the methodological level, it is necessary to validate some of the existing proposals for evaluating the degree of inclusion of a university or defining vulnerable collectives; at the operational level, it is necessary to evaluate the impact of the many institutional and social policies and actions being developed.

This chapter addresses, in general terms, conceptual and practical aspects related to the inclusion and support of vulnerable collectives at universities. First, it highlights the commitment of universities to social development and, thus, to the promotion and development of more inclusive organisations. Second, it provides guidance for the identification of vulnerable collectives in the university while identifying some of the problems and challenges that their consideration entails. In this sense, it takes up and studies in greater depth some of the aspects already discussed in previous publications (Gairín & Suárez, 2012, 2013, 2014, 2015, 2016; Gairín & Rodríguez-Gómez, 2019).

2   Higher Education and Its Social Orientation

The importance of education is beyond question, given its recognised importance in the progress of people and societies. In addition to providing us with knowledge, it enriches culture, the spirit and everything that characterises us as human beings while also supporting higher levels of social and economic development. In these circumstances, it is no surprise that there should be talk of education for all, that goals should be set such as how to "achieve educational equality and overcome all forms of discrimination in education" (OEI, 2010, p. 148) and that the topic should be a UN Sustainable Development Goal.[1]

We might think, in the same vein, that the importance of higher education (HE, hereinafter) is also beyond question, although in practice not everyone has access to it, not everyone wishes to have access to it and not everyone should have access to it if we think, beyond the right to education, about social needs and personal and institutional possibilities.

The restrictive sense of which we speak necessarily forces us to consider some of the key issues on the topic that Tolosana (2014, p. 25) had already raised:

- Who is higher education for? For all those who wish to have access to it, for the best, for those who can afford it, etc.?
- Do we prioritise the transmission or creation of knowledge?
- Do we prepare citizens for their personal and social emancipation or should our priority be their employability based on market demands?
- Is excellence our only goal or do we believe that it should be harmonised with equal opportunities?

The answers are not simple, if we manage to escape the predominant orientations and the clichés that may accompany them. For Hugo Casanova (2012), the contemporary university emerges in the mid-1940s (post-World War II) and takes as its reference the US university, which (Tolosana, 2014, p. 26):
- changes the relationship with society:
  - in response to the huge demand, there is a process of expansion; and
  - it responds to market demands;
- in its internal organisation:
  - provides a differentiated stimulus to research and is organised by departments; and
  - implements external evaluation mechanisms.

It implies, in a way, a break with the German model promoted by philosopher and linguist Wilhelm von Humboldt, where freedom and scientific knowledge were fundamental, and with the Napoleonic model of creating uniformity and professionalisation. The hegemony of the American model has remained until today and, while its positive contributions should be recognised, it has not provided specific answers to many questions (what are a university's own purposes and what is its social function?) and has had unwanted side effects:
- The historical and cultural features of different contexts have been omitted in the attempt to mimic the US model to the fullest.
- The commercialisation of research has been encouraged.
- The State's commitment to the university and its role as a provider of social services and a guarantor of equity and equal opportunities has been reduced.
- Upon decreasing public regulation, the expansion of the private sector – in some cases of doubtful quality – has been bolstered.

We live in times that are ephemeral (Bauman, 2007), uncertain and confusing – times that promote the crisis of the solid social structures of the past and call into question the pre-eminence of political power over economic, religious or other structures.

For many authors, this situation necessitates the establishment of a new relationship between the University, the State and Society. There is talk of a new pact and a greater orientation of the university towards social problems,

thus recovering some of its legitimacy. In this regard and for Santos (2005), there would be five areas of action:
1. *access*: to achieve the democratisation of access, overcoming the discrimination factors of class, race, sex and ethnicity;
2. *extension*: to assign to universities active participation in the building of social cohesion;
3. *research-action*: to link scientific interests and the production of knowledge with the satisfaction of the needs of society;
4. *ecology of knowledge*: to promote dialogue between the scientific and humanistic knowledge produced by the university and the popular, traditional, indigenous, non-Western cultures, etc. that exist in society; and
5. *university and state school*: to make it necessary to link basic and secondary education with intermediate and higher education in a generalised educational project.

A proposal such as this forces us to think of high-quality higher education for everyone who is capable of responding to its demands; also, to answer some questions such as the quantity-quality, quality-equity and equity-excellence relationships in higher education, overcoming some of the existing platitudes such as those related to the ability (or lack thereof) to achieve the development of certain competencies in this educational stage or the chance of certain vulnerable collectives of gaining access to higher education.

For some authors (e.g., Gairín & Suárez, 2015), HE is a fundamental tool of progress and social growth and the individual development of each and every citizen making up a nation. It is conceived as a public good and forms part of such an approach as a right. Its importance is increasing nowadays, if we consider the particular scenario of democratic societies in the knowledge society, which forces us to provide intellectual resources to all citizens if we do not wish to strengthen marginal groups; also, if we think in terms of a trend rather than a completed and finalised project.

3 The Inclusive University

The Declaration of the Regional Conference of HE in Latin America and the Caribbean (CRES, 2008) and the World Conference on HE (UNESCO, 2009) highlighted the need to guarantee access to HE as a real right for all citizens and, at the same time, for this to contribute effectively to democratic coexistence, tolerance, the strengthening of a spirit of solidarity and cooperation, and the creation of knowledge for the social and productive transformation of societies.

These declarations highlight the university's commitment to educational inclusion, are associated with the strengthening of a democratic society and seek the achievement of quality educational opportunities for all students, with special consideration for those in situations of vulnerability. Regardless of social origin, race, ethnicity, gender, disability or other circumstances, all students who are prepared should have the opportunity to participate and succeed in HE.

At the regulatory level, international standards offer specific orientations that have driven changes of a constitutional and legal order, which, accompanied by legislative developments, recognise and guarantee the rights of vulnerable groups. The following are some examples in this respect: the United Nations Convention on the Rights of Persons with Disabilities, which contains a specific article on the education of such persons (article 24); the European Disability Strategy 2010–2020; the Declaration on the Rights of Persons Belonging to National or Ethnic, Religious and Linguistic Minorities (1992); Convention 169 of the International Labour Organisation (ILO, 1989); and the Declaration on the Rights of Indigenous Peoples (2007).

These orientations promote and drive the construction of full citizenship, providing inclusive and respectful legislative frameworks for diversity. In any case, they should be accompanied, given that this is not always the case, by social, cultural or other measures. It is particularly important to guarantee the acquisition of knowledge and competencies defined as fundamental and relevant, to allow all citizens to participate and fully exercise their political, social and cultural rights (Gairín & Suárez, 2014, p. 36).

The processes of educational inclusion represent, in this context and today, an important challenge for the university. Sustained in social justice and equity (Forlín, 2013) and with a strong ethical component (Reindal, 2016), it pursues the successful learning and full participation of all students in a standardised educational context (Ainscow, 2015), unlike the integration that affects people's disabilities and their location in less restrictive contexts (Sanahuja, Muñoz, & Gairín, 2020).

In particular, it is important to highlight the effort that can be made in relation to traditionally marginalised collectives, while maintaining the individualised attention that every citizen needs. It's clear that, owing to geographical, social, cultural or other circumstances, there are collectives that are less represented than they should be in a university; their integration into university dynamics is one of the most important challenges that the institution faces. In the Eurydice Report (2011), *underrepresented collectives* are identified as those students who belong to certain collectives that, owing to their vulnerability and situation of exclusion, are not represented or do not participate in or have access to HE due to criteria such as socioeconomic status, gender, disability, ethnicity and age.

Building inclusive universities is about supporting the visibility and recognition of these collectives, which tend to remain "invisible" inside their institutions despite having gained admission. Beyond the philosophical and epistemological debate that might be held on concepts such as normality, the right to difference, stereotypes and stigmatisation, among others, it is important to recognise, assess and act in relation to existing differences. We should remember that these collectives are not vulnerable per se but, rather, are groups in vulnerable situations as a result of historical, social and political conditions and processes. These are groups that have suffered a history of discrimination and exclusion in which different circumstances and their violated rights are combined yet which nevertheless maintain a certain autonomy and are active in claiming full participation in the society in which they are located (Gairín & Suárez, 2014, p. 36).

The university must find the appropriate mechanisms to facilitate inclusive processes; in this regard, a set of services, plans and support actions is usually structured with the aim of improving access, participation and learning for these students. In line with Moriña (2017), this network of actions should start from a holistic approach in which institutional and organisational aspects, as well as material and human resources (teachers, students with and without disabilities and administrative staff), intermingle to provide an efficient answer to the challenges of the inclusive university. At the same time and in line with the bioecological model of inclusive education (Hewett, Douglas, McLinden, & Keil, 2017), the university must be able to identify the potential range of barriers that – on an academic level –impede an inclusive university within the university microsystem and as a sociocultural community (Fleming, Plotner, & Oertle, 2017).

There are many barriers that must be overcome, including: students' own barriers (low self-esteem, lack of experience in autonomy, etc.), social barriers (discriminatory attitudes, barriers to physical autonomy, etc.) and institutional barriers (invisibility, lack of training for faculty and staff, inappropriate spaces and insufficient time, limited orientation and advising programmes, etc.). It is true that universities and government systems are responding, more and more, with specific policies, strategies and actions to the new demands of students and society. However, the challenge remains – as some HE institutions have begun to recognise – in the progress, completion of studies and transition into the working world of vulnerable collectives. New and better knowledge, skills and abilities are increasingly necessary to complete educational levels, but also to perform personally and professionally in society.

Tiana (2010) synthesises, as an example, the current situation of Ibero-American HE as a balance in which, on the one hand, there are prominent positive aspects such as the democratisation of access and the diversification of course and degree offerings, while on the other hand there are also negative aspects worth mentioning, such as the processes of privatisation and commercialisation and the dearth of educational offerings. In the words of Henríquez (2015), the challenge of equity and inclusion implies not only opening up HE institutions to those collectives that have traditionally been excluded therefrom but also and mainly guaranteeing all citizens the full implementation of the "virtuous circle of access-retention-achievement" (p. 12).

The main challenge, then, is to promote a university education not only as a formal or administrative procedure, which is reflected in a numerical expansion, but also as a process that guarantees all students the learning, skills and competencies they need: in short, the knowledge needed to perform as citizens in various social areas (economic, productive, political, health, cultural, etc.).

4 Defining Situations of Vulnerability in Higher Education

The diversification of social class in the university as a consequence of greatly increased enrolment, the social composition of the students, university internalisation and the diversity in the number of institutions leads to a new scenario for the development of HE (Brunner & Ferrer, 2011; Rama, 2009). Part of this involves addressing students' problems and avoiding the reproduction and intensification of social inequality and the underrepresentation of vulnerable groups (Chiroleu, 2010).

The increase in social representation in the student body as well as the change in the student profile and the admission of traditionally underrepresented collectives (including students with low socioeconomic status, women, students with disabilities or displaced students) form a complex panorama in which significant advances are discovered in terms of representation, as already mentioned, but in which inequality is also expressed in terms of the existence or insufficiency of options and the feasibility of educational opportunities (Aponte-Hernández, 2008). Moreover, on many occasions is, according to Ezcurra (2008), an "exclusionary inclusion" is produced, if we consider how processes such as dropping out or failing mainly affect students in situations of vulnerability and detract from the very idea of inclusion. In a similar vein, Sverdlick, Ferrari, and Jaimovich (2005) affirm that the massive increase in HE enrolment does not indicate a causal relationship with respect democratisation at this educational level.

An inclusive educational system welcomes all students and considers cultural and social diversity as an element that makes the teaching-learning process simultaneously more complex and enriching, minimising the barriers that hinder participation, especially for students in situations of vulnerability and those at a higher risk of marginality and exclusion. Diversity as a challenge and opportunity thus constitutes a call for growth and learning – for the universities themselves and their actors – to innovate and develop new competencies (Sebastián & Scharager, 2007). In this sense, recognising diversity implies inclusion and vice versa, starting from the creation of real, concrete conditions that provide for the access and, fundamentally, the retention and completion of studies for all students.

An earlier study (Gairín & Suárez, 2012), considers and analyses five axes of social inequality (socioeconomic and urban-rural; gender; ethnic and racial; disability; and age) as criteria to define collectives in situations of vulnerability in HE (e.g., students located in quintiles I and II, women in certain fields and courses, indigenous people, Afro-descendants and Gypsies – among other ethnic minorities – people with disabilities, and adults with low qualification levels). Exclusion and vulnerability today manifest themselves in varied ways which may change over time, resulting in a complex scenario in which universities need to adapt to students but also to themselves, modifying their structures, academic and administrative staff, among other aspects.

The definition and analysis of these axes coincides, furthermore, with other contributions from the field of sociology and the performance of HE institutions in diverse contexts. Thus, for example, Subirats (2004) analyses inequalities on three axes: age, gender and ethnicity or place of origin: These axes identify as possible collectives in situations of vulnerability and/or exclusion young people, the elderly, women, immigrants or people from poor countries, whether or not they are in an irregular situation. Accordingly, the factors of exclusion or vulnerability in education would be illiteracy or low educational levels, school failure, early school leaving and lack of knowledge of the vehicular language.

For its part, the Inter-American Development Bank (IDB) in its report *Outsiders? The Changing Patterns of Exclusion in Latin America and the Caribbean* (Márquez et al., 2007) mentions as collectives at risk of social exclusion indigenous collectives, physically disabled people, the population with a very low human development index (HDI) and women.

Likewise, the Communiqué issued by the 2007 Conference of European Ministers responsible for HE drew attention to students with the greatest difficulties in taking part in university education, including those who, owing to their particular individual, social or family circumstances, constitute a smaller proportion of university students than the rest of the groups. These are people with some type of disability, those who come from lower socioeconomic strata, immigrants, people with family responsibilities, those who work and other collectives that have not traditionally been part of the conventional university student population.

It should be made clear that the differentiation between the various axes has an analytical meaning, in that it recognises that, in reality, there are combined situations of inequality, for example in the case of women belonging to an indigenous group who also have precarious income levels, resulting in situations of extreme vulnerability. In societies with high levels of inequality, these axes are closely associated, and it is pertinent to indicate that exclusion and vulnerability shift between two levels that are difficult to separate: on the one hand, their own characteristics and the internal features of HE systems, and on the other hand external conditions in which they are located and develop (Sverdlick, Ferrari, & Jaimovich, 2005).

5 Working for Equity in Higher Education

Achieving inclusion in HE is tied to the quality of the universities: that is, the challenge of achieving equity and equal opportunities for all students and especially those who have been excluded – and still are even today – from the right to education, is considered to be one more element that identifies the quality of university institutions. As Dias Sobrinho (2008) indicates, quality is thus linked to the principle of belonging, social responsibility, cultural diversity and the contexts in which HE institutions find themselves and are developing. In fact, quality universities can only be so if they are also inclusive.

As some authors suggest (Díaz-Romero, 2010; Dias Sobrinho, 2008), analysing equity and social justice in relation to the concept of education as a public good implies accepting that it is impossible to envision quality universities that are not inclusive, and vice versa, or educational systems that leave out sections of the population. This idea is reinforced, for example, in studies such as that developed by Whiteford, Shah, and Si Nair (2013), who argue that increasing equity in the access and participation of disadvantaged students, apart from being a matter of quality, would not imply a negative impact on academic standards.

The movement for inclusion is structured, in this sense, around three pillars (Jurado, 2007): as its basis, around principles and values that go beyond the framework of integration; in its philosophical and ideological base, considering the university as an agent of change and progress framed in a new model of society; and in its practical development, educational strategies focused on interaction and for the benefit of quality teaching for all and free from any type of exclusion (e.g., bringing together all the aspects that comprise a class and its setting, cooperation by all, educational rather than merely academic objectives, curricular redesign, diversity as a source of learning, education in values and attitudes or evaluation depending on the work performed by each student).

In the words of Renaut (2008), one ought to think of a form of complex equality, of equal opportunities in the sense that each student has the possibility of embarking on his or her trajectory with a reasonable chance of success. In fact, we often talk about the fact that the educational process must have ecological validity (acquisition of useful competencies for solving real problems), educational validity (functional learning), personal validity (assumption of individuality as a pivot of the educational project) and normalisation (attention within the ordinary system). Therefore, it is necessary to continually ask oneself: what type of university is needed to respond to the diversity of students? What are the most appropriate strategies for addressing the heterogeneity of collectives? What changes do the teaching and learning processes require? All these, and other issues must be elucidated (Gairín & Suárez, 2014, p. 52).

Equity is needed, leaving aside debates about the term in the field of social and public policy, which are often more concerned with the negative (inequity and inequality) than with the positive (equity or social justice in a society characterised by inequity). And we do so by accepting the Multidimensional Equity Model proposed by Espinoza (2013) because it gives an idea of the complexity and diversity of approaches that must be considered and which are also reflected in Table 1.1.

At the classroom level, it is important to ascertain whether the classes and teaching activities are accessible to all students, if students are involved in developing them, whether the activities promote the understanding of individual or group differences as well as cooperative methodologies and whether they encourage differentiated evaluation models. At the institutional level, it is crucial to identify whether the support systems (psycho-pedagogical, tutorials or others) promote autonomy and respect diversity, positive actions to avoid discriminatory processes, coordination between teachers and other teaching agents, development of universal accessibility, and linkage with the community and action research on the responses to existing needs. In short, whether they support the promotion of universal designs for learning (which respect the principles of equity, flexibility, information and accessibility, among others) and the development of inclusive institutions (Gairín & Suárez, 2014, p. 54).

TABLE 1.1 The Multidimensional Equity Model (from Espinoza, 2013, p. 28)

Concept	Dimensions	Resources	Access	Retention	Performance	Outcomes
Equity	Equity for equal needs	Guarantee that all people with the same needs obtain the same amount of financial, social and cultural resources.	Provide access at both individual and group levels based on need.	Ensure that students with equal needs have equal academic progress	Ensure that students with equal needs have similar academic performance	Ensure that those with equal needs obtain similar jobs, income level and political power
	Equity for equal capabilities	Ensure that all people with a certain level of potential have the same amount of financial, social and cultural resources	Ensure that all people with similar abilities and skills have access to quality education	Ensure that students with equal potential have equal educational progress	Ensure that students with equal skills have similar educational performance	Ensure that those with the same potential at birth obtain similar jobs, income level and political power
	Equity for equal achievement	Ensure that people who reach or whose parents reach the same educational level have equal resources	Provide equal access to quality education	Ensure that students with equal grades remain in the same system	Facilitate equality of achievement for those who have achieved the same academic performance in the past	Ensure that people with similar academic achievement obtain similar jobs, income level and political power

Making progress on issues of inclusivity not only entails classroom and institutional measures towards the other but also involves accepting, participating in and becoming aware of different people; in fact, we could well say that it is linked to the pedagogy of alterity (Ortega, 2014) and takes into account all the elements that come into play in the educational process, as well as those that have been ignored, such as the teacher as a generator of expectations and the teaching material as a cultural mediator. It is also important to analyse the subject with a future-facing perspective and take into account international reports that examine it and the publications that disseminate these reports.

Achieving the above purposes is not easy but it can be considered as a challenge to be progressively overcome. It is necessary to act, but it is equally – or perhaps more – important to do so in a coordinated and systematic way. In this regard, it is important to promote orientation and advising plans in universities that – at a general, departmental or study level – provide the support that all students need to guarantee the maximum usefulness of their studies. Actions in this regard are incipient, and not for lack of generic proposals (see, for example, the contributions of Gairín et al., 2003, 2004, 2009, or the publications mentioned on the attention given to vulnerable groups) or specific ones focused on advising plans for students with disabilities (Galán & Gairín, 2013) or who are underrepresented at the university (Egido, Fernández, & Galán, 2014).

6   Some Problems and Limitations to Be Overcome

We are currently in a situation that, although far from satisfactory, reflects the progress that has been made in the field of inclusion; the primary challenge is continuing to make progress in the achievements obtained while still overcoming the remaining challenges (Tiana, 2010). We consider as progress the aspects identified by the scientific literature as such and/or improvements regarding HE and collectives in situations of vulnerability. As for the remaining challenges, these are ones related to the knowledge society, although sporadic actions in this area have been recorded. For our analysis, we will consider earlier studies in this field (Gairín & Suárez, 2015).

6.1   *Progress in Regulatory and Legislative Frameworks*
Progress in legislation – related to guaranteeing access, retention and the completion of studies of all HE students, particularly of those in situations of vulnerability – has unquestionably been recorded in almost all countries. However, the first issue to examine is the difference in approaches mentioned

in the Eurydice Report (2011). Some approaches promote specific measures aimed at the participation of vulnerable collectives while others apply overall strategies aimed at increasing general participation with the intention of expanding the participation of these collectives. The report indicates that the third option is that of countries that opt for a mixed approach, which is characterised by a general policy approach reflected in the legislation and the implementation of specific measures for collectives defined by each country as groups in a situation of vulnerability.

For Terigi (2010), understanding inclusion as an educational policy problem makes it necessary to broaden the meaning of exclusion in education, to propose educational policies that effectively address the complexity of the causes of school exclusion (which is related to multiple factors and is not only linked to the school trajectory) and for the initiatives implemented to involve requirements such as physical space, allocation of materials, evaluation and monitoring strategies, as well as teacher assistance.

6.2   *Progress in Institutional Actions*

The panorama of progress on the institutional level is varied and diverse, since the actions implemented by each institution respond to the dynamics of each university, its resources and the possibilities dictated by its context.

In this sense, the six symposia developed at the II International Congress on University and Vulnerable Collectives (Gairín, Palmeros, & Barrales, 2014) are very significant as the closure of the European ACCEDES Project.[2] Each of these focused on a vulnerable collective (people with disabilities, indigenous people, students with a low Human Development Index, students in rural settings, those belonging to minority groups, and immigrants), and presented papers that systematised, with great precision, the actions implemented by the universities participating in the project in relation to the access, retention and completion of studies of these collectives. On the other hand, Gairín, Castro and Rodríguez-Gómez's 2014 study brings together, in individual booklets, a selection of generic and specific organisational development strategies suited to these collectives and capable of being applied in universities.[3] Along the same lines are contributions from the ACCESS4ALL Project[4] or the ORACLE Project,[5] in addition to specific actions such as those incorporated into bilateral agreements[6] or specific developments such as the Tutorial Action Plan for university students with disabilities.[7]

Reviewing the intervention strategies, the following may be highlighted (Gairín & Suárez, 2015):
– *Orientation and tutorial*: This strategy can especially support those students who have difficulties in their academic development. It can take many

forms: between peers, with teachers, with advanced students, as an institutional, face-to-face or virtual action plan; and it can refer to academic as well as, in some cases, social and personal aspects.
- *Scholarships and financial aid*: Universities sometimes provide this type of aid to students who are in unfavourable socioeconomic situations. The aid may be for enrolment fees, maintenance costs or bibliographic material, among other things; the selection criteria are usually associated with the socioeconomic level and, occasionally, with the student's performance and merit.
- *Elimination of architectural barriers*, especially in the case of students with visible physical disabilities. It must be made clear that this is the most general of the actions for this vulnerable collective. It is also necessary to include actions aimed at overcoming other tangible barriers in the classroom as well as the intangible barriers that affect this group and that are common to others, such as stereotypes and prejudices.

These three types of strategies cover three main areas, which are usually the most problematic among students in a situation of vulnerability. First, those related to academic aspects concerning student performance; second, the financial difficulties that are a common condition among students of low socioeconomic level but also among indigenous and Afro-descendant students, among others; and lastly, those that directly and visibly affect students with some type of physical disability.

Similarly, other strategies that have been implemented by universities and may be mentioned are all those preparatory or induction activities aimed at ensuring that future and even first-year students become familiar with the campus and the university structures. This allows students to get to know, first hand, the institution, its spaces, and how it is organised and operated – all of which serves as essential knowledge as part of the adaptation process in the early years of study.

In other cases, specific teacher training strategies are implemented for welcoming students who come from vulnerable situations into the classroom and to ensure the quality of learning as well as its relevance and suitability to their needs. Some institutions are also considering the possibility of beginning to undertake processes that include reviewing the curriculum and study plans in order to incorporate new skills and knowledge. Other universities have chosen, in addition, to create student care offices offering social services such as medical attention and assistance with student residence or psychological support.

It should be made clear that these are not the only strategies being implemented, but rather just those that have been noted as recurrent both in the publications mentioned and in the references cited. It is not our concern here to assess the development and implementation of these strategies, but rather to use them to illustrate universities' investment in the inclusion of vulnerable collectives, whether these be students with disabilities, those belonging to ethnic minorities, immigrants or those with a rural background, etc.

In summary, it is important to emphasise that the progress in achieving the inclusion of vulnerable students should be analysed as a cross-cutting issue for the institution itself. It involves incorporating strategies and programmes that have an impact on the institution's structures, dynamics and professionals and whose targets are not only students in a situation of vulnerability.

6.3 *Challenges in the Inclusion of Vulnerable Collectives in the University*
The challenges to be considered, common to many of the universities that promote inclusion programmes, are summarised below.

a *Gathering accurate information regarding collectives in situations of vulnerability and their educational circumstances.* The rigorous and systematic development of systems for the collection of relevant information and with precise indicators, far from stigmatising these collectives, would make it possible to identify new collectives in situations of vulnerability affected by current contextual and social conditions and that reach beyond frequent indicators such as gender, socioeconomic status and place of residence. New social and contextual conditions have modified the situation of families and students in the region: for example, situations of economic crisis, the incorporation of refugees or of workers in search of new specialisations.

b *Developing specific actions for all collectives in situations of vulnerability.* The proposed diagnosis would not only allow the collectives to be made visible but also enable the development of actions and strategies.

c *Systematising the actions and strategies developed by universities.* The diversity and variety of actions carried out have already been mentioned. However, it is also important for the universities themselves to develop their systematisations and promote, for example, knowledge creation and management processes (debates, exchange of experiences, demonstrations etc.). On the other hand, it is to be hoped that this systematisation should lead to the institutionalisation of these actions, thereby improving inclusion.

d *Incorporating strategies aimed at overcoming the digital divide.* The reference to the essential incorporation of technologies in university classrooms is necessary in the knowledge society. As Blanco (2014) points out, there is a digital divide that constitutes a factor of exclusion and mainly afflicts socioeconomically vulnerable students and/or those who are in rural areas. Information technology in HE should be oriented to promote the teaching-learning processes and be implemented as a tool available to all students.

The aforementioned challenges could be related to preventing the expansion of universities from affecting equity, the development of their own inclusive capacity in the universities and the fostering of a permanent dialogue between the university, vulnerable collectives and society.

7 Final Considerations

Defending inclusion and diversity as axes of HE implies recognising that they are, at the same time, a goal and a challenge for the educational system, universities and the institutions and players involved. Referring to these concepts, understood as social processes, leads in turn to a related concept: that of situations of vulnerability. It is therefore necessary to consider three complex and multidimensional notions that are still debated and interpreted in different ways.

Diversity is conceived as an intrinsic characteristic of societies, no longer as a negative aspect needing to be homogenised or excluded from educational institutions, but as a value and an opportunity: a positive aspect whose value must be reassessed. Inclusion is understood as a process that aspires to achieve the full, active and critical participation of all citizens, on equal terms and in all areas of society (education, work, health and housing, among others). It is not, therefore, a process of adaptation or integration in which you must relinquish something of your own in order to be a part of it.

Many universities have developed initiatives to improve the situation of vulnerable groups and to provide inclusive education in their respective institutions. Supported by organisations that deal with higher education, they design projects to establish collaborative networks, exchange experiences and build useful and effective new instruments of intervention. However, the challenges and projects for improvement still have a long way to go, if we accept education as a public and social good and continue to aspire to it being available to all citizens.

Reacting and responding to these unfair situations is necessary but does not seem to be sufficient. We must be proactive in the transformation of our institutions, as well as in that of society, in order to reach a desirable situation in which educational institutions do not need specific policies to support vulnerable groups because society as a whole would provide them with the attention and resources necessary to develop their lives, as is the case with each and every citizen of the nation (Tolosana, 2014).

Finally, and by way of synthesis, we must not forget that three important ideas emerge from the principle of education for all: (a) that promoting and driving inclusive processes may be the most effective way to combat discriminatory and exclusive attitudes; (b) that training institutions must be restructured to ensure proper attention is given to all students; and (c) that, sometimes, school exclusion is the prelude to certain trajectories of social exclusion. Although we may be able to find different nuances concerning the concept of inclusive educational centres, the fact is that they all share a broader concern for creating an inclusive society based on the values of social justice, equity and democratic participation.

Acknowledgement

This document has been produced as a part of the project "ACCESS4ALL – Laboratory for Policies and Practices of Social Development in Higher Education" (Ref. 2015-1-ES01-KA203-015970) co-funded by the European Union (Erasmus+ Programme).

Notes

1. Sustainable Development Goal 4 has seven outcome targets and three means of implementation to achieve them. It speaks, in this regard, of primary, secondary and university education; early childhood development and universal preschool education; equal access to technical, vocational and tertiary education; adequate skills for decent work; gender equality and inclusion; universal literacy for youth; citizenship education for sustainable development; effective learning environments; scholarships; and teachers and educators.
2. See http://projectes.uab.cat/accedes/
3. Open access publications at: http://projectes. uab.cat/accedes/
4. See https://access4allproject.eu/
5. See https://observatorio-oracle.org/
6. IDEAS project: http://projectes.uab.cat/ideas/
7. PATdis: https://ddd.uab.cat/record/147452

References

Ainscow, M. (2015). *Towards self-improving school systems: Lessons from a city challenge*. Routledge.

Aponte-Hernández, E. (2008). Desigualdad, inclusión y equidad en la ES en América Latina y el Caribe: tendencias y escenario alternativo en el horizonte 2021. In A. L. Gazzola & A. Didriksson (Eds.), *Tendencias de la ES en América Latina y el Caribe* (pp. 113–154). IESALC – UNESCO.

Bauman, Z. (2007). *Temps líquids. Viure una època d'incertesa*. Viena Edicions.

Brunner, J. J., & Ferrer, R. (2011). *ES en Iberoamérica. Informe 2011*. Centro Interuniversitario de Desarrollo (CINDA) – Universia.

Casanova, H. (2012). *El gobierno de la universidad en España*. NETBIBLO S.L.

Chiroleu, A. (2010). Políticas de educación superior en América Latina en el siglo XXI. ¿Renovación, ambigüedad o continuismo? In *Congreso de la Asociación de Estudios Latinoamericanos* (pp. 1–18). Toronto, Canada.

CRES. (2008). *Tendencias de la Educación Superior en América Latina*. https://www.oei.es/historico/salactsi/cres2008.htm

Dias Sobrinho, J. (2008). Calidad, pertinencia y responsabilidad social de la universidad latinoamericana y caribeña. In A. L. Gazzola & A. Didriksson (Eds.), *Tendencias de la ES en América Latina y el Caribe* (pp. 87–112). IESALC – UNESCO.

Díaz-Romero, P. (2010). *Universidades de calidad: Universidades inclusivas* (pp. 1–6). Fundación Equitas.

Egido, I., Fernandez, M. J., & Galan, A. (2014). La dimensión social del proceso de Bolonia: Apoyos y servicios para grupos de estudiantes poco representados en las universidades españolas. *Educacion XXI, 17*(2), 57–81.

Espinoza, O. (Coord.). (2013). *Equidad e inclusividad en la Educación Superior en los países andinos: los casos de Bolivia, Chile, Colombia y Perú*. Red Iberoamérica de Investigación en Políticas Educativas (RIAPE).

Eurydice. (2011). *La modernización de la educación superior en Europa*. EACEA.

Ezcurra, A. M. (2008). Educación Universitaria: Una Inclusión Excluyente. In *Conferencia en III Encuentro Nacional sobre Ingreso Universitario*. Fundación Ideas.

Fleming, A., Plotner, A., & Oertle, K. (2017). College students with disabilities: The relationship between student characteristics, the academic environment and performance. *Journal of Postsecondary Education and Disability, 30*(3), 209–221.

Forlín, C. (2013). Changing paradigms and future directions for implementing inclusive education in developing countries. *Asian Journal of Inclusive Education, 1*(2), 19–31.

Gairín, J. (2003). Un modelo para la generalización de un programa de tutoría universitaria. In *Simposio de Estrategias de Formación para el cambio organizacional*. Universitat Autònoma de Barcelona, diciembre.

Gairín, J. (2004). Elementos para la elaboración de planes de tutoría en la universidad. *Contextos educativos, 6-7*, 21–41.

Gairín, J. (2009). La transición secundaria-universidad y la incorporación a la universidad. La acogida de los estudiantes de primer curso. *Revista Española de Pedagogía, 242*, 27–44.

Gairín, J., Castro, D., & Rodríguez-Gómez, D. (2014). *Acceso, permanencia y egreso en la universidad de colectivos vulnerables en Latinoamérica: Intervenir y cambiar la realidad.* Santillana. http://accelera.uab.cat/documents_edo/pdf/ACCEDES2014_Estrategias.rar

Gairín, J., & Rodríguez-Gómez, D. (2019). La atención a colectivos vulnerables como reto de la universidad inclusiva. In P. Figueras (Ed.), *Trayectorias, transiciones y resultados de los estudiantes en la universidad* (pp. 225–257). Laertes.

Gairín, J., & Suárez, C. I. (2012). La vulnerabilidad en Educación Superior. In J. Gairín, D. Rodríguez-Gómez, & D. Castro Ceacero (Eds.), *Éxito académico de colectivos vulnerables en entornos de riesgo en Latinoamérica* (pp. 39–58). Wolters Kluwer.

Gairín, J., & Suárez, C. I. (2013). La vulnerabilidad en Educación Superior. In J. Gairín, D. Rodríguez-Gómez, & D. Castro Ceacero (Eds.), *Éxito académico de colectivos vulnerables en entornos de riesgo en Latinoamérica* (pp. 39–58). Wolters Kluwer.

Gairín, J., & Suárez, C. I. (2014). Clarificar e identificar los grupos vulnerables. In J. Gairín (Ed.), *Colectivos vulnerables en la universidad. Reflexión y propuestas para la intervención* (pp. 33–61). Wolters Kluwer.

Gairín, J., & Suárez, C. I. (2015). XIII. Avances y retos en la inclusión de colectivos en situación de vulnerabilidad en la educación superior. In J. Gairín (Ed.), *Los sistemas de acceso, normativa de permanencia y estrategias de tutoría y retención de estudiantes en educación superior* (pp. 281–296). Wolters Kluwer.

Gairín, J., & Suárez, C. I. (2016). Inclusión y grupos en situación de vulnerabilidad: orientaciones para repensar el rol de las universidades. *Sinéctica, 46*, 1–15.

Galán, A., & Gairín, J. (2013). *Plan de acción tutorial para estudiantes universitarios con discapacidad (PATdis).* Ministerio de Educación, Cultura y Deporte. https://sede.educacion.gob.es/publiventa/detalle.action?cod=16097

Henríquez, P. (2015). Responsabilidad Social de la Universidad: Uno de los Requisitos para ser Universidad. In A. Aponte Hernández (Ed.), *La Responsabilidad Social de las Universidades: Implicaciones para América Latina y el Caribe* (pp. 15–24). UNESCO-IESALC.

Hewett, R., Douglas, G., McLinden, M., & Keil, S. (2017). Developing an inclusive learning environment for students with visual impairment in higher education: progressive mutual accommodation and learner experiences in the United Kingdom. *European Journal of Special Needs Education, 32*(1), 89–109.

Jurado, P. (2007). *Integración educativa y socio-laboral* (Materiales para la Docencia). Universidad Autónoma de Barcelona.

Márquez, G., et al. (2008). *Los de afuera. Patrones cambiantes de exclusión en América Latina y el Caribe.* Banco Interamericano de Desarrollo.

Moriña, A. (2017). Inclusive education in higher education: Challenges and opportunities. *European Journal of Special Needs Education, 32*(1), 3–17.

OEI. (2010). *Metas Educativas 2020. La educación que queremos para la generación de los Bicentenarios.* Author.

Ortega, P. (2014). Educar en la alteralidad. *Boletín Redipe, 3–4,* 6–20.

Rama, C. (2009). La tendencia a la masificación de la cobertura de la ES en América Latina. *Revista Iberoamericana de Educación, 50,* 173–195.

Reindal, S. M. (2016). Discussing inclusive education: An inquiry into different interpretations and a search for ethical aspects of inclusion using the capabilities approach. *European Journal of Special Needs Education, 31*(1), 1–12.

Renaut, A. (2008). La Universidad frente a los desafíos de la democracia. *Temas y debates, 16,* 153–161.

Sanahuja-Gavaldà, J. M., Muñoz-Moreno, J. L., & Gairín-Sallan, J. (2020). Tutoring students with disabilities at the university. *Culture and Education.* doi:10.1080/1135640 5.2019.1709392

Santos, B. de S. (2005). *La universidad en el siglo XXI. Para una reforma democrática y emancipadora de la universidad.* Miño y Dávila.

Sebastián, C., & Scharager, J. (2007). Diversidad y Educación Superor: Algunas reflexiones iniciales. *Calidad en la Educación, 26,* 19–36.

Subirats, J. (Dir.). (2004). *Pobreza y exclusión social. Un análisis de la realidad española y europea* (Colección Estudios sociales No. 16). Fundación La Caixa.

Sverdlick, I., Ferrari, P., & Jaimovich, A. (2005). *Desigualdad e inclusión en la ES. Un estudio comparado en cinco países de América Latina.* Laboratorio de Políticas Públicas.

Terigi, F. (2010). La inclusión como problema de las políticas educativas. *Quehacer educativo, 100,* 75–78.

Tiana, A. (2010). El espacio iberoamericano del conocimiento como marco para la cooperación en educación superior. In A. Marchesi & M. Poggi (Eds.), *Presente y futuro de la educación iberoamericana* (pp. 67–90). AECID.

Tolosana, C. (2014). La atención de grupos vulnerables: un reto educativo y social. In J. Gairín (Ed.), *Colectivos vulnerables en la Universidad. Reflexiones y propuestas para la intervención* (pp. 19–32). Wolters Kluwer.

UNESCO. (2009). *Directrices sobre políticas de inclusión en la educación.* Author.

Whiteford, G., Shah, M., & Sid Nair, C. (2013). Equity and excellence are not mutually exclusive. *Quality Assurance in Education, 21*(3), 299–310. www.emeraldinsight.com/0968-4883.htm

CHAPTER 2

Diversity, Access, and Success in Higher Education: A Transnational Overview

Fabio Dovigo

Abstract

In the last twenty years, there has been growing interest internationally in the increase and diversification of the population of students attending Higher Education. Higher Education is one of the most important factors that can foster social mobility, by reducing disadvantages and poverty across generations and having a broad impact across all of society. Widening participation in Higher Education, usually referred to as the "social dimension" of the Bologna Process in Europe, aims to promote equality of opportunities concerning: access, retention, participation and successful completion of studies; living and studying conditions; student guidance and counselling; financial support; equal opportunities in mobility; and supporting student participation in Higher Education governance. These objectives are in line with the idea that the diversity of the population should be reflected by the student body, and that students' participation in Higher Education should not be limited by their different backgrounds. The chapter will offer an analysis of the way the social dimension has been developed in the European context over the years, as well as an overview of the results achieved and the next challenges to be faced by the Higher Education institutions.

Keywords

social dimension – widening participation – Bologna Process – diversity – equality – equity – inclusion – under-represented groups – quality – higher education access

1   **Introduction**

In the last twenty years, there has been growing interest internationally in the increase and diversification of the population of students attending Higher Education (HE) (OECD, 2001). The focus on widening participation is justified by institutional, economic and social justice factors related to the development of what has been defined as a "knowledge society", where knowledge has moved from being a substructure for production to becoming the core structure of work itself (Delanty, 2001; Hargreaves, 2003). In terms of social justice, HE is one of the most important factors that can foster social mobility, by reducing disadvantages and poverty across generations and having a broad impact across all of society. Nevertheless, HE can, on the contrary, also contribute to strengthening inequalities deeply, as this level of education is not compulsory and therefore not accessible to everyone (Vignoles & Murray, 2016).

As for Europe, the notion and principles of widening participation in HE are usually referred to as the "social dimension" of the Bologna Process, which has led to building a European Higher Education Area (EHEA) composed of a group of 48 countries cooperating to achieve comparable and compatible HE systems across the continent. One of the EHEA's objectives is to promote equality of opportunities in HE concerning: access, retention, participation and successful completion of studies; living and studying conditions; student guidance and counselling; financial support; equal opportunities in mobility; and supporting student participation in HE governance (Curaj et al., 2012; Crosier & Parveva, 2013). These objectives are in line with the idea that the diversity of the population should be reflected by the student body, and that students' participation in HE should not be limited by their different backgrounds. The social dimension has been recognised and often cited as part of the Bologna Process. Acknowledging that the EHEA encompasses a wide variety of social, economic and cultural conditions, over the years the common orientation has been to leave each country free to identify which features should be considered when the composition of the student body is compared with the total population. Accordingly, the categories of under-represented students usually vary according to the country examined.

The first mention of the social dimension in the Bologna Process dates to 2001, when the Conference of Ministers responsible for HE endorsed the call from the European Student Union to include the topic in the Bologna agenda. Accordingly, the Conference mentioned it in the Prague Communiqué (2001), underlining that HE should be considered a public good and remain a public responsibility. Four years later, the Bergen Ministerial Conference confirmed the willingness of the participant countries to support the goal of widening access to HE (Ministerial Conference Bergen, 2005). However, the contents and purposes of the social dimension were defined more precisely only starting with the London Communiqué (2007), which describes them as "the societal aspiration that the student body entering, participating in and completing higher education at all levels should reflect the diversity of our populations" and reaffirms "the importance of students being able to complete their studies without obstacles related to their social and economic background" (Ministerial Conference London, 2007, p. 5). According to the document, the starting point for participating countries to develop national strategies and action plans based on the identification of specific groups excluded from or under-represented in the academic context was to delve into the social dimension of HE.

At the following meeting in Yerevan, the EHEA countries took stock of the progress made and restated their willingness to support the development of the social dimension of HE, as part of a wider strategy to improve inclusion in European society. The Communiqué issued by the Conference committee members to fostering "relevant learning activities in appropriate contexts for different types of learners, including lifelong learning", as well as permeability and articulation between different education sectors, gender balance, access and completion for students from disadvantaged backgrounds, and international mobility for students and staff (Ministerial Conference Yerevan, 2015). In addition, the Ministerial Conference launched a new plan called "Widening Participation for Equity and Growth" (EHEA, 2015a) and approved the report from the Bologna Follow-Up Group (BFUG) Working Group (EHEA, 2015b). Both documents emphasised the need to develop a coherent set of policy measures and national plans or strategies to address participation in HE. They also underlined the need to provide guidelines to set national targets for under-represented groups, collect relevant data in each country, and follow up with specific actions undertaken.

Shortly after, advances made towards the objective of widening participation were summarised by the Bologna Process Implementation Report (2015), which highlighted that, despite the efforts made by the EHEA countries, the goal of ensuring equal opportunities for all students in HE was far from being achieved in most areas: gender balance, opportunities to access different fields of study, take-up of students from families with a low educational background, access to HE for immigrants and children of immigrants. Notwithstanding the commitments made by governments to set measurable targets for widening overall participation and increasing participation of under-represented groups in HE, according to the report, most EU countries set targets for increasing overall participation, but less than 20% defined quantitative objectives regarding these groups (European Commission/EACEA/Eurydice, 2018b; Łibacka, 2015).

Twenty years after the launch of the Bologna Process, the idea of improving inclusion in HE for students from more disadvantaged backgrounds is still compelling, but its achievement has proved more difficult than expected. Translating the social, economic and cultural profile of vulnerable students from diverse countries into a coherent European framework for action has been especially challenging. As has recently been noted, many questions still await a precise answer concerning broadening participation in HE: "Who has access to higher education? To what extent does young peoples' socio-economic background or gender influence their chances of becoming higher education students? Do admission systems reduce or reinforce existing societal inequalities?" (European Commission/EACEA/Eurydice, 2018a).

2   Widening Participation in Higher Education

Since the beginning, the debate about the social dimension of HE has focused on the concept of widening participation, setting it as a pivotal priority that involves filling the gap between different social groups in the enrolment of students in HE. Three main views, which reflect different perspectives on the question of inclusion in HE, have emerged regarding the way participation should be ensured (European Commission, 2015; Eurydice, 2011).

According to the first approach, facilitating students' enrolment and success in tertiary education is a goal that should be pursued on its own. The more students access HE and get a degree – reducing the number of those who drop out and delay the completion of studies – the better the chances they will have of obtaining early and good employment in the future. Even though it is attractive, this "open door policy" is not free from contradictions. In the face of widespread funding cuts, a growing number of universities are now obliged to adopt a grant scheme in which funding is strictly related to the number of students who are enrolled and graduate on time. Therefore, in escalating student take-up and urging students to end their careers without delays, universities are not led by a sense of equity, but the need to ensure an ongoing and stable funding base that will help them survive. Consequently, this approach is highly vulnerable to the risk of pushing the system towards adopting low-standard, massified teaching and learning procedures, in which quantity and speed replace a focus on student diversity and individual needs.

A second discourse on participation in HE, on the contrary, assigns a prominent role to efficiency, accountability and, more generally, quality. Participation is thus primarily interpreted as ensuring that students can take advantage of HE by providing them access to excellent teaching. According to this viewpoint, efficiency is seen as the best way to guarantee all students an equitable and quality educational experience based on meritocratic grounds, at a time when public funding in HE is increasingly being cut. However, although inclusion in HE should not be seen as incompatible with delivering quality education, this view emphasises a competitive (instead of cooperative) approach to HE, perceived as "a hierarchical system characterised by quality rankings and prestige markers" (Harwood et al., 2016). In this system, merit is an abstract entity detached from the analysis of the role students' economic and cultural capital plays in deciding who can actually access (or even consider accessing) HE (Brennan, 2018; Holmegaard et al., 2017). Consequently, within this framework students from a disadvantaged background are usually not accepted or re-oriented towards lower-level institutions (as defined by reputation and rankings). This way, the stratification of the system remains unchallenged (Duru-Bellat, 2008; Triventi, 2013).

Finally, a third perspective underlines that the university system should pay special attention to supporting students from under-represented groups, starting with raising their aspirations and educational attainment concerning HE, both before and during their enrolment in tertiary education (Harwood, 2016). This viewpoint recommends helping disadvantaged students by supporting expectations regarding access to HE, as well as providing specific support during the study programme, to foster enrolment and maintain retention and course completion rates. This perspective on broadening participation also includes initiatives aimed at mature students who, within a lifelong learning programme framework, want to start or resume a career in HE.

These three views, which can respectively be described as a quantitative, qualitative, and inclusive approach to widening participation, show that different perspectives can be adopted in considering the role that the social dimension plays in democratising European policies about tertiary education. In this regard, expanding access and guaranteeing quality learning experiences for students is not enough. Ensuring that as large as possible a proportion of the population will have a real opportunity to take advantage of HE entails that students from different economic, social and cultural backgrounds are systematically supported to achieve and succeed on their educational path. Therefore, it implies that different strategies – economic, social, pedagogical, psychological, cultural and linguistic – are put in place to improve the organisation of HE as an inclusive environment that contributes to achieving a more inclusive society (ESU, 2019b).

While the purpose of the social dimension ("reflecting diversity of the population", as stated in the London Communiqué) is straightforward, its implementation poses manifold questions in terms of data collection, establishing cause and effect relationships, enabling generalisation of outcomes, and maintaining a coherent, not manipulable, definition of equity (Usher, 2015). Moreover, it is subject to the particular ways each European government interprets the task of widening participation by identifying under-represented student groups.

3   Under-Represented Groups in Higher Education

Attempts to define tertiary education learners according to broad categories often risk labelling students or confining them to an over-simplistic classification that can do more harm than good to the progress of inclusive practices in HE. Binary classifications such as "traditional/non-traditional" or "native/immigrant" tend to underestimate the complex nuances of students' identities, personal development and choices regarding HE. For instance, if we take a closer look at the so-called non-traditional students, we will find that this category encompasses features related to, among other things, gender, socio-economic background, ethnic origins, cultural capital, disabilities, and being a mature and/or working-class student. It is easy to see how the combination of these minorities adds up to a majority that doesn't match the typical image of a student as a Western white man, without physical and intellectual impairments, and free from the constraints of needing to economically support himself or dependents (Hinton-Smith, 2012). What these kinds of definitions actually have in common is the reference to minority students as lacking one or more characteristics compared to this ideal model. As a consequence, this emphasis on deficits overshadows a much of the knowledge and abilities these students have acquired through their life experience, which cannot be undervalued only because they do not fit into the conventional set of academic skills (O'Shea et al., 2016).

As we have mentioned, the definitions of under-represented groups in HE differ from country to country. However, some shared themes emerge regarding the priorities and approaches considered. The most common questions concern the students' socio-economic background, gender, disabilities, migration, ethnic differences, and mature students. Moreover, these questions often overlap, resulting in a combination of factors that make the goal of including those learners even more challenging. An elitist view of HE, supported by the relentless spread of neoliberal dogma across education in Europe and beyond, identifies those groups as the scapegoat for the supposed declining quality of university education (Maher & Thompson Tetreault, 2013; Olssen & Peters, 2005). On the contrary, the data shows that the path leading to exclusion from participation in HE can be found in the way the secondary school system is still stratified in many EU countries, differentiating schools according to their ranking level and/or reputation (Allmendinger, 2016). In turn, school stratification produces the phenomenon of early tracking, through which students are assigned to separate school tracks depending on their performance or supposed abilities. As a result, students with a disadvantaged background are usually nudged to opt for vocational training courses that are deemed more "compatible" with their profile, but actually make it much more difficult for them to access tertiary education (Dupriez et al., 2008; Orr et al., 2017).

To tackle this issue, in recent years some EU countries have promoted and diversified access to HE for students with vocational (or other non-standard) educational qualifications. This usually takes the form of bridging programmes or Higher Vocational Education and Training pathways (Auzinger et al., 2016). However, most European students still enter HE directly, usually within two years of leaving upper secondary school (Eurostudent, 2019). 14% of students postpone HE enrolment by over 24 months. This delayed transition is more common among students whose parents do not have a HE background. Moreover, students who delay the transition to HE often have regular work experience before enrolling in HE. They usually depend on their own income to finance themselves and can experience serious economic difficulties compared to other students (Eurostudent, 2016). In nearly all countries, the ratio between secondary education graduates and HE entrants is higher among the female population than the male one (European Commission/EACEA/Eurydice, 2018a).

Finally, the number of students enrolled part-time in HE across the Bologna Area does not show a regular trend compared to full-time students. Data shows that, in 2014/15, over one quarter of all students were part-timers in half of all EHEA countries, and most of these were mature and low study intensity students (European Commission/EACEA/Eurydice, 2018a). However, the term "part-time studies" has different meanings in different EU countries and follows different organisational patterns depending on national regulations. Consequently, it is not uncommon for learners formally classified as full-time students by government statistics to actually be recorded as part-time students in other surveys.

4   Factors Affecting Participation of Under-Represented Groups

Of the factors that affect the participation of under-represented groups in HE, the socio-economic and cultural background of students has been the most frequently analysed. Research emphasises that the parental educational background plays a pivotal role in the chance of attaining a HE qualification, as children of highly educated parents are still much more likely to achieve a HE degree than children of low- or medium-educated parents (Croll & Attwood, 2013; European Commission/EACEA/Eurydice, 2015). Even though the situation is slowly improving, with young people from lower educational family backgrounds having better opportunities to obtain a degree than their elders did in the past, students from these families are still largely under-represented among new HE entrants, as well as being more likely to enter HE with a remarkable delay. Furthermore, the prevalence of new entrants from highly educated households is even more conspicuous in countries where the share of people with HE degrees within older age cohorts is already relatively high. As a consequence, learners from less educated families will have only a marginal chance of entering tertiary education unless the HE sector is further expanded (European Commission/EACEA/Eurydice, 2018a).

However, explanations based on parental educational background are in some ways limited. Under-representation of students from these families is often ascribed to poor educational performance, a lack of motivation to complete secondary school (as well as to attend university), and insufficient family experience regarding the benefits of HE (Crosier & Parveva, 2013). Evidence shows that, beyond economic capital and educational background, working-class families frequently lack the cultural capital that would enable them to look at attending HE as a natural aspiration. Accordingly, some European countries have launched special programmes to encourage students from these families to consider HE enrolment as a legitimate and viable option. Nevertheless, it has been argued that working-class groups are rightly more inclined than middle-class groups to perceive choices related to participation in HE as inherently risky, costly and uncertain (Archer & Huchings, 2000). Consequently, there is "an enormous difference between such established middle class familial habituses in which going to university is part of a normal biography, simply part of what people like us do, and often too obvious to articulate, and working-class familial habitus, characterised by uncertainty, unfamiliarity, lack of knowledge and often confusion in relation to the field of higher education" (Reay et al., 2005, p. 61).

Another important area of interest in the social dimension is the gender gap between men and women who participate in HE (Barone, 2011; Kreissl et al., 2015; Morley, 2013). In this regard, a major issue concerns the under-representation of men in HE in nearly all European countries. Even though this gap has decreased in the last ten years, female enrolment in tertiary education is still greater than male enrolment in most countries. However, while female students are in the majority, especially in the second cycle of HE, the gender gap clearly reverses in the third-cycle programmes, a worrisome sign that ensuring that women participate at the level required to qualify to start an academic career remains an unresolved problem. Moreover, this question is also connected to the strong gender imbalance that continues to affect some disciplines in HE. While women are strongly represented in the education, health and welfare fields of study, engineering, manufacturing and construction, information and communication technologies are still largely male-dominated areas (European Commission/EACEA/Eurydice, 2017).

Regarding students with disabilities, EU surveys have found that the share of learners indicating any type of disability or impairment ranges, depending on the country examined, from 7% to 39%. These wide variations may correspond to actual differences in the way the inclusion of disabled students is managed in different European countries but could also be explained by the wider or more narrow definition of impairment adopted by each member state (Riddells et al., 2005; Riddell & Weedon, 2014). Among the most frequently cited barriers that prevent access to HE for young people with disabilities are a lack of suitable infrastructure, an insufficient adaptation of teaching and learning materials, and budget problems. Nevertheless, other, more nuanced but equally important deterrents are rarely mentioned, such as the psychological barriers produced by perceived negative attitudes or stereotypes, for example, as well as the lack of a more widespread culture of acceptance of disability (Crosier & Parveva, 2013). Physical chronic diseases are one of the most frequently named functional limitations by students. However, not all impairments (e.g. learning disabilities) are immediately visible and noticeable, nor do all students with impairments need or want support from the university structure, as some prefer not to disclose their condition. Student ratings regarding the support they receive from HE institutions are not homogeneous, as in some countries (Albania, the Netherlands, Ireland, and Georgia) it is deemed satisfactory, whereas in others (Denmark, Italy, Estonia, Malta, Iceland, Austria, Serbia, Slovenia, and Hungary) it is considered inadequate, especially by students with a severe impairment (Eurostudent, 2018).

An additional question regarding inclusion in HE is whether students with a migrant background, especially those whose parents have a low educational level, have the same opportunities to access and achieve HE as native students. However, collecting and comparing data on this important group of students poses some important questions (Griga & Hadjar, 2014). On the one hand, EU surveys assign students to this category based on their country of birth. This makes it difficult to differentiate between permanent migrants who enrol in HE and other students who moved to the country specifically for the purpose of accessing HE. On the other hand, the category does not account for second-generation immigrant students. Keeping these limitations in mind, the data indicates that, in most EU countries, the participation of the foreign-born student population in HE is lower compared to that of native-born students. Moreover, the share of HE students with both parents born abroad (thus presumably with a second-generation immigrant background) is lower than 10%. Consequently, as the foreign-born group in EU reports frequently also encompasses international students, participation rates for first-generation immigrants are presumably even lower (European Commission/EACEA/Eurydice, 2018a).

Mature learners are another important under-represented group in HE (Brooks, 2012; Kenny et al., 2010). They are usually defined as students aged 30 or older who, due to a lack of information or resources, did not have the opportunity to enter HE immediately after leaving secondary school. However, it is important to note that the mature student category does not necessarily overlap with the group of delayed transition students, who enter HE two years or more after leaving school, as taking gap years or studying for a longer period of time has become increasingly common in some European countries. On the whole, in the last few years the number of mature students has decreased in Europe, but there are sizeable differences between member states in this regard. The highest share of mature students can be found in Nordic countries, which also have a large proportion of delayed transition students who take longer to complete their tertiary studies. In contrast, other countries, such as France and Germany, have a relatively low share of mature students, but also few learners who postpone the conclusion of their study pathways. In the remaining countries (such as the Czech Republic, Hungary, Poland and Slovakia) students are likely to graduate earlier, so the group of mature students coincides with those who have delayed transition (European Commission/EACEA/Eurydice, 2018).

However, the description of the under-represented in HE groups currently provided by EU research reports is limited in many respects. First, information is collected at a different pace and with different survey methods in each country. This significantly hinders the smooth aggregation and analysis of data. As a consequence, the final picture provided by EU reports often describes an outdated situation, preventing a timely understanding of the trends that are influencing the highly dynamic HE sector. Secondly, member states differ in the way groups of under-represented students are defined and investigated. Consequently, transnational comparisons of conditions and progress made are especially problematic, as with the case of second-generation immigrant students we mentioned. Thirdly, the analysis of under-represented groups does not account for students who deal with multiple barriers at the same time (Banerjee, 2018). For example, both mature students and those with a migrant background frequently struggle because of competing pressures that require that they manage working and studying at the same time (Antonucci, 2016). Finally, while some categories (such as students from a low socio-economic background) are usually analysed in-depth, other specific groups (such as learners with psychosocial disabilities or LGBTQ students) are little or not at all represented in surveys. Even though they are actually as vulnerable or at-risk as other groups, these categories are usually considered too problematic or politically sensitive to be managed by the academic institutions in charge of collecting data (ESU, 2019a).

Lastly, it is worth noting that many EU member states have not yet put in place a national policy or plan to identify under-represented groups in tertiary education. Efforts in this direction, as well as to systematise data collection, are still inadequate. Whereas most EU countries have carried out a set of actions to widen access to HE, although generally in a partial and heterogeneous way, much less attention has been paid to the measures that would guarantee the effective inclusion of vulnerable students throughout their academic careers until the completion of studies. The analysis of these measures will help to further understand their connection with the social dimension goals emphasised by the Bologna Process.

5   Measures Undertaken to Favour the Participation of Under-Represented Groups

As a consequence of the implementation of the Bologna Process, the number of students entering HE in Europe has increased over time, although the dynamics of this trend have been different in each country. However, taking up more students does not automatically translate to improving the social dimension of HE, as the actual impact of this growth on young people's access to tertiary education has been scarce or minimal for some specific groups.

Over the years, European countries have developed a variety of policy strategies to overcome these limitations. They encompass both policy actions that address all students and measures designed to improve the inclusion of selected groups. The former aim to support and widen overall student participation in HE, whereas the latter focuses on distinct under-represented groups through various actions, such as financial support, targeted outreach and information programmes, special admission to reserved places, and the provision of services for guidance and counselling. However, plans in this direction are usually undertaken by each HE institutions autonomous way. Consequently, most initiatives are not included in the national monitoring activity or, if they are, provide only scarce information about their implementation.

A typical example of action meant to benefit all students is housing policy. For many universities, especially in capital cities and large towns, ensuring the right to housing for students is traditionally problematic. In many EU countries, programmes to increase the number of places available for students was systematically behind the number of students potentially entitled to them, due to the recent expansion of the HE sector. This particularly affects young people whose residence is far from the university site, as the supply of accommodation is rarely able to meet the large demand (ESU, 2019a).

Another increasingly common measure concerning access, which is especially popular in countries where admittance to university is relatively unrestricted, regards programmes that aim to help prospective students explore in advance the degree course they would opt to enrol in, so as to understand whether it would actually be a good match. This matching activity is developed through online self-assessment tests, trial lectures at university, interviews, counselling activities and so on. These initiatives are part of the more general effort EU universities make to support access through information and guidance related to the academic and career options, as well as the development of induction programmes and the organisation of preliminary visits to the university site for prospective students. Furthermore, HE institutions normally grant students guidance services related to their academic and career options within and beyond the access phase. These services are regularly integrated by psychological or counselling activities, especially for students with special educational needs. Nevertheless, all these actions are usually designed and administered at the local level by each institution, making it difficult to understand the extent and effectiveness of these interventions, especially regarding the population of disadvantaged students.

Moreover, to favour wider access to HE, some EU member states have created new kinds of degrees and modified the curriculum of existing academic programmes. In this regard, the Netherlands and Portugal launched short degree programmes designed for students who want to get on a fast track towards a profession, but also retain the option to achieve a first-level degree. Austria, France, Germany and Norway provide open-subject first level programmes that facilitate students' gradually focusing on the choice of academic topic they prefer to specialise in. This aims to reduce the high number of learners who leave university or switch degrees because they make the wrong choice during the first year (Schaeper, 2020).

To facilitate access to HE, most EU countries created alternative routes that provide different, and often integrated, kinds of approaches beyond traditional enrolment. They include, for example, work-based learning opportunities, standardised tests, specific access courses, foundation degrees, and recognition of prior learning (McGrath et al., 2014). As for the latter, recognition of non-formal or informal learning is an important part of the Bologna Process, as it strongly impacts the opportunities that under-represented students have to access HE. However, many EU countries still lack regulations on the way this type of learning should be regarded. Even where regulations are in place, HE institutions' approaches to managing the validation process vary widely within the same country.

Several platforms have been created through cooperation between EU countries concerning good practices that aim to favour under-represented students' access to HE. These various platforms have in common the goal of collecting and sharing practices that have proved effective in facilitating student enrolment, retainment and success on their academic paths. Among the many existing platforms, it is worth mentioning the European University Association database, the IDEAS website, the EASLHE online observatory, and the ACCESS4ALL bank of good practices (Rodríguez-Gómez, 2019; Tupan-Wenno et al., 2016). Beyond student access, online platforms have also been put in place to share outcome data regarding study success at the European level. This activity is part of an international effort made by HE institutions to develop quality assurance processes that include providing information related to students' careers, such as access, retention, time-to-degree, completion and drop-out rates. While collecting study success rates is a mandatory part of the periodic reaccreditation procedure of each institution, the publication of data enables prospective students to acquire relevant information with regard to their academic choices. This in turn helps raise HE institutions' awareness of the importance of supporting students' success as a critical component of the university's reputation and quality.

Over the last few years, measures designed to guarantee better social integration of students as a way of strengthening the social dimension have generated increasing interest. Research shows that study success rates are closely associated with students developing a sense of belonging to the HE environment (Hoffman, 2002; Johnson, 2007). This factor is critical in the first year and for learners from under-represented groups, especially in universities where attending academic courses risks becoming a massified and anonymous experience. To this end, many HE institutions have undertaken specific actions to provide students with more individualised and tailored support throughout their academic careers, as a way to strengthen students' affiliation with the university environment and to sustain engagement with learning activities. In this regard, the ability of the institution, and more precisely the teaching staff, to build personal relationships with vulnerable students from the beginning of their university pathways plays a very important role in ensuring that this affiliation link is established and nurtured, thereby preventing disaffection and drop-out (Schömer, 2014).

Building a peer group support culture among students is also an important component of this process. Students from under-represented groups especially benefit from being in contact with and getting information and guidance from other students, as it increases their opportunities to feel integrated into the HE environment and to acquire deeper knowledge of the university culture and rules (Clark et al., 2013; Latino & Unite, 2012). This opportunity is particularly relevant for students who come from families without an academic background, or those who cannot take part in formal activities such as study groups, student societies and sporting associations. Encouraging the establishment of informal connections and forms of cooperation greatly helps disadvantaged students perceive themselves as legitimate and active members of the academic community.

Even though these are less eye-catching, HE institutions' actions to promote systematic monitoring of learners' activities can play a significant role in helping vulnerable students to persist and succeed in their academic careers (Kristensen, 2010; Jarvis, 2014). While social integration and peer support programmes contribute to building a welcoming and supportive environment for all students from their enrolment onwards, monitoring specific aspects (such as attendance rates, exams passed and marks obtained) makes it easier to identify in advance students who will potentially be at risk and implement targeted supportive actions through personal mentoring, coaching and counselling activities. Nevertheless, effective monitoring implies developing a high level of coordination between academic staff, especially those directly involved in supporting student learning. Coordination is mandatory to ensure that all curriculum components (course objectives, teaching and learning practices, and examination and assessment activities) will be coherent and adequately aligned, as this aspect especially affects the retention and success of disadvantaged students.

Finally, among the various means of supporting the social dimension, financial support for vulnerable students undoubtedly plays a key role. The most widely used method to provide this for learners from a low socio-economic background are grants and scholarships established through public support schemes. They are generally provided on a universal or compensatory basis, and also, less frequently, based on meritocratic criteria (European Commission/EACEA/Eurydice, 2018c; Herbaut & Geven, 2019). In most European countries, financial aid is based conditionally on the social and economic profile of the students' family (income, size of the family unit, etc.). However, this approach excludes vulnerable students whose circumstances do not strictly fit the profile identified by the administration, as the universalistic scheme that is usually employed cannot target specific groups. Moreover, in many countries the portion of the budget that is allocated to this purpose does not suffice to ensure that all students who are formally entitled to receive financial support will obtain it. In addition, while grants guarantee that students will receive funding as a form of non-repayable support, some countries, such as the United Kingdom, Iceland, Norway and Sweden are gradually shifting to a system based on student loans. This involves the risk that students will relinquish the opportunity to enrol in HE to avoid the debt they could incur for several years after graduation.

A growing number of member states are enacting regulations that connect a share of academic sector funding to study performance. Accordingly, governments use the economic lever to pressure universities to pay more attention to student retention and graduation rates and, indirectly, to adopt policies that favour learners' success. As we have mentioned, this approach can have the unintended consequence of lowering the quality of the academic career. In fact, the risk is that ensuring wider access to HE could be achieved by massification, reducing university careers to an impoverished experience that leads to students acquiring inflated degrees. Conversely, effective inclusion in HE requires that student support services be available to all, through the provision of public funding, as this proves to be a major factor in reducing disparities related to the academic success of students from disadvantaged socio-economic backgrounds. Unfortunately, at present these services remain inadequately funded and supported in most European countries.

An evaluation of the above measures has illustrated that their effectiveness is limited if they are undertaken in the form of disconnected or temporary actions. Success in promoting the inclusion of under-represented students clearly requires a systemic and enduring approach. The evidence shows that the most effective programmes are based on a policy mix, which combines and complements several instruments that aim to foster academic integration and study completion for under-represented groups (Thomas, 2012). Actions aimed at clarifying and facilitating study options in terms of access, retention and progress need to be coupled with an effort to guarantee quality learning experiences, to support social integration in collaboration with academic staff and peers, as well as to provide suitable counselling services and monitoring programmes. All these activities should be interconnected and promoted consistently to ensure they have a positive impact on the way diversity is currently managed in HE, so that supporting under-represented groups can be seen as an important opportunity to improve education for all.

6   Access, Retention and Success

Most EU policies regarding the achievement of wider and more equitable participation in HE focus on reducing barriers that hinder access to tertiary education. However, although facilitating take-up among under-represented students is a pivotal element of fostering the social dimension, its actual effectiveness relies on the way those policies are embedded in a more comprehensive approach concerning inclusion in HE. Research emphasises that students from underprivileged groups usually opt for part-time education programmes, as well as for shorter and less creditable degrees that provide fewer opportunities in relation to future employment or opportunities to pursue further third-level education education (Belfield et al., 2018; Jerrim & Vignoles, 2015; Koucký & Bartušek, 2013). This phenomenon is especially evident in countries where, as a result of the Bologna Process, the increasing number of students enrolling in tertiary education has been managed through the creation of a more stratified HE structure, often diversified into research universities, university colleges, and short-cycle colleges. Data show that colleges usually enrol the largest share of young people from disadvantaged backgrounds, while fewer students are able to access and, above all, complete their studies at research universities (Arum et al., 2012; Cahalan et al., 2019; Santiago et al., 2008). This indirect selection mechanism favours the reproduction of the existing imbalance in terms of educational and working opportunities and, in turn, social disparities. Consequently, an inclusive approach to HE requires a more precise focus on rebalancing the opportunities for disadvantaged students not only to be admitted to more prestigious universities, but also to strengthen their retention and success rates through adequate support from these institutions.

Non-completion of HE has a strong impact both on the educational system and students' lives. On the one hand, it is a drain on valuable public finance and resources. On the other hand, it both prevents students from acquiring a better social and economic position and damages the way young people perceive themselves as competent learners and individuals. Student drop-out in HE has been examined in relation to a number of specific socio-cultural, structural, policy, institutional, personal, and learning factors (European Commission/ EACEA/Eurydice, 2015; Quinn, 2013). Even though they all have a different role and weight in the process of dropping out, the decision to withdraw is usually the result of a combination of elements, which are strictly interconnected and should be considered from a holistic perspective (Chen, 2012). In this regard, we can broadly differentiate between individual and structural factors. The former include students' financial obligations, health problems, family reasons, and a mismatch with the programme or study subject selected. Structural factors relate to the institutions' inability to implement effective measures to address the needs of students from a disadvantaged background, who are especially at risk during the first year of their academic path.

Structural factors are frequently linked to the lack of efficient tracking procedures concerning students' early leaving. While institutional strategies issued by European universities regularly mention the need to ensure retention and that students complete their academic careers, policy documents rarely specify what the desired retention rates are in terms of explicit and specific targets. Completion and drop-out rates are therefore not consistently monitored or quantified. Even universities that put in place actions to strengthen student retention and completion lack a systematic analysis of the profiles and characteristics of at-risk learners, as well as of the effectiveness of policies for reducing non-completion rates (Carlhed, 2017). When data on retention and completion are included in quality assurance processes (often as a part of performance-based funding mechanisms), they are prevalently considered in terms of statistics and analysed through indicators that help assess institutional viability and programme effectiveness. Conversely, the same information is seldom used to complete a more detailed examination of the reasons why students drop out of HE, or to outline possible strategies for preventing early leaving (European Commission/EACEA/Eurydice, 2018a; Mountford-Zimdars & Harrison, 2016).

Many academic institutions have undertaken initiatives to stimulate students to complete their studies within the set period of time through a system of incentives and/or sanctions. Moreover, most universities offer information, advice and guidance services, especially for learners deemed more 'at risk' of dropping out. However, only a few countries have implemented structured and systematic prevention actions in the form of counselling, additional funding, peer and social support groups, and flexible learning tracks. Yet, surveys indicate that those actions are not adequately designed and funded to meet growing demand from students, and especially to specifically address under-represented groups (ESU, 2019a).

Students' success in HE is also a problematic topic to investigate, as the way this construct is conceived differs across European countries. Depending on the member state, estimates of study completion rates can include the time stipulated to achieve a degree, as well as a calculation of the retention or drop-out percentages. Therefore, national indicators of student success vary, as some countries take into account the prescribed study period plus one extra year, while others prefer to prioritise retention and drop-out rates during the first academic year. Moreover, some researchers criticise the common assumption that participation in HE is always beneficial in terms of students' quality of life and future opportunities (Corliss et al., 2020; Walker & Fongwa, 2017). Graduates from certain areas may find it more difficult to get a job in line with their level of education. In addition, they may be entrusted with the same responsibilities as those with a secondary school diploma, but at a lower salary due to their delay in joining the workforce (Souto-Otero & Whitworth, 2017). While it is widely recognised that in the long term getting a degree usually helps individuals improve their economic and social status, this is not true for all students, especially for those from a disadvantaged background, whose options are more limited. Consequently, the completion of studies cannot be linked to an automatic reduction in the social or economic stratification of the population (MacMillan et al., 2014).

7 Comparing the Social Dimension in Europe

The Bologna Process is the attempt to create a European Higher Education Area as a common framework developed by member states through structural reforms and shared tools regarding the various dimensions of HE. Comparing national policies and academic structures to harmonise the activities involved in tertiary education as much as possible has been an important part of this process. However, the analysis of the social dimension poses some specific challenges to this comparison exercise (Bleiklie & Michelsen, 2013; Curaj et al., 2015). On the one hand, while other dimensions, such as the recognition of qualifications and credits throughout the EHEA are only moderately influenced by the socio-economic and cultural context of each country, the role that specific local and national factors play in identifying and promoting under-represented groups in HE is pivotal. On the other hand, the effort to foster a European agenda to improve equity in HE has clear implications for political decision-making, concerning the measures that should be adopted to facilitate academic access and the success of young people from disadvantaged backgrounds.

Over the years, the examination of the dynamics of the social dimension has mostly been based on quantitative approaches that aimed to classify and measure the evolution of the university system with regard to the inclusion of an increasing population of diverse learners. This classification gave rise to the concept of "non-traditional students", as a generic label encompassing a large number of students with heterogeneous characteristics who shared the condition of being vulnerable or at risk regarding their opportunities to attend and conclude post-secondary studies. This analysis produced a valuable set of quantitative data that helped to define the disadvantaged groups more clearly – in terms of age, gender, ability, socio-economic background and ethnic origins – as well as their potential needs and paths in HE (Curaj et al., 2018; Finnegan, 2014). Nevertheless, this description, provided by data collected at the national level, has increasingly revealed its limitations in terms of providing an in-depth understanding of the current state of the social dimension from a European perspective. Comparisons built on broad categories, such as "non-traditional students" have been able to offer only an initial representation of the phenomenon, whose complexity is reflected in the multiplicity of categories used in each country to define this large and heterogeneous group of learners (Crozier et al., 2008; EUA, 2019).

In this regard, research faces several equally important problems. Firstly, although the goal of promoting the social dimension is to help universities to reflect the whole range of diversity of Europe's population (EHEA, 2012), most of the data mainly focus on disadvantaged students who enrol in HE. Consequently, we have much less information on the potential students who turn down this opportunity, and the reasons why they take different courses of action. Therefore, the available knowledge is disproportionally concentrated on the side of the equation concerning the individuals who have already been persuaded to enter HE, whereas it would be equally (or even more) important to delve into the motivations of those who dismiss this option. Secondly, HE surveys usually provide us with a snapshot of students' careers at different points in time (access, progress, completion). However, far less information is available regarding the mechanism and dynamics that ensure some universities do better than others in fostering student retention and success. Positive results in favouring the inclusion of under-represented students are rarely supported by evidence concerning the adoption of organisational or pedagogical strategies. Hence, the institutional activity related to promoting the social dimension is often regarded as a "black box", without a clear connection between input and output. Finally, as data collection mostly focuses on the academic careers of students as individuals, we lack comparative research on the role that institutional policies in Europe play in helping students – especially those from a disadvantaged background – to achieve academic success. Information on retention and completion rates in European countries, as well as the drop-out level and the average time to graduation, is scarce and heterogeneous. Whereas international inquiries, like the OECD survey "Education at a Glance", at first sight may indicate that these dimensions are consistently parallel across HE systems at the global level, a closer look shows that these exercises should be regarded with caution, due to the different ways the related indicators are designed and used in most of the countries considered (OECD, 2019).

However, it should be noted that the variety of indicators is also a direct expression of the cultural and organisational peculiarities of the HE structures in each European country. Since the beginning, the impulse towards unification initiated by the Bologna Process has dealt with evidence that the social dimension is definitely less standardisable than academic credits, since questions related to the national (and sometimes local) specific features of tertiary education are highly relevant in this respect. In view of this complexity, the European Union, after acknowledging the principle of promoting the participation of under-represented students in HE, has wisely adopted a liberal approach to the question, by leaving member states free to determine what groups and measures should be targeted in relation to the national context. Nevertheless, this autonomy has not been complemented with a similar effort to gradually integrate and align the multiplicity of local strategies brought about to improve equity in HE by promoting transnational policy learning across Europe. Accordingly, the story of developing the social dimension in the European Union clearly shows that ensuring respect for diversity is only the first step in the process of inclusion, which also requires managing differences and putting them into practice through cooperation.

In this regard, the emphasis that the Lisbon Strategy, concurrently with the Bologna Process, has placed on strengthening the measurement of European indicators regarding education has mostly been a missed opportunity regarding the social dimension of HE. Certainly, the purpose of the strategy of monitoring the impact of actions undertaken to promote and improve the quality of tertiary education in Europe is commendable. In theory, it would be helpful to not only support effective practices, but also discover underestimated problems related to students' experiences in HE. However, this emphasis on measurement as a synonym for improving quality has contributed to diverting attention from the central question of fostering access and success for disadvantaged students, as the level of complexity involved in quantifying the manifold aspects and local variations of the social dimension has proved to be especially challenging (Daly, 2008; Holford, 2008). Following the Lisbon Strategy, most European countries have implemented monitoring systems that aim to examine the distinctive attributes of the HE student population in terms of age, gender, social and economic background, and so on. Reports that are regularly published at the national level provide an analysis of the profiles and learning paths of students in connection with their academic performances.

Nevertheless, the impact of actions taken to tackle exclusion from HE is not assessed systematically in every member state. Moreover, even when it is, the information offered rarely goes beyond a simple description of the variety of measures undertaken, let alone providing a detailed account of their efficacy. Even when national governments, such as the Flemish Community in Belgium, have created steering mechanisms by setting targets in relation to specific vulnerable groups, the outcomes are evaluated more in terms of efficiency that effectiveness (Haezendonck et al., 2017).

Furthermore, a large part of the monitoring system developed by countries relies on the activity of quality assurance agencies, which do not analyse the way admission procedures affect students according to their different backgrounds or features. Nor do the agencies delve into the strategies adopted by HE institutions to guarantee access and success for disadvantaged students, but simply verify that the admission process matches the programme requirements, as defined by the institution. This question also concerns the small number of member states that have created alternative entry routes to encourage access to HE for under-represented students. Moreover, only a few countries have put in place and made public a tracking system of national indicators concerning the completion and average time to graduation, as well as the monitoring of measures to prevent students dropping out of HE (ESU, 2018). Finally, the monitoring activity often lacks information (or collects only very poor information) on important aspects concerning student diversity, e.g. the socio-economic or ethnic backgrounds of learners, or their occupational status prior to entry into tertiary education. Due to this lack of data, actions taken to promote the participation of under-represented students cannot be evaluated systematically and, as a result, further sustained and disseminated.

Recent reports on the social dimension support this view, indicating that 27 of the 48 member states participating in the EHEA have not yet defined national targets regarding under-represented groups, while less than 20% have so far identified quantitative targets (European Commission, 2019; European Commission/EACEA/Eurydice (2018a). Instead of specifying clear-cut objectives and benchmarks, European countries usually prefer to promote initiatives aimed at encouraging overall student participation in HE, assuming that this general strategy will also help include young people from disadvantaged backgrounds. Nevertheless, in the last few years a few countries have been able to create compelling policies that target specific under-represented groups. Ireland, for example, set specific objectives regarding mature learners, young people with disabilities, and students from disadvantaged socio-economic groups. Between 2015 and 2019, the Flemish Community in Belgium has focused on enrolling first-generation students whose parents do not have a HE degree. Over the same period of time, Finland put in place specific measures to reduce the gender gap by favouring male participation in HE, while Lithuania aimed to rebalance the same gap by encouraging female students to pursue a career in the STEM sectors.

Overall, while the decision-making processes of governments and institutions concerning HE over the last few years have been increasingly connected to information provided by monitoring systems, the social dimension has progressively been left out of this process. This can be partly explained by the complexity of gathering, analysing and comparing the multiple facets of under-representation in HE. However, the recurring plea to acquire more data regarding this question can also be interpreted as a way of postponing (or worse, covertly dismissing) the adoption of appropriate measures in favour of this large population of students (Kajser et al., 2015). Although the collection and analysis of data are not carried out as systematically as might be hoped for, the information that is already available clearly indicates that investments made in programmes that aim to widen participation in HE remain inadequate. Getting and comparing data from across Europe more precisely would help clarify how much stronger a commitment from EU governments and institutions is required to fill the huge gap between repeated declarations on equity in HE and interventions that are actually put in place to achieve it. Evidently, this is not just a technical question, as it involves taking a clear political stance and, consequently, concrete actions towards inclusion in HE. However, this would interfere with the neoliberal trend currently spreading in Europe and beyond, in which tertiary education plays a crucial role in determining the reproduction of the existing socio-economic stratification (Marginson, 2016; Olssen, 2016; Raaper, 2016).

8 Conclusions

Over the last twenty years, promoting the participation of disadvantaged students in HE has been an important goal of the Bologna Process. However, nowadays the objective of creating a more inclusive university environment, in which the diversity of the population is actually reflected by the student body, is far from being achieved. The situation has only improved slightly with regard to young people from a low socio-economic background being able to access HE, opportunities being created for mature students to get degrees through flexible study arrangements, as well as the need to reduce the gender gap in tertiary education, both as a whole and in relation to some scientific areas. Other important questions, such as, for example, widening access for students from a migrant background or the recognition of prior non-formal and informal learning, are still largely overlooked by policies concerning HE (European Commission, 2019).

Investments in the development of the social dimension have been hindered by funding cuts that have affected the university sector, especially following the 2008 economic crisis. In an era of scarcity, the quest for equity has been replaced rapidly by an elitist narrative of HE based on competition and ranking, which has dismissed most of the demands made to fulfil more equitable conditions in tertiary education (Locke, 2014; Hazelkorn, 2015). To help re-centre the inclusion of disadvantaged students in the debate on the HE we want in Europe, it is paramount that we clarify what specific goals and concrete measures member states should focus on to set a possible agenda for the future. To this end, four main themes emerge from the research as deserving special attention.

Firstly, the approaches that have proven most effective in strengthening opportunities for inclusion for under-represented students are those based on comprehensive strategies aimed at identifying and removing barriers to participation in HE. These strategies bring about policies that integrate various areas of intervention (information, finance, organisation and pedagogy) and promote positive change both at the institutional and at the student levels. Moreover, effective strategies can link this with the overall process of modernisation of HE in Europe, e.g. quality assurance procedures and the dissemination of good practices to a wider audience. This would help identify the patterns that favour the sustainability of successful policies and practices regarding inclusion in tertiary education.

Secondly, the recognition that different national conditions and cultural variations exist in Europe should not be a hindrance to finding an agreement on a core set of definitions and benchmarks that would improve the collection and comparison of information about the social dimension in the EHEA. In this regard, member states must make an effort to further clarify the criteria and priorities of policies concerning HE participation for students from disadvantaged backgrounds, by also developing national access plans devised for this purpose.

Thirdly, actions to generate inclusion should track students' academic paths more accurately. Evidence from several universities across Europe indicates that this monitoring activity plays a key role in identifying and preventing under-represented students from dropping out. Moreover, monitoring has proved to be especially effective in promoting the success of vulnerable students when combined with specific programmes that provide regular counselling, mentoring and peer support activities.

Fourthly, student tracking should be part of a wider and stable system of indicators that would enable member states to collect and analyse critical data regarding the study path of disadvantaged students. These indicators should help not only to take stock of the progress students make and the milestones they reach, in terms of access, retention, time-to-degree and completion, but also to understand what factors are responsible for effectively preventing dropout and promoting the success of under-represented students in HE.

Finally, this interpretative process should be connected to a general effort made by EU governments and academic institutions to provide more transparent access to information, as a way of fostering the critical debate on policies concerning equity in HE. Indicators related to social dimensions should regularly be included in institutional strategic plans, as well as analysed and popularised both at the institutional and national levels. This would promote a culture of accountability for governments and HE institutions that, in turn, would enable disadvantaged students to determine and maximise their academic options. Furthermore, it would help to recognise the participation of under-represented groups in HE not only as a question of equity, but also as a valuable resource for strengthening the role of European universities as democratic institutions.

Acknowledgement

This document has been produced as a part of the project "ACCESS4ALL – Laboratory for Policies and Practices of Social Development in Higher Education" (Ref. 2015-1-ES01-KA203-015970) co-funded by the European Union (Erasmus+ Programme).

References

Allmendinger, J. (2016). Good and bad education systems: Is there an ideal? In A. Hadjar & C. Gross (Eds.), *Education systems and inequalities* (pp. 321–334). Policy Press.

Antonucci, L. (2016). *Student lives in crisis: Deepening inequality in times of austerity*. Policy Press.

Archer, L., & Hutchings, M. (2000). "Bettering yourself": Discourses of risk, cost and benefit in ethnically diverse, young working-class non-participants' constructions of higher education. *British Journal of Sociology of Education, 21*(4), 555–574.

Arum, R., Gamoran, A., & Shavit, Y. (2012). Expanded opportunities for all in global higher education systems. In L. Weiss & N. Dolby (Eds.), *Social class and education* (pp. 15–36). Routledge.

Auzinger, M., Fellinger, J., Luomi-Messerer, K., Mobilio, L., Ulicna, D., & Zaidi, A. (2016). *Study on international sectoral qualifications frameworks and systems*. Publications Office of the European Union.

Banerjee, P. A. (2018). Widening participation in higher education with a view to implementing institutional change. *Perspectives: Policy and Practice in Higher Education, 22*(3), 75–81.

Barone, C. (2011). Some things never change: Gender segregation in higher education across eight nations and three decades. *Sociology of Education, 84*(2), 157–176.

Belfield, C., Britton, J., Buscha, F., Dearden, L., Dickson, M., Van Der Erve, L., Sibieta, L., Vignoles, A., Walker, I., & Zhu, Y. (2018). *The relative labour market returns to different degrees*. Research report, June 2018. https://dera.ioe.ac.uk/33025/1/The_relative_labour_market-returns_to_different_degrees.pdf

Bleiklie, I., & Michelsen, S. (2013). Comparing HE policies in Europe. *Higher Education, 65*(1), 113–133.

Brennan, J. (2018). The social dimension of higher education: Reproductive and transformative. In *Handbook on the politics of higher education*. Edward Elgar Publishing.

Brooks, R. (2012). Student-parents and higher education: A cross-national comparison. *Journal of Education Policy, 27*(3), 423–439.

Cahalan, M., Perna, L. W., Yamashita, M., Wright-Kim, J., & Jiang, N. (2019). *Indicators of higher education equity in the United States: 2019 historical trend report*. Pell Institute for the Study of Opportunity in Higher Education. https://vtechworks.lib.vt.edu/handle/10919/96092

Carlhed, C. (2017). Resistances to scientific knowledge production of comparative measurements of dropout and completion in European higher education. *European Educational Research Journal, 16*(4), 386–406.

Chen, R. (2012). Institutional characteristics and college student drop-out risks: A multilevel event history analysis. *Research in Higher Education, 53*, 487–505.

Clark, R., Andrews, J., & Gorman, P. (2013). Tackling transition: The value of peer mentoring. *Widening Participation and Lifelong Learning, 14*(1), 57–75.

Corliss, M., Daly, A., & Lewis, P. (2020). Is a university degree still a worthwhile financial investment in Australia? *Australian Journal of Education, 64*(1), 73–90.

Croll, P., & Attwood, G. (2013). Participation in higher education: Aspirations, attainment and social background. *British Journal of Educational Studies, 61*(2), 187–202.

Crosier, D., & Parveva, T. (2013). *The Bologna process: Its impact in Europe and beyond*. UNESCO.

Crozier, G., Reay, D., Clayton, J., Colliander, L., & Grinstead, J. (2008). Different strokes for different folks: Diverse students in diverse institutions–experiences of higher education. *Research Papers in Education, 23*(2), 167–177.

Curaj, A., Deca, L., & Pricopie, R. (Eds.). (2018). *European higher education area: The impact of past and future policies.* Springer.

Curaj, A., Matei, L., Pricopie, R., Salmi, J., & Scott, P. (Eds.). (2015). *The European higher education area: Between critical reflections and future policies.* Springer.

Curaj, A., Scott, P., Vlasceanu, L., & Wilson, L. (Eds.). (2012). *European higher education at the crossroads: Between the Bologna process and national reforms.* Springer.

Cureton, D., & Gravestock, P. (2018). Supporting students' learning: The power of the student–teacher relationship. In M. Shah, A. Bennett, & E. Southgate (Eds.), *Widening higher education participation* (pp. 51–71). Palgrave Macmillan.

Daly, M. (2008). Whither EU social policy? An account and assessment of developments in the Lisbon social inclusion process. *Journal of Social Policy, 37*(1), 1–19.

Delanty, G. (2001). *Challenging knowledge: The university in the knowledge society.* Open University Press.

Dupriez, V., Dumay, X., & Vause, A. (2008). How do school systems manage pupils' heterogeneity? *Comparative Education Review, 52*(2), 245–273.

Duru-Bellat, M., Kieffer, A., & Reimer, D. (2008). Patterns of social inequalities in access to higher education in France and Germany. *International Journal of Comparative Sociology, 49*(4–5), 347–368.

EHEA. (2012). *Making the most of our potential: Consolidating the European Higher Education Area.* EHEA. http://www.ehea.info/Upload/document/ministerial_declarations/Bucharest_Communique_2012_610673.pdf

EHEA. (2015a). *Widening participation for equity and Growth. A strategy for the development of the social dimension and lifelong learning in the European Higher Education Area to 2020.* Author. http://www.ehea.info/media.ehea.info/file/2015_Yerevan/71/5/Widening_Participation_for_Equity_and_Growth_A_Strategy_for_the_Development_of_the_SD_and_LLL_in_the_EHEA_to_2020_613715.pdf

EHEA. (2015b). *Report of the 2012–2015 BFUG working group on the social dimension and lifelong learning.* Author. http://www.ehea.info/media.ehea.info/file/2015_Yerevan/71/3/Report_of_the_2012-2015_BFUG_WG_on_the_Social_Dimension_and_Lifelong_Learning_to_the_BFUG_613713.pdf

ESU. (2019a). *Bologna with student eyes 2018: The final countdown.* Author.

ESU. (2019b). *Social dimension policy paper 2019.* Author.

EUA. (2019). *Diversity, equity and inclusion in European higher education institutions.* Author. https://eua.eu/downloads/publications/web_diversity%20equity%20and%20inclusion%20in%20european%20higher%20education%20institutions.pdf

European Commission. (2015). *Dropout and completion in higher education in Europe: Main report.* Publications Office of the European Union.

European Commission. (2019). *Education and training monitor 2019.* Publications Office of the European Union.

European Commission/EACEA/Eurydice. (2015). *The European higher education area in 2015: Bologna process implementation report*. Publications Office of the European Union.

European Commission/EACEA/Eurydice. (2017). *Modernisation of higher education in Europe: Academic staff – 2017 Eurydice report*. Publications Office of the European Union.

European Commission/EACEA/Eurydice. (2018a). *The European Higher Education Area in 2018: Bologna process implementation report*. Publications Office of the European Union.

European Commission/EACEA/Eurydice. (2018b). *Structural indicators for monitoring education and training systems in Europe – 2018*. Eurydice report. Publications Office of the European Union.

European Commission/EACEA/Eurydice. (2018c). *National student fee and support systems in European higher education – 2018/19. Eurydice – Facts and figures*. Publications Office of the European Union.

European Commission/Education, Audiovisual and Culture Executive Agency/Eurydice. (2014). *Modernisation of higher education in Europe: Access, retention and employability 2014*. Publications Office of the European Union. http://commit.eucen.eu/sites/commit.eucen.eu/files/Eurydice_AccRetEmpl_May2014_165EN.pdf

Eurostudent. (2016). *Delayed entry into higher education*. Author. https://www.eurostudent.eu/download_files/documents/IB_delayed_transition.pdf

Eurostudent. (2018). *Social and economic conditions of student life in Europe: EUROSTUDENT VI 2016–2018: Synopsis of indicators*. W. Bertelsmann Verlag.

Eurostudent. (2019). *The plurality of transitions into and within higher education*. Author. https://www.eurostudent.eu/download_files/documents/EUROSTUDENT_INTELLIGENCE_BRIEF_32019.pdf

Eurydice. (2011). *Modernization of higher education in Europe: Funding and the social dimension*. EACEA.

Finnegan, F., Merrill, B., & Thunborg, C. (Eds.). (2014). *Student voices on inequalities in European higher education: Challenges for theory, policy and practice in a time of change*. Routledge.

Griga, D., & Hadjar, A. (2014). Migrant background and higher education participation in Europe: The effect of the educational systems. *European Sociological Review, 30*(3), 275–286.

Haezendonck, E., Willems, K., & Hillemann, J. (2017). Doing good while performing well at Flemish universities: Benchmarking higher education institutions in terms of social inclusion and market performance. *International Journal of Inclusive Education, 21*(1), 31–47.

Hargreaves, A. (2003). *Teaching in the knowledge society: Education in the age of insecurity*. Teachers College Press.

Harwood, V., Hickey-Moody, A., McMahon, S., & O'Shea, S. (2016). *The politics of widening participation and university access for young people: Making educational futures.* Taylor & Francis.

Hazelkorn, E. (2015). *Rankings and the reshaping of higher education: The battle for world-class excellence.* Springer.

Herbaut, E., & Geven, K. M. (2019). *What works to reduce inequalities in Higher Education? A systematic review of the (quasi-)experimental literature on outreach and financial aid.* The World Bank. http://documents.worldbank.org/curated/en/650601554221255443/pdf/What-Works-to-Reduce-Inequalities-in-Higher-Education-A-Systematic-Review-of-the-Quasi-Experimental-Literature-on-Outreach-and-Financial-Aid.pdf

Hinton-Smith, T. (Ed.). (2012). *Widening participation in higher education: Casting the net wide?* Palgrave Macmillan.

Hoffman, M., Richmond, J., Morrow, J., & Salomone, K. (2002). Investigating "sense of belonging" in first-year college students. *Journal of College Student Retention: Research, Theory & Practice, 4*(3), 227–256.

Holford, J. (2014). The lost honour of the social dimension: Bologna, exports and the idea of the university. *International Journal of Lifelong Education, 33*(1), 7–25.

Holmegaard, H. T., Madsen, L. M., & Ulriksen, L. (2017). Why should European higher education care about the retention of non-traditional students? *European Educational Research Journal, 16*(1), 3–11.

Kaiser, F., Maoláin, A. Ó., & Vikmane, L. (2015). No future for the social dimension? In A., Curaj, L., Matei, R., Pricopie, J., Salmi, & P., Scott (Eds.), *The European higher education area: Between critical reflections and future policies* (pp. 449–466). Springer.

Kenny, A., Fleming, T., Loxley, A., & Finnegan, F. (2010). *Where next? A study of work and life experiences of mature students (incl. disadvantaged) in three higher education institutions* (Combat Poverty Agency, Working Paper 10/02). Ireland. https://arrow.tudublin.ie/cgi/viewcontent.cgi?article=1043&context=beschreoth

Koucký, J., & Bartušek, A. (2013). *Access to a degree in Europe. Inequality in tertiary education attainment 1950–2011* (Working paper). Education Policy Centre – Charles University in Prague. https://pdfs.semanticscholar.org/7e17/dc0aa5d2641339bf64442bde06f0846c6ec0.pdf?_ga=2.104037440.1137904621.1587373360-892996249.1587025948

Kreissl, K., Striedinger, A., Sauer, B., & Hofbauer, J. (2015). Will gender equality ever fit in? Contested discursive spaces of university reform. *Gender and Education, 27*(3), 221–238.

Kristensen, B. (2010). Has external quality assurance actually improved quality in higher education over the course of 20 years of the 'quality revolution'? *Quality in Higher Education, 16*(2), 153–157.

Jarvis, D. S. (2014). Regulating higher education: Quality assurance and neo-liberal managerialism in higher education – A critical introduction. *Policy and Society, 33*(3), 155–166.

Jerrim, J., & Vignoles, A. (2015). University access for disadvantaged children: A comparison across countries. *Higher Education, 70*, 903–921.

Johnson, D. R., Soldner, M., Leonard, J. B., Alvarez, P., Inkelas, K. K., Rowan-Kenyon, H.T., & Longerbeam, S. D. (2007). Examining sense of belonging among first-year undergraduates from different racial/ethnic groups. *Journal of College Student Development, 48*(5), 525–542.

Latino, J. A., & Unite, C. M. (2012). Providing academic support through peer education. *New Directions for Higher Education, 157*(2012), 31–43.

Łibacka, K. (2015). *Follow-up on the implementation of the Bologna process*. European Parliament. Committee on Culture and Education.

Locke, W. (2014). The intensification of rankings logic in an increasingly marketised higher education environment. *European Journal of Education, 49*(1), 77–90.

Macmillan, L., Tyler, C., & Vignoles, A. (2014). Who gets the top jobs? The role of family background and networks in recent graduates' access to high-status professions. *Journal of Social Policy, 44*(3), 487–515.

Maher, F. A., & Tetreault, M. K. T. (2013). *Privilege and diversity in the academy*. Routledge.

Marginson, S. (2016). The worldwide trend to high participation higher education: Dynamics of social stratification in inclusive systems. *Higher Education, 72*(4), 413–434.

McGrath, C. H., Henham, M. L., Corbett, A., Durazzi, N., Frearson, M., Janta, B., Kamphuis, B. W., Katashiro, E., Brankovic, N., Guerin, B., Manville, C., Schwartz, I., & Schweppenstedde, D. (2014). *Higher education entrance qualifications and exams in Europe: A comparison*. European Union. https://www.rand.org/pubs/research_reports/RR574.html

Ministerial Conference Bergen. (2005). *Communiqué. The European Higher Education Area. Achieving the goals*. EHEA. http://www.ehea.info/media.ehea.info/file/2005_Bergen/52/0/2005_Bergen_Communique_english_580520.pdf

Ministerial Conference London. (2007). *Communiqué. Towards the European Higher Education Area: Responding to challenges in a globalised world*. EHEA. http://www.ehea.info/media.ehea.info/file/2007_London/69/7/2007_London_Communique_English_588697.pdf

Ministerial Conference Prague. (2001). *Communiqué. Towards European Higher Education Area*. EHEA. http://www.ehea.info/media.ehea.info/file/2001_Prague/44/2/2001_Prague_Communique_English_553442.pdf

Ministerial Conference Yerevan. (2015). *Yerevan Communiqué*. EHEA. http://www.ehea.info/media.ehea.info/file/2015_Yerevan/70/7/YerevanCommuniqueFinal_613707.pdf

Morley, L. (2013). The rules of the game: Women and the leaderist turn in higher education. *Gender and Education, 25*(1), 116–131.

Mountford-Zimdars, A., & Harrison, N. (Eds.). (2016). *Access to higher education: Theoretical perspectives and contemporary challenges*. Taylor & Francis.

OECD. (2019). *Education at a glance 2019: OECD indicators*. Author.

Olssen, M., & Peters, M. A. (2005). Neoliberalism, higher education and the knowledge economy: From the free market to knowledge capitalism. *Journal of Education Policy, 20*(3), 313–345.

Olssen, M. (2016). Neoliberal competition in higher education today: Research, accountability and impact. *British Journal of Sociology of Education, 37*(1), 129–148.

Orr, D., Usher, A., Haj, C., Atherton, G., & Geanta, I. (2017). *Study on the impact of admission systems on higher education outcomes*. Final report. European Commission.

O'Shea, S., Lysaght, P., Roberts, J., & Harwood, V. (2016). Shifting the blame in higher education–social inclusion and deficit discourses. *Higher Education Research & Development, 35*(2), 322–336.

Quinn, J. (2013). *Drop-out and completion in higher education in Europe among students from under-represented groups. An independent report authored for the European Commission*. NESET, European Commission.

Raaper, R. (2016). Academic perceptions of higher education assessment processes in neoliberal academia. *Critical Studies in Education, 57*(2), 175–190.

Reay, D., David, M. E., & Ball, S. J. (2005). *Degrees of choice: Class, race, gender and higher education*. Trentham Books.

Riddell, S., Tinklin, T., & Wilson, A. (2005). *Disabled students in higher education: Perspectives on widening access and changing policy*. Routledge.

Riddell, S., & Weedon, E. (2014). European higher education, the inclusion of students from under-represented groups and the Bologna Process. *International Journal of Lifelong Education, 33*(1), 26–44.

Rodríguez-Gómez, D., Gairín, J., Dovigo, F., Clements, K., Jerónimo, M., Lucas, L., Marin, E., Mehtala, S., Pinheiro, F. P., Timmis, S., & Stîngu, M. (2019). Access4All: Policies and practices of social development in higher education. In J. Hoffman, P. Blessinger, & M. Makhanya (Eds.), *Strategies for facilitating inclusive campuses in higher education: International perspectives on equity and inclusion* (pp. 55–69). Emerald Publishing Limited.

Santiago, P., Tremblay, K., Basri, E., & Amal, E. (Eds.). (2008). *Tertiary education for the knowledge society. Special features: Equity, innovation, labour market, internationalisation* (Vol. 2). http://www.oecd.org/education/skills-beyond-school/41266759.pdf

Schaeper, H. (2020). The first year in higher education: The role of individual factors and the learning environment for academic integration. *Higher Education, 79*(1), 95–110.

Schömer, F. (2014). Non-traditional students and barriers to participation in German universities. Student voices on inequalities in European higher education. Challenges for theory, policy and practice in a time of change. In F. Finnegan, B. Merrill, & C. Thunborg (Eds.), *Student voices on inequalities in European higher education: Challenges for theory, policy and practice in a time of change* (pp. 86–97). Routledge.

Souto-Otero, M., & Whitworth, A. (2017). Adult participation in higher education and the 'knowledge economy': A cross-national analysis of patterns of delayed participation in higher education across 15 European countries. *British Journal of Sociology of Education, 38*(6), 763–781.

Thomas, L. (2012). Building student engagement and belonging in higher education at a time of change. *Paul Hamlyn Foundation, 100*, 1–99.

Triventi, M. (2013). Stratification in higher education and its relationship with social inequality: A comparative study of 11 European countries. *European Sociological Review, 29*(3), 489–502.

Tupan-Wenno, M., Camilleri, A. F., Fröhlich, M., & King, S. (2016). *Effective approaches to enhancing the social dimension of higher education*. The IDEAS Consortium.

Usher, A. (2015). Equity and the social dimension: An overview. In A. Curaj, L. Matei, R. Pricopie, J. Salmi, & P. Scott (Eds.), *The European higher education area: Between critical reflections and future policies* (pp. 433–447). Springer.

Vignoles, A., & Murray, N. (2016). Widening participation in higher education. *Education Sciences, 6*(2), 13–16.

Walker, M., & Fongwa, S. (2017). *Universities, employability and human development*. Springer.

Weedon, E., & Riddell, S. (2016). Higher education in Europe: Widening participation. In M. Shah, A. Bennett, & E. Southgate (Eds.), *Widening higher education participation* (pp. 49–61). Chandos Publishing.

PART 2

Fostering Good Practices for Inclusion

∴

CHAPTER 3

Good Practices and Experiences for Inclusion in Finland

Saana Mehtälä, Kati Clements and Tiina Mäkelä

Abstract

This chapter presents inclusion practices and their state in a Finnish higher education institution. First, six good practices of inclusion that are used in the university are presented. These include, for example, practices that promote accessible education as well as the physical and mental health of all students. The goal of this section is to provide an overall picture and present different perspectives of the work that has been conducted at the HEI in collaboration with various internal and external stakeholders. Second, the inclusion self-assessment tool created by ACCESS4ALL project is briefly introduced together with the results received by the university on their self-evaluation through the tool. The results suggest that there is a need for better integration of inclusion practices to the daily life of staff and students. Finally, the possible future actions to promote inclusion in Finnish HEIs, such as student involvement, are discussed.

Keywords

good practices – inclusion – Finland – self-assessment – accessibility – mental health – physical health

1   Introduction

In Finland, the Ministry of Education and Culture sector numbers fourteen universities today. Two of them are foundation universities, while the rest are public corporations. The National Defence University, a military institution of higher education that is part of the Defence Forces, also provides university-level education. From the beginning of 2010, universities have had the status of independent legal entities and been separated from the state. However, the state continues to be the primary financier of the universities. Direct government funding covers an approximate of 64% of university budgets. In addition, universities are encouraged to acquire private donations. Moreover, there are twenty-four polytechnics (University of Applied Sciences, UAS) in the Finnish Ministry of Education and Culture sector. From the beginning of the year 2015 they have had the status of independent legal entities and operate as limited companies. The State is the primary financier of the polytechnics. Furthermore, two other higher education institutions, the Åland University of Applied Sciences in the self-governing Province of Åland and the Police College of Finland, are subordinate to the Ministry of the Interior. The steering of polytechnics based on financing and statutes, as well as operating licenses, has been renewed through the polytechnics reform. The final part of the reform took effect from the beginning of 2015.

University education in Finland is divided into twenty fields of study: Agriculture and Forestry, Art and Design, Dentistry, Economics, Educational Sciences, Engineering and Architecture, Fine Arts, Health Sciences, Humanities, Law, Medicine, Music, Natural Sciences, Pharmacy, Psychology, Social Sciences, Sport Sciences, Theatre and Dance, Theology, and Veterinary Medicine. Polytechnic education is provided in the following fields: Business and Administration, Culture, Humanities and Education, Natural Resources and the Environment, Natural Sciences, Social Sciences, Social Services, Health and Sport, Technology, Communication and Transport, and Tourism, Catering and Domestic Services. First cycle programs are offered both by universities and by polytechnics. The extent of a university Bachelor's level degree is 180 ECTS credits and takes three years. The extent of a Polytechnic Bachelor's degree is generally 210–240 ECTS credits, which means 3.5–4 years of full-time study. The extra 30–60 ECTS credits in the Polytechnic degree come from a job placement period, which is a mandatory part of the degree.

In comparison to many other countries, Finnish state provides lots of economical support for students in the high education. There are, however, challenges such as balancing work life and studies and feelings of loneliness and social exclusion to be tackled. Study Grant is a government financed benefit, which is paid to the student's bank account monthly. Students are eligible for the Study Grant only for the months when they study (when they gain about five ECTS credits per month). The amount is approximate €340 per month for most students. In addition, a student may be entitled to the Housing Supplement, which is maximum €200. Government also guarantees student loans up to €400 per month if certain conditions are met.

In this chapter, six good practices of inclusion are presented from Finnish Higher Education Institute, to provide both an overall picture and different perspectives of the work that has been conducted at the HEI in collaboration

GOOD PRACTICES AND EXPERIENCES FOR INCLUSION IN FINLAND 65

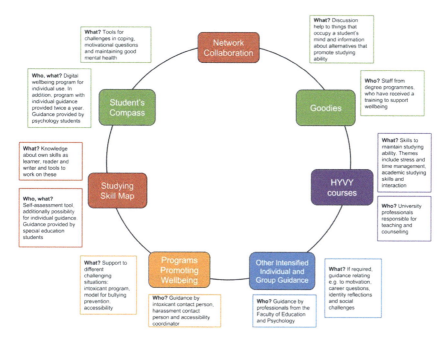

FIGURE 3.1   Student Life Support for Inclusion in Finnish HEI (Source: https://www.jyu.fi/studentlife)

with various internal and external stakeholders (see Figure 3.1). Information was collected either by asking people in charge of the practice to fill up the template or by interviewing them. Additionally, different documents were used as support materials for collecting information of the practices.

2   Good Practises from Finnish HEI – Six Cases

2.1   *Gender Equality*

The mission of the faculty is to holistically integrate the perspectives of technology, information, organisations, business and people. In the recruitment phase, teams in charge of recruiting students (teachers, administrative staff and student ambassadors in the faculty) communicate studying opportunities by visiting schools and participating in student fairs and organising other events. The holistic mission is presented to upper secondary school students. The team questions, for example, ideas female students may have on IT as being separate from working with people. Studies on IT are presented broadly so that people, male and female, can find their own areas of interest within the human-computer interaction, which currently takes place in all sectors of society. In the selection process, unlike many other universities in Finland, the faculty does not only look for grades in science and math studies but considers aspirants' high grades in languages and any other subjects they excel in.

In the beginning of studies, there is 6-month period during which students, males and females alike are supported in integrating into the student community by means of various group-activities and events. During the studies, teachers invite ex-students (alumni) and other experts working in the IT sector to talk about their work. Both male and female representatives are selected. Both genders are invited to present in faculty events, seminars and celebrations. Specific events such as sauna nights with faculty women (students and staff) have also been organised.

The broad perspective of IT is brought up during the studies: Everyone, no matter of personal interests or gender-based preferences, can find something motivating in these studies. Instead of letting traditional gender boundaries influence their decisions, everyone is encouraged to make them based on their individual preferences. Female students are encouraged to take more part in the coding, designing and developing of IT. As additional support work, the faculty has also participated in projects such as a project for Understanding and Providing a Developmental Approach to Technology Education (UPDATE) aiming at examining why girls drop out from Technology Education at different stages of their education and create new educational practices to encourage them to continue with a technology-enhanced personal curriculum.

It has been more usual to have women highly represented in the faculty since the 1970's. Particularly in Masters' studies, there is a relatively high percentage (around 30%) of female students. However, the proportion of female students still varies between subjects. For example, having more female coders is a relatively new phenomenon. Since the definition of a broad faculty mission (approximately 5 years), more systematic work has been made in highlighting the importance of different and complementary perspectives in IT from all individuals representing both genders.

Similar practices can be scaled up or down. There may be, however, a need to better model these practices and be more systematic so as to assure the scalability. At this moment, practices are still more based on general culture and natural ways of working providing all participants with autonomy and trusting that they consider gender equity aspects in their individual practices.

In relation to the effectiveness of the practice, there are some statistics of student access and retention, which are used to evaluate the gender balance within the faculty. In addition, past projects such as UPDATE and students surveys have provided evaluation data. However, it should be noted that gender-issues have not been explicitly evaluated in these surveys. Open-ended questions give, nevertheless, students the opportunity to express concerns related to gender. However, no such issues have been expressed by the students.

While the proportion of female students is relatively high, the proportion of female faculty teachers and research professors is still quite low. Gender equity could still be better in these groups. Some practices such as considering not only math and science subjects but also other subjects within which aspirants excel, could be transferred to other faculties, institutions and societal contexts so as to foster diversity in IT students. The same principles of valuing differences can be applied to any issues related to equity. Transferring practices to other cultural contexts may be challenging as these practices reflect societal values related to gender equity and equity in general. Due to societal and cultural contexts, many things work automatically without a need to pay excessive attention to these issues. In other cultural contexts, there may be a need for a more systematic approach to these issues.

2.2   *Accessible Education*

In 2014, Rector's decision was made on the arrangement of accessible education. The purpose of the decision is to ensure that all the university practices and actions are conducted according to the national equality law (see Finlex, 2014). The responsibilities of the university include e.g. being able to offer every student the possibility to use the university's physical and ICT environments. In addition, the university needs to make sure that enough information is provided to staff and students to ensure accessibility. Faculties and departments are responsible for the equality of entrance examinations, accessibility of communication and learning materials and creating individual arrangements to students in collaboration with university services.

In the accessibility decision, roles have been defined for applicants and students as well. The applicant's responsibilities include informing the university about possible barriers and applying for individual arrangements for entrance examination if necessary. Similarly, every student is responsible for informing the university about possible barriers and applying for individual arrangements. This ensures that the exams and education correspond to the student's needs. Individual arrangements are especially important in the light of student rights, since individual arrangements are parallel to the reasonable adjustments presented in the national equality law. The neglect of the reasonable adjustments, in turn, is viewed as discrimination.

In the accessibility decision, accessibility is considered from the point of view of social, personal, physical, and ICT learning environments. Information is distributed through HEI website, including an online form to report possible barriers to accessibility. In the case there is either a permanent or a temporal need, all applicants and students at the Finnish HEI can apply for individual arrangements from University Services. Recommendations have been made to approximately 100 applicants and 50 students per academic year. Individual arrangements related to student admission and studies include, for example, assistive technology, individual guidance and study planning, expert interpreters or other personal assistants, additional time and breaks during the exams. To the extent permitted by the student, a person named by the head of the unit informs personnel about the arrangements in a centralised manner according to the agreement with the student.

The maturity level of the practice is yet initial but arrangements have been made to assure its implementation and continuity in a long run, for example, with the distribution of responsibilities between different stakeholders. At this time, arrangements are scaled up at the institutional level and scaled down at the level of individual units and people. Individual study arrangements have been further developed based on the practices at the University of Turku (Finland). Their transfer has thus already proved possible. Principles apply to all types of individual needs and can be applied to different types of target groups as long as a statement from an expert assessing individual's needs are provided. Same principles can be applied in different institutions and societies as long as enough training, information, and resources are addressed to their application.

Even though students are an important target group of the accessibility decision, it is noteworthy that all university community members can report accessibility challenges through the online form provided. The execution plan and actions taken are presented on the university webpage and can be openly commented by anyone. The actions taken are also reported each year to the university heads and student association. In addition, equity committee evaluates accessibility as a part of their equity planning. Within the limits of data privacy laws, quantitative and qualitative information is gathered on applicants' and students' wishes and needs to further develop the work. Presentations and trainings have increased knowledge and consciousness of students' rights and university's obligations. The increased awareness can be seen on increased contacts made, new initiatives and development projects. Knowledge of students' experiences of individual study arrangements as well as experiences of people in charge of these issues in each unit are collected via surveys. This information is used to improve practices. Additionally, Finnish Student Health Service evaluates health, safety and wellbeing in educational institutions.

Individual arrangements are a crucial part of improving accessibility among students. However, in their current form, these arrangements are merely repairing actions carried out to adapt physical, social and ICT environments to everyone's needs. Ideally, all environments should be designed to be inclusive. At the level of the HEI, accessibility practices have improved. Yet, there is always a need for continuous development. For example, it would be important to take accessibility into account already in the staff's know-how and education planning, since this could decrease the need for repairing actions. Inclusion could be improved by increasing collaboration with national and international parties, since many countries are already ahead of Finland with inclusion practices. Additionally, providing materials promoting inclusion supports inclusive operation. However, it is important to provide training alongside with materials, so that the institutions could better commit to continuous operations. Ultimately, it is essential for inclusive operations to initiate an organisation wide change in thinking.

2.3 *Student Health Service*

During the first year of university studies, students (including exchange students) fill out an online health survey. It consists of a wide range of questions (e.g. life management, sleep, mood, oral healthcare, exercise, use of alcohol or narcotics, relationships). Based on survey results, respondents with possible health problems are offered an appointment with Student Health Service. In addition, other students are given the opportunity to get an appointment, if they wish so. The results from the survey are used to support decision making. As an emerging practice, results are being analysed faculty by faculty so as to provide guidance to faculties based on somewhat differing needs of their student groups. During their years of studies, students use services both for every day matters (contraception, allergies) and for more severe problems. Students are growingly directed towards nurses, who further direct students to doctors when needed. In addition to individual guidance, specific group activities (peer support) are organised.

There is two-directional collaboration between Student Health Service and faculties' Goodie wellbeing advisors. The Goodies meeting students may further direct them to health professionals or health professionals meeting students may direct them to wellbeing advisors. Additionally, meetings are arranged between health professionals and Goodie advisors, and a health working group (Student Health Service, University Sports, Pastoral care, student members …) holds meetings around different health themes. The group designs, for example, theme days or weeks such as wellbeing weeks. Student Health Service collaborates with other student health service providers within the city (e.g. services for polytechnics and vocational schools). Health inspections are made at the university facilities together with health inspectors, with student members participating in the analysis. Approximately half of the fees collected from students (around 54 euros per student per academic year) are directed towards Student Health Service. Based on this fee, most of the services are free of charge. However, a visit to a specialist costs around 24 euros per visit.

Finnish Student Health Service has been functioning for 60 years. In recent decades, its services have become diverse. More attention is given to prevention and health promotion instead of focusing on illnesses. More responsibility is given to nurses. Students are encouraged to take responsibility of their own health and wellbeing. Additionally, digital tools are used to a greater extent: students can manage their own appointments digitally and there is remote testing for sexually transmitting diseases. Some appointments can even be carried out remotely.

All of the around 12,000 university students (excluding doctoral students) can use the student health services. Some students may choose to use other services, for example, when they have private insurance. However, the services are generally used by all students needing them. General health services are used for various purposes, such as flu, contraception, vaccination and counselling for travelling. Oral health services are particularly used among students, since it is known that the services are much more expensive after university years. Mental health services, in turn, are used by a small percentage of students, but this number appears to be increasing in recent years.

The effectiveness of Student Health Service is evaluated in many ways. For example, there is a satisfaction survey for service users and feedback can be provided online. In addition, there is an electronic emoji-quick response tool to express satisfaction. The feedback is collected and analysed systematically with the aid of a program gathering the data. The feedback received is analysed and discussed once a month. By doing this, it is assured that the professionals receive feedback concerning their own work. Additionally, students in the Student Health Service board have organised surveys for students such as The Finnish Student Health Survey ("The Finnish Student Health Survey", n.d.).

In terms of scalability, there has been discussion of extending Student Health Service to cover Polytechnics. Scaling up services could be possible but would require changes in the administration, employee structure, working spaces, and naturally, more human and economic resources. Transfer to similar high education institutions such as polytechnics is seen as relatively easy. When considering transfer to other societies, some issues should be considered. For example, it is important to assure that the nurses are highly educated, as they are given a lot of responsibility. Divisions in work and hierarchies between doctors and nurses may also obstruct this working model. The work is based on collaboration and trust between different professionals. There is a need to view health holistically from various perspectives. In some societies, doctors are very specialised in one area, while general health care perspective may be more difficult to obtain. In some cultures, focus on prevention instead of curing illnesses may also be challenging. Finally, society's economic structure differing from Finland may cause some challenges (the Finnish Centre for Pensions, "KELA", is a major funder of these services).

2.4 *University Sports*

University Sports is a university unit in charge of organising sport activities both for students and for university staff members. The unit works in close collaboration with the student association, which is a member of the Finnish students sport association. Other important external stakeholders are Finnish sport associations. University sports works closely with Finnish Student Health Service, for example, in Health work group (internal and external stakeholders). There is internal collaboration with the subject associations within the university, student services, space services and the department of communication. Collaboration with faculties is based on Goodie operating model, providing support for students. Additionally, some students conduct Master's thesis work and job training at University Sports. There is collaboration at an international level, for example, in the form of different exchange projects. In addition to university students, University Sports offers some courses to members of polytechnics in the same city.

From the university students' perspective, students can buy a sport sticker (approximately 65 euros), which will give them access to all group fitness and ball game activities. Separate courses can be attended based on course fee, which is around 20–50 euros per course. There is a free sport course, which students can take as a part of their studies (up to 4 credits). In another course (2 credits), students can choose among 30 different types of activities. The student receives the course credits once a total of 15 sessions of sports activities have been completed. Students have the possibility to use the university gym free of charge.

University Sports supports student and staff in selecting activities they are interested in and by providing information related to them. All students, regardless of their social, financial or health status, are encouraged to participate in sports activities. The University Sports has been working nearly 45 years, and the free sports course for students has existed nearly since the beginning of the operation. Historically, the focus of University Sports was more on ball games.

However, in recent decades, the offerings have been expanded significantly. It seems that the practices are quite well stabilised and will continue to remain that way in the future.

Academic sports (group fitness, ball games and gym) is available for both the university and polytechnics in the city, but the course offerings are only available to university members. Based on the ongoing Master's theses, the most active users at the university are from the Faculty of Sport Science (approximately 80% of their students participate) and the least active users are from the IT faculty (approximately 29% of students participate). The percentage of users within other faculties is around 50–60%. In collaboration with Finnish Student Health Service, University sports aims at identifying services for physically more passive students or students, who are not oriented to group sports or ball games.

In terms of evaluation, University Sports gathers feedback in many ways. This includes a wide board where users can leave their messages. Messages written during one week are photographed and saved for further analysis. Additional channels for feedback include Facebook and surveys that are carried out to evaluate services. In addition to internal surveys, surveys conducted by Finnish Student Health Service at national level provide feedback to the parties involved in student health. Student association, in turn, has organised theme weeks for expressing complains or providing positive feedback. Participants of the sports course keep learning diaries and provide general feedback at the end of the course. University Sports organises coffee sessions with trainers to discuss and share feedback and concerns. Finally, studies such as Master's theses focusing on this theme support the development work. Feedback and evaluation results are used in order to improve the program. Overall, University Sports is very open to suggestions. For example, the sport course contents can be modified during the academic year based on suggestions made by the students.

As established, University Sports has been scaled up to offer services to other higher education institutes in the city. Scaling up the services require, however, further resources, such as time, money and personnel. Target groups of the practice, in turn, are quite wide: students, staff members, people with varying ages, varying sizes and varying health conditions participate in academic sports. In fact, the model has been partially transferred to other higher education institutions. Good practices are exchanged in collaboration with various stakeholders at national level. There has also been exchange with countries such as Malta, Italy, Spain and Germany. Based on these experiences, there may be cultural differences obstructing the transfer. For example, in some countries university sports may be more focused on professional sports than physical exercise for nonprofessional people. Additionally, some activities may be more expensive, fixed and closed.

2.5 The Goodie Model

The development of wellbeing advisor concept and the Goodie Model started as an attempt to support the students in their diverse daily challenges affecting their study ability. Organisational responsibility for study ability and the active participation of other stakeholders were found to be prerequisites to successful and sustainable change. The Goodie Operating Model aims to promote student wellbeing and study engagement. The model consists of (1) Goodie wellbeing adviser services for all students who encounter challenges, (2) academic study ability course for first year students, and (3) Student Compass, an internet-based program to enhance the general mental health and overall functioning of students.

The Goodie wellbeing advisers are university staff members who have been selected and trained to support the wellbeing of students, but they are not therapists or psychologists. A student can come to Goodie with any issue or problem and discussions are always kept confidential. Goodie advisers help to find information on how to promote and enhance student's (social, physical, emotional, cognitive, educational, etc.) wellbeing, put them in touch with available peer support groups and share ideas on how to build their own support network. If needed, the advisers will guide the students further to aid them in reaching the right services. The Academic study ability course for first year students includes academic reading and writing skills, study planning, time management, self-exploration, emotional self-regulation, interaction skills and everyday life management skills.

The Student Compass is an internet-based self-help program to enhance the general mental health and overall functioning of students. It aims at providing practical tools and coping strategies for student's daily life, with a basis on the principles and processes of Acceptance and Commitment Therapy (ACT). The program includes three themes: Stress, anxiety and depression. The Student Compass may be used independently online without coach support, in the student's own pace. However, there is also coach support available, where the student receives personal contact in the form of two face-to-face meetings with the coach and five weeks online.

During years 2011–2013 the practice was a pilot with Finnish students. From year 2013, it has worked as an established practice. Since year 2015, there has been a pilot phase for international students. The Goodie wellbeing activities for Finnish students are based on 72 trained staff members (from which 48 are active) in 19 departments. Therefore, the maturity level of the practice is intermediate for Finnish students and initial for the international students. Between 2013–2016 and from the student body of 15,000, 1017 students have found their way to Goodie guidance. In terms of scalability, the Goodie guidance has already been scaled up to include not only Finnish students but also international students. Scalability may be successful as long as the network characteristics of the Goodie model remain active. In regard to transferability, the Goodie operating model could be used in any HE institution in order to develop low threshold counselling at department level. It requires relatively little resources as agency is given to university teachers and students themselves instead of external stakeholders.

According to the university accessibility coordinator, the Goodie model has produced smooth cooperation with Goodies when planning the individual arrangements for the students with disabilities and learning difficulties. The developers have documented student feedback and Goodie adviser reports to be analysed for quality assurance. Goodie wellbeing advisors have reported to have better knowhow for responding to students' challenges. They have also received support in advisors' work from their peers, decreasing the feelings of working alone with these challenges. Finally, they have experienced that the limits of advising and guidance work has become clearer for all participants.

Students, in turn, have reported that Goodie operational model enables searching for help in an early stage and makes approaching Goodies easy as they are near the student community and conversations are kept as confidential. In general, the operational model has led to more proactive ways to improve the wellbeing of students and eased the advisors work by means of shared working models. In addition, the Goodie model has supported the students' readiness to maintain and improve their ability to learn.

According to a faculty student counsellor, most higher education students do not have notable problems with their study ability. Dyslexia, for example, might not be problematic to a student until the end of bachelor's studies, when it is time to perform the maturity exam. However, it becomes harder to meet the needs of an individual when problems start to accumulate. In these situations, it is important to consider the role of university in supporting the students, and similarly what kind of support the student needs to be able to cope with everyday life. Thus, when the studying ability is strong, it is quite effortless to find solutions. Once the studying ability decreases, solving accessibility problems might not be enough to ensure the continuity of studies. The needs of students might have great variance when life situations change and thus, it is important to be able to inspect the student's situation in a more comprehensive way instead of trying to find solutions to different problems. It is also crucial to realise that not all challenges faced by students are permanent, which emphasises the significance of timely support, such as the one provided by Goodies.

2.6 Student Compass

The development of the Student Compass wellbeing program promoting students' psychological wellbeing was based on good results received from online-based interventions and research evidence. The goal was to create a new type of an easy access guidance practice that would help the students to increase their wellbeing and to support the work of Goodie wellbeing advisors, who are trained university staff members supporting students' wellbeing. The Student Compass includes online-based coach-guided Acceptance and Commitment Therapy (ACT) program with blended face-to-face and online sessions. The Department of Psychology developed the online program and trained the 4th year students to work as coaches in face-to-face meetings and in online exercises.

Piloting the Student Compass started in Spring and the research in Autumn 2012. In 2013, the Student Compass was available for all students at the HEI. The maturity level of the practice is intermediate. Between 2013–2016, there have been 2600 log-ins and 231 students have met a coach in a face-to-face session. The whole student population is around 15,000. The feedback from the students who have participated in the coach sessions is gathered with an online questionnaire. With a scale of 1–10, the participants' average satisfaction with the program has been 7.8. Further, self-evaluation shows that the Student Compass increases wellbeing and satisfaction with life. The results were maintained at the 12-month follow-up. Additionally, the coaches have found their work meaningful and useful for their own professional development (Räsänen et al., 2016).

In terms of scalability, a self-guided and independently used online program can be quite easily scaled. Regarding guided online ACT intervention, it is recommendable to organise the coach support in work community or locally. The Student Compass program has the potential to be transferred to other universities and be used by young adults in general in various communities and societies.

3 Methodology: Self-Assessment of HEI Inclusion in Finland

Based on previous inclusion research, European Union Erasmus+ programme funded "ACCESS4ALL" project (2018) has created tools for HE inclusion self-assessment, development and good practise sharing. With these tools HEIs can identify their level of Inclusion and plan development activities as well as for sharing those within their communities. The A4A Institution Self-Assessment Tool has been developed for analysing the current level of inclusion within the HEI. The tool is meant to be used for HEIs to improve their inclusion policies. Based on the answers provided, the tool creates an institutional profile regarding six dimensions:

1. HEI organisational maturity
2. Institutional innovation management culture
3. Knowledge sharing
4. Inclusion shared understanding
5. Policies for inclusion and
6. Actions for inclusion.

The organisational maturity dimension is based on organisational development theories focusing on development through planned interventions using both individual and whole organisation approach (e.g. Waddell, Cummings, & Worley, 2016). The change management culture dimension, in turn, focuses on the occurrence and nature of different values within the organisation. The knowledge sharing dimension attempts to portray the effects that explicit and tacit information sharing processes have on inclusion. The fourth dimension, inclusion shared understanding, covers the various factors affecting the achievement of shared understanding about inclusion. Policies for inclusion are considered in terms of budget management, training provided for staff, institutional structures that support inclusion and strategic actions aimed at enhancing the readiness to meet the needs of students from vulnerable groups (consistent with the Index for Inclusion guidelines; Booth & Ainscow, 2011).

FIGURE 3.2   Results of A4A self-assessment in Finnish HEI

Finally, the actions for inclusion dimension is based on the view of inclusion as a process to reduce inequality, which, in turn, relates to creating equity promoting conditions e.g. in terms of participation and academic completion (Espinoza & González, 2009). Figure 3.2 presents the results of a Finnish HEI received by using the A4A Self-Assessment Tool.

4   A4A Self-Assessment Tool Results: Finnish HEI

4.1   *Organisational Maturity*
The overall score of this dimension is 3.0. The institution should develop strategies and mechanism of knowledge management that allow a constant interconnection between its members and a better capacity to generate processes of constant innovation. In this sense, among other proposals, a distributed type of leadership should be promoted that allows different organisational units (research teams, institutes, departments or faculties) to propose their own proposals. Thus, a flexible and more adaptive structure, based on internal and external knowledge, will have to be provided.

4.2   *Institutional Innovation Management Culture*
The institution received a score of 3.4 from this dimension. Streamlining the change and reviewing innovation processes must become an institutional value, explicit and disseminated. In addition, some mechanisms should be available to agree on levels of contingency planning that are capable of adapting to different situations and scenarios. To reach satisfactory levels of contingent planning, barriers and resistances must be foreseen and open spaces for debate and collaboration between teams and persons should be generated.

4.3   *Knowledge Sharing*
The score received from this dimension is 3.6. It is appropriate to boost joint work and encourage regular cooperation among professionals with different profiles and levels of experience, to generate new knowledge. Thus, it would be possible to institutionalise the frequent use of the technological tools, resources, spaces and times that the organisation facilitates, guaranteeing the necessary formation for it whenever it is required. It would also contribute to the promotion of a climate conducive to the encounter, the sharing and the cooperation between the different professionals. On the other hand, the HEI has to maintain strategic alliances with other institutions – local, national and international – in relation to how to improve the attention to vulnerable groups through the internationalisation of knowledge.

4.4 *Inclusion Shared Understanding*

The overall score for this dimension is 3.4. To guarantee the implication of all the agents (teachers, students, administrative staff, etc.) for the improvement and increasing of the inclusion in the institution, the institution has to promote actions addressed to the implication and compromise of all the agents towards inclusion. These actions have to facilitate all the agents' active and participative action in the different institutional areas, facilitating the access to information and the good use of all the available resources and services, as well as the better interaction among them towards the strengthening of an inclusive culture.

4.5 *Policies for Inclusion*

The institution received a score of 3.2 from this dimension. In order to improve or to promote more suitable policies for inclusion, the HEI should put in place strategies to follow up and evaluate the policies for inclusion. The focus in this phase is to collect evidences and data of the implementation of the policies for inclusion (e.g. level of impact of training programs, adaptability of facilities, among others) and evaluate them according to the HEI strategic plans. In addition, measures to make decisions based on these evidences are also recommended.

4.6 *Actions for Inclusion*

The score received from the final dimension is 3.4. The design and development of a plan to improve the income, permanence and egress of the students in the university have to contemplate the different services and programs that the institution has and puts at the service of educational inclusion. On the other hand, this plan for improvement must require the commitment and participation of the university community in decision-making and in the reflection of the design and development of the plan. As a result, it is possible to respond to the set of needs that were detected and be consistent with the purposes and priorities that were set. It would also be desirable to incorporate indicators for a follow-up evaluation and permanent self-assessment to ensure that the responses to the reality are adequate.

5   Conclusions

This book chapter presented six good practices on how to tackle inclusion aspects in Finnish HEI. The A4A self-assessment tool showed that despite of the good practises rising from Finnish HEI, there are still areas to improve in, even though the situation seems quite positive. To be able to start a process of self-development of this kind in HEI, the management of the organisation must be actively involved and willing to proceed. There might be ideas and motivation at the worker level, but changes such as this one need to come top down to be effective. For example, the working group of the HEI found it hard to find space and time for the inclusion work. Thus, management should make people participate – that is the only way to find time from busy schedules. Motivation and time spent to the self-assessment are the real challenges. If there is no legislation or funding for inclusion, there is a real chance that inclusive actions are left undone.

Goals for Finnish HEI:
- Planned time for inclusion and development of staff's understanding
- Try to develop policies top-down to ensure that each staff member has to develop inclusion skills as part of their job description.
- To gain bottom-up approaches, include students' views more when improving the instruments for supporting inclusion

Acknowledgement

This document has been produced as a part of the project "ACCESS4ALL – Laboratory for Policies and Practices of Social Development in Higher Education" (Ref. 2015-1-ES01-KA203-015970) co-funded by the European Union (Erasmus+ Programme)

References

ACCESS4ALL project. (2018). http://access4allproject.eu/

Booth, T., & Ainscow, M. (2011). *Index for inclusion: Developing learning and participation in schools*. Centre for Studies on Inclusive Education.

Espinoza, O., González, L. E., & Latorre, C. L. (2009). Un modelo de equidad para la educación superior: Análisis de su aplicación al caso chileno. *Revista de la educación superior, 38*(150), 97–111.

Finlex. (2014). *Yhdenvertaisuuslaki* [Equality law]. http://www.finlex.fi/fi/laki/alkup/2014/20141325

Kunttu, K., Pesonen, T., & Saari, J. (2016). *Student health survey 2016: A national survey among Finnish university students*. https://1285112865.rsc.cdn77.org/app/uploads/2020/03/KOTT_2016_ENG.pdf

Räsänen, P., Lappalainen, P., Muotka, J., Tolvanen, A., & Lappalainen, R. (2016). An online guided ACT intervention for enhancing the psychological wellbeing of university students: A randomized controlled clinical trial. *Behaviour Research and Therapy, 78*, 30–42.

Waddell, D., Creed, A., Cummings, T., & Worley, C. (2016). *Organisational change: Development and transformation*. Cengage AU.

CHAPTER 4

Fostering Good Practices for Vulnerable Students in Higher Education: Suggestions from Italy

Fabio Dovigo

Abstract

The positive advantages of diversity in the Higher Education environment have been largely documented by research. Nevertheless, face to the apparent benefits of diversity, current attempts to widen and reinforce HE participation still deal with a number of challenges. Even though European governments repeatedly committed to the goals of increasing graduation rates and fostering diversity in HE, the lack of financial support, combined with unfavourable demographic patterns, prevents them to reach such ambitious objectives. Consequently, universities still tend to be open to students that are likely to succeed from the outset more than those that are affected by economic, social or cultural drawbacks. To counter this trend, good practices concerning favouring the access, retention and success of underprivileged students to Higher Education have been brought about in many European countries. The chapter will provide an examination of the socioeconomic, organisational and educational factors that influence the development of good practices in Italy, as well as an evaluation of the advantages and limitations of the good practices approach applied to Higher Education.

Keywords

widening participation – inclusion – good practices – diversity – underprivileged students – equality – equity – quality – higher education organisation

1   Facing Diversity in Higher Education

The positive advantages of diversity in the Higher Education (HE) environment have been largely documented by research. Drawing on people with different skills and experiences not only enhances ability in problem solving, but also improves learning more than when it occurs among homogeneous and more uniform groups (Younger et al., 2019). Investigation shows that students who interact with peers from different socio-economic and cultural backgrounds develop more positive personal and academic self-esteem, graduate earlier and better, acquire leadership competences and higher commitment towards community engagement, as well as prove to be less exposed to stereotypes and prejudice biases (Bowl & Bathmaker, 2016; Bowman, 2011; Engberg & Hurtado, 2011; Espenshade & Radford, 2013; Fabricius & Preisler, 2015; Hurtado & Deangelo, 2012).

Nevertheless, face to the apparent benefits of diversity, current attempts to widen and reinforce HE participation still deal with a number of challenges. Even though European governments repeatedly committed to the goals of increasing graduation rates and fostering diversity in HE, the constant lack of financial support, combined with unfavourable demographic patterns, prevents them to reach such ambitious objectives (Mok & Neubauer, 2016; Huisman & van Vught, 2009). Consequently, universities still tend to be open to students that are likely to succeed from the outset more than those that are affected by economic, social or cultural drawbacks, so evading the duty of providing fair opportunities to all on an equity basis. Official national statements about the significance of adopting equity policies that would favour the enrolment of students from less traditional social and economic backgrounds are not followed by the implementation of congruent financial measures (Codling & Meek, 2006; Dakka, 2015; Hazelkorn, 2015). University administrations emphasise that supporting vulnerable students is more expensive as, on the one hand, it entails more help and tutoring than traditional students and, on the other, vulnerable students are more at risk in terms of early leaving rates, which in turn affect universities ability to get funded. As a consequence, more economic funds would be required to guarantee that HE institutions can promote effective actions in order to ensure access, retention, and completion of disadvantaged students (Haigh, 2014; Teichler, 2008; Van Vught, 2009).

Beyond the financial issue, the aim of widening diversity of the students' profile raises several additional questions. Diversity cannot be assumed as desirable *per se,* nor we can't take for granted that everyone sees it as an advantage from the educational point of view, unless it is assumed and communicated as an intentional goal. Diversity can usually raise tensions and conflicts, as welcoming and accommodating vulnerable students implies a purposeful effort to tackle socio-economical, cultural and linguistic hindrances (Booth & Ainscow, 2011; Chun & Feagin, 2019). Hence, it only becomes a desirable condition when it is considered as a value shared throughout the academic community. Furthermore, in an academic world dominated by the mantra of excellence, many universities are predictably afraid that expanding the share of vulnerable students would lower their overall academic scores and, consequently, jeopardise the ability to enrol high potential students, who are commonly attracted by the good reputation apparently secured by the ranking systems so popular nowadays. Accordingly, universities are currently trapped in a double bind, as European and national policies, on the one hand regularly emphasise the need for widening access of citizens to HE by increasing the number of vulnerable students enrolled, on the other are putting growing pressure on ranking and performance as the only way of justifying resources governments have been investing in HE (Archer, 2007).

This trend concerns as well the increasing population of mature students, which represents a relevant portion of vulnerable learners currently attending university studies. The demographic decline of young population leads to intensifying competition among HE institutions to secure enrolment of the decreasing number of students and, at the same time, encourages to consider mature students as a promising market segment that could balance for the drop of younger learners (Coertjens et al., 2017; Crozier et al., 2007; Wilcox et al., 2005). The need for ongoing training and reskill in an increasingly dynamic work environment concurs to focus the attention of universities on the same direction, through the development of postgraduate degrees and lifelong learning programs. However, HE institutions conceived for young students struggle to adapt to the needs of mature students, which are considerably different in terms of time, personal drives, professional goals, learning abilities, and work time balance. Systematic enrolment of mature students requires considerable reworking from universities in terms of course organisation and flexible timetable, as well as an extensive review of existing teaching programmes and the adoption of alternative learning methods. Accordingly, even though mature students are seen as a crucial opportunity for HE institutions involved in consolidating and expanding the population of learners, so far this vision has not been really implemented. Consequently, its impact on actual academic practices in European universities is still limited.

2   The University System Organisation in Italy

Except for a limited number of institutions, originally set up by private entities and later formally recognised by the government, most of the existing universities in Italy were directly established by the State and currently rely on the Ministry of Education administration. Nowadays, in Italy there are 56 state universities, 3 state polytechnics, 17 private universities, 3 universities for foreigners, 6 "special system high schools", offering qualifications only at the master and PhD levels, and 11 on-line universities.

Until the Bologna agreement was signed in 1999, only one kind of four years degree was offered in all Italian universities. The only exceptions were the course studies in Architecture, Engineering, Chemistry (which lasted five years) and Medicine (six years). After 1999 the Italian HE sector, as most European universities, experienced a major review process aimed to align Italian HE curricula to the European model defined by the Bologna reform. As a result, the current Italian HE system is organised into three separate sectors: university tertiary education, non-university tertiary education (offered by the Higher level Arts and Music Education system), and higher technical education and training (or post-secondary non tertiary education). Tertiary education is currently defined by a three-tier structure, consisting of a first-level bachelor degree ("laurea triennale", 3 years), a second-level master degree ("laurea magistrale", 2 years) and doctoral studies (3 years). Some course studies (e.g. medicine, law, architecture) are based on a single cycle degree lasting 5 to 6 years.

To be admitted to HE, students must own an upper secondary school certificate that allows them, except for vocational training course certificates, a direct transition to any kind of university course. Equivalent foreign qualifications may also be accepted, after recognition from the university administration. University credits (ECTS) usually consist of a minimum of 25 working/studying hours, including contact hours and student workload. An average annual workload for full-time students is generally quantified in 60 credits.

Compared to other university systems, the organisation of HE in Italy displays some relevant peculiarities (Ballarino & Perotti, 2012). Firstly, in the last forty years, due to socioeconomic factors, the participation rate to tertiary education has been low, despite the expansion of secondary school and the demographic decrease of the young population. Secondly, the Italian academic organisation is quite homogeneous, as the tertiary education sector is still entirely managed by universities. Differently from other countries, where tertiary education is based on a dual or (as in Germany) and diversified system (e.g. in USA), HE in Italy is based on a unitary structure. In particular, there is not an established offer of technical and vocational education at the tertiary level as we commonly find, for example, in the Nordic Countries. Finally, despite multiple attempts to modernise the university governance, the self-government style of academic oligarchies in Italy has been preserved over time. Accordingly, even though the administration is highly centralised at the national level, professors still have full power in determining how internal university polices and careers are managed at the local level.

These features of the academic system largely shaped the way the Bologna reform has been adopted in Italy. Two relevant measures were associated with the introduction of the reform (Di Pietro, 2011). On the one hand, universities were urged to bring about more systematic information strategies addressed to potential students. Those strategies, developed as orientation sessions or open days, have thus become a stable part of the effort HE institutions make to enrol new freshmen every year. As such, they have played an important role in making the academic perspective attractive, especially to students from disadvantaged background, whose families often lack information and previous experience in this regard. On the other hand, the reform indirectly pushed academic institutions to lower the threshold for accessing HE, by reducing grading standards and selection criteria. This policy encouraged students from disadvantaged backgrounds or with low performance in secondary education, who usually would have dismissed the idea of enrolling in HE, to favourably consider the opportunity of entering tertiary education (Bratti et al., 2010).

However, these actions also highlighted the risk that the goal of widening up HE would have been achieved at the cost of severely undermining the quality of academic provision. This reflection, combined with a concern for the increasing fragmentation of local policies and the impact of the 2008 economic crisis on the Italian economy, led the Ministry of Education to limit the moderate autonomy granted by the reform to the university administrations. Accordingly, starting from 2010 the Ministry regained stronger control of the sector through the adoption of a set of norms addressed to both reduce national financing and decrease the hiring of academic positions.

In the long term, this unresolved dialectic between the national and local administrations, combined with the persistent effect of the crisis, produced a downward effect on the academic system in Italy. While the positive growth spurred by the reform at the beginning of 2000 has gradually declined in most universities, the opportunity to develop more functional governance and administration mechanisms has been seized in a very limited way. In this regard, adopting the conceptual lens proposed by Trow (1973, 2006), researchers emphasise that the Italian HE organisation "has undergone a transition from mass to universal in terms of expansion, whereas it is still changing from élite to mass in terms of functioning mechanisms" (Turri, 2013, p. 102). This conclusion is in line with most of the data emerging from recent investigations concerning the condition of disadvantaged students in HE in Italy.

3 Inclusion in Higher Education in Italy after the Bologna Reform

Similar to other European countries, following the introduction of the Bologna process (the so-called 3+2 reform) also in Italy the enrolment in HE of students coming from disadvantaged social backgrounds has increased, in parallel with the multiplication of curricula offered, which nearly doubled from 2001 to 2003 (Geuna & Muscio, 2008). Ten years later (2013), 74% of first-level graduates were the first in their families to get a degree (Cammelli & Gasperoni, 2015). Correspondingly, the percentage of vulnerable students increased from 20% in 2004 to 26% out of the total in 2013. However, in the following years, Italian universities lost on average 20% of first-year students, while rules overseeing the allocation of public funds to universities have been considerably transformed, putting more pressure on HE institutions to compete for enrolling more of the decreasing population of students (Ballarino & Panichella, 2016). Beyond the widespread demographic decline that affects many European countries, other elements that contribute to this situation in Italy are the ongoing economic crisis, which hinders families' ability to shoulder the costs of university education, and the worsening of graduates' employment opportunities. This combination of factors, as well as the lack of effective student support policies, explains why Italy has a very low rate of graduates (19%) compared to the average 37% in the OCSE area (OECD, 2019). In summary, shorter courses promoted by reform that aimed to expand the population of students attending HE were able to increase enrolment only in the very first years, while drop-out rates are still relevant spite the many initiatives undertaken at the national and local level. Research shows that cultural capital possessed by the students' family is the main factor associated with the decision of enrolling in university. More precisely, children from parents that own only compulsory schooling are less likely to enrol in HE (Checchi et al., 2013; Contini & Scagni, 2013). Family incomes also have a role in the decision of students, but only in the lowest tail of the distribution. Therefore, the influence of cultural (and sometimes also financial) limitations produces disaffection of vulnerable children from HE, generating long-term disinvestment in human capital that in turn reinforces the transmission of marginalised conditions from one generation to the other, especially in students from lower social classes or migration background (Aina et al., 2011; Azzolini & Barone, 2013). This trend cannot be inverted simply through reforms aimed to transform HE by redesigning curricula and courses. The Bologna process proved to be able to provide access, but not the retention of disadvantaged learners. As a consequence, we need to acknowledge that "although the Italian university system has virtually no entry barriers, tuition fees are low and there are a large number of public universities, which, in principle, should give the same opportunities to children regardless of family background, the inequalities emerge both in the university attendance and in the likelihood of withdrawal" (Aina, 2013, p. 454). Family cultural and economic context still overcomes such positive features of Italian universities, contradicting the recurring narrative of equity and fair opportunities usually recalled in official statements. Additionally, students from lower social classes or with a migration background are systematically directed to enrol at vocational or technical high schools, so excluding them from the possibility to attend HE. Hence, measures as adopting a more flexible and comprehensive high school system, as well as reducing the financial gap by ensuring students that credit would be equally available to different income groups, are mandatory to guarantee that good practices aimed at fostering inclusion in HE in Italy could be effective and sustainable, especially in the long run.

4 Unprivileged Students in He in Italy: An Overview

As we mentioned, Italy has a longstanding tradition of low participation rate to HE compared to other European countries. Consequently, while in 2013 the European Union set the objective of 40% of all 30–34 years-old young people obtaining a degree (or equivalent qualification) by 2020, the Italian government preferred to indicate a more prudential goal of 26–27%. This goal has been already achieved in 2016, although with a large gender gap – 34.0% women against 21.7% of men, according to Eurostat (2019a). However, the number of Italian graduates is still very far from that of the other European Higher Education Area (EHEA) member states. The difference is mainly due to the lower number of bachelor students, as well as the lack of an established technical and vocational HE system. Conversely, the amount of Italian master's graduates is in line with the EHEA average data, thanks to the high rate of enrolment in master courses (ANVUR, 2018).

Filling the gap with the other European countries in the HE sector is difficult because of the inadequate investment Italy makes in tertiary education. Compared to the OECD countries, where the average expenditure on tertiary education accounted for 1.5% of GDP in 2017, Italy invested only 0.3% in the same year (OECD, 2019). The cut in public spending also caused a relevant decrease in the number of university teachers, who declined by 14.9% between 2008 and 2017. Beyond increasing the average age of teachers (20% over the age of 60 and only 14% under 40), the funding cut raised the teacher-student ratio (1 to 31 in 2017), as well as the number of teaching hours per teacher, with a 7% increase from 2014 to 2017 (ANVUR, 2018).

The dearth of investment in HE has differently affected Italian geographical areas, with a deeper negative impact on the South and the islands. In the last few years, the number of enrolments has significantly decreased in Southern universities (−26% between 2003 and 2018). At the same time, the dropout rate between bachelor and master courses is 2 to 4% higher compared to the corresponding courses in Northern universities (ANVUR, 2018). As a consequence, in 2018 the number of graduates was only 21.2% in Southern Italy, while the national figure was 27.8% (Istat, 2019b). The decrease in investment in tertiary education is also correlated to the increase of young people not in employment, education or training (NEET). In 2018, 23.4% of young people in Italy were NEET, of which 25.4% women and 21.5% men (Istat, 2019a). This figure is the highest in the European Union, whose NEET percentage in the same year was 12.9% (Eurostat, 2019c).

Concerning the EHEA objective of widening participation to HE of learners from diverse conditions and backgrounds, social class of origin and parental education still play a pivotal role in influencing the access of Italian young people to HE. These two factors acquired special relevance in the aftermath of the 2008 economic crisis. In 2018, graduates from working class or petty bourgeoise families were 21.6%, of whom 23.3% at the bachelor level, 20.9% at the master level, and only 15.4% at the single cycle degree level. On the opposite, graduates from bourgeoise or white collar families were 22.4% (20.3% at the bachelor level, 22.0% at the master level, and 33.0% at the single cycle degree level). This difference can be further understood if we consider parental education (Ballarino & Panichella, 2016). Compared to 2015, in 2018 the share of students whose parents hold an upper secondary school diploma or a university degree has increased by 17%, whereas enrolment of young people whose parents hold a primary or lower secondary school diploma has decreased by almost 30%. Moreover, research shows that underprivileged students – living in Southern Italy and/or coming from a vocational track school – are disadvantaged with regard not only to the enrolment, but also persistence in HE, with large cumulative differentials from the other students (Contini et al., 2018).

5   The Role of Parental Education

The beneficial effect the Bologna reform initially had on the inclusion of underrepresented students in the Italian university system has lost momentum over the years. More precisely, parental education is still a good predictor of the opportunities young people are provided concerning entering HE in Italy. The most advantageous educational paths with higher expected occupational returns (e.g. medicine degree) are still the prerogative of students from upper classes (Triventi et al., 2016; Vergolini & Vlach, 2016). Accordingly, the ability of the university system to help young people from disadvantaged groups to improve their socioeconomic condition is still too limited. In 2012, only 13.9% of graduates between 30 and 44 years-old had parents without a degree (Istat, 2018a; OECD, 2017b). More precisely, after the initial surge (+19%) following the adoption of the 3+2 organisation in 2000 (especially due to the intake of mature students attracted by the new study system), during the 2003–2018 period the number of students enrolled in HE in Italy has decreased by 13%, i.e. over 40,000 students (Almalaurea, 2019). Moreover, socioeconomic disparities affect access rates also concerning master studies. In 2018, the enrolment gap in master level education between students whose parents had or not an academic degree was 26%.

Reduction in enrolment rates can be partly explained by the decline of young people population in Italy, which has decreased by 40% in the last thirty years (Istat, 2018b). Another important factor is the lower enrolment rate in HE of students from upper secondary school, which went from 54.4% in 2011 to 49.1% in 2015 (MIUR, 2017; Istat, 2018c). Furthermore, the wave of mature students' enrolment, which characterised the first years after the university reform, has gradually faded out. While in the 2000–2009 years the number of mature students raised from 2.8 to 7.4% (also as a consequence of the recognition of past working qualifications in terms of university credits), the rate has then decreased to 2.4%, less than it was before the beginning of the reform (ANVUR, 2016).

In the last few years, the students' ability to complete university exams within set time period – an endemic problem in Italy – has definitely improved, going from 39.4% in 2008 to 53.6% in 2018 (ETM, 2019). The condition of working while studying is the factor that mostly affects the timely completion of the academic career. Learners who work full time and part-time respectively take 50.5% and 10.3% longer than expected in getting a degree. However, in spite of these advances in the average duration of studies and completion rates, the attainment rate of HE in Italy is still not the same as the other European countries. More precisely, in 2018 the number of 30–34 years-old with a HE degree was the second-lowest in the EU (26.9%), far below the EU average (39.9%). As we noted, graduation rates are strictly interrelated with the students' family background. In 2018, 30% of graduates (and, notably, 43% from the single cycle courses) had at least one parent possessing a degree (Almalaurea, 2019).

6 Study Completion and Dropout

Another important element to understand the condition of disadvantaged students in Italian HE is the role of dropout from education. This phenomenon doesn't affect only university studies, but can be identified already in secondary school. In 2018, the number of 18–24 years-old individuals that left education and training earlier than expected was 14.5%, with a remarkable difference between men and women (16.5% against 12.3%) (Eurostat, 2019b). While this number has decreased from 2005, when early leavers amounted to 22.1% of the same population, Italy still lags behind the average rate in the European Union (10.6%).

As for the university, although the number of students enrolling in HE after secondary education is already low (3 out of 10), a relevant share of them are not able to complete their studies. In 2016, the dropout rates of bachelor, master and single cycle degree students were, respectively, 12.2%, 5.9% and 7.5% (Istat, 2016; Almalaurea, 2019). Research emphasises that the decision to leave university is usually connected to the students' educational background and pre-enrolment profile (Zotti, 2015). Female, younger and full-time learners are less prone to drop out, as well as with those who enrol in HE immediately after the secondary school. Conversely, students with a lower score on high school diploma and those coming from vocational secondary education are more likely to drop out. This data aligns with the literature on the way early tracking of students from disadvantaged families affects their secondary school choices, which in turn influence their future chances to complete HE in Italy (Checchi et al., 2013).

The students' propensity towards enrolling in master studies after completing the bachelor level, which declined in the years following the 3+2 reform, has recently gathered momentum, with 60% of students stating their willingness to enter a master level course (Eurostudent, 2018b). Compared to previous years, when most of the students opted for deferring the enrolment in the next study level, this preference is also associated with a direct transition from bachelor to master studies. This choice can be partially explained as a consequence of the economic crisis and the connected reduction in job opportunities for graduates. In this regard, getting further qualification can be interpreted as a way to achieve better occupational perspectives. However, in the uncertain economic situation that currently affects Italy, this option can also be interpreted as a way of using the university as a "temporary parking space", which eventually produces a negative effect in terms of over-education (Maiolo et al., 2013).

This concern is confirmed by the difficult transition from education to work many Italian students undergo after graduation. A common explanation of this problem is the lack of congruence between the skills certified by the university courses and those required by the world of work (Kottmann et al., 2015a, 2015b). However, the dimensions of the phenomenon suggest that, beyond this potential mismatch, more structural economic questions lay behind this situation. In 2018 the employment rate of Italian HE graduates, which sharply fell following the economic crisis and has been slowly recovering only in recent years, is still one of the lowest (62.8%) compared to the EU average of 85.5%. The inability to find a position that lives up to the investment made in education is also reflected by the increasing number of Italian graduates that move abroad to find a job: 28,000 of them emigrated in 2017, with an increment of 3.9% since 2016 (41.8% since 2013) (European Commission, 2019).

7   Financial Support in Italian Tertiary Education

The described low returns on education are combined with a growing high cost of HE in Italy, as university fees are among the highest in the EHEA and not adequately compensated by student support. In 2017, the average yearly fee was €1345 for bachelor studies and €1520 for master studies. In the same year, only 11.6% of students received a grant based on their financial condition and academic results. The percentage of publicly-financed study loans is almost nil (1%) (European Commission/EACEA/Eurydice, 2018b). A recent government initiative brought about in 2017 allows students whose indicator of the family economic condition is up to €13000 to be exempted from paying fees. However, university fees have in general increased in Italy over the last few years. While in 2005 the economic contribution required from families was 26.8%, in 2015 it raised to 35.4%, well beyond the OECD average rate (30.6%) (OECD, 2018).

Students with a low socio-economic background are provided scholarship grants defined at the regional level and financed by a combination of funds from regional authorities and the Ministry of Education. However, unlike most European countries, a very low share of Italian HE students (10.9%) actually manages to get a scholarship (European Commission/EACEA/Eurydice, 2018a). Moreover, interventions addressed to provide grants to students have been gradually replaced over time by schemes based on tax exemption. As for support in terms of housing, although the accommodation offer provided by the HE institutions has recently increased, it is still not proportioned to the growing number of off-campus students. Therefore, only around 20% of learners can find a place in a university residence. Finally, a relevant gap between Northern and Southern Italy can be identified concerning the overall support academic institutions can grant students, as universities in the South are less able to offer scholarships or housing to disadvantaged students. This situation contributed to strengthening students' emigration from South to the North of the country in recent years (Eurostudent, 2018b).

Because of the insufficient provision from the institutions, students' subsistence in Italy is still largely based on family support. This support often persists even beyond the completion of studies, as many young people struggle to become economically independent in a labour market that mostly offers temporary or underpaid positions. The prolonged downturn of the labour market, together with the reduced enrolment rates of mature students, has also determined a decrease in the number of graduates with working experience (from 74.7% in 2008 to 65.4% in 2018). As a consequence, in 2018 only 6.1% of graduates were working in permanent employment during their university studies. Research shows that both low and high intensity working activities negatively affect study retention and completion (Triventi, 2014). Despite these hard circumstances, most students express moderate satisfaction with their academic path. Only 15% experienced some difficult situation that could have put at risk their career (Eurostudent, 2018b). However, while the limited share of students that face serious problems during their studies is encouraging, this result can also be explained by the dropping enrolment rate in HE that affected underprivileged learners over the last few years. Accordingly, self-selection mechanisms would contribute to keeping away from HE young people that deem they won't fit with the current university system requirements.

8 A Snapshot of Underprivileged Groups in the Italian University

Investigation shows that in recent years the students' population age (both in terms of average and median) has increased by about a year. The ageing of HE learners may be explained by the lower enrolment rates of younger students in the last ten years, as well as by the increased number of students that opt for continuing education at the master level (Eurostudent, 2018a). Conversely, the delay in enrolling in HE both at the bachelor and master level has clearly decreased, as we mentioned, as a consequence of the declining offer from the world of work and the growth of university fees.

In the last ten years, women have been in the majority of Italian graduates (OECD, 2019). In 2018 they were 58.7% of the graduates' population, more precisely 58.6% at the bachelor level, 56.3% at the master level, and 64.5% from single cycle degree courses. Women are also less affected by dropout and achieve a HE qualification more quickly (57.5%). Furthermore, data indicate a strong differentiation by gender regarding scientific disciplinary areas. At the bachelor and master level, women are a strong majority in the teaching (93.3%), linguistic (83.8%), psychological (80.4%), and health professions (70.3%) disciplines, while they are a minority in the engineering (26.6%), scientific (26.9%), and physical education (32.7%) courses. Women clearly prevail in all disciplinary groups at the single-cycle master courses: from 96.0% in teaching courses to 53.3% in medicine and dentistry. However, women are noticeably still at a disadvantage concerning access to the academic career in Italy. While they outnumber men as for university intake and graduation, the ratio of PhD and post-doc positions is equally balanced in terms of gender. However, this balance starts breaking from the hiring of lecturer and associate professors, who are prevalently males, whereas the gap becomes even wider at the full professor level.

Students with children are 1% of the population (Eurostudent, 2018a, 2018b). Their number has decreased over time, highlighting a lack of support from Italian institutions towards this category of learners, which only recently started being made up. Due to family care commitments, the rate of students with children is especially high among learners who report experiencing financial difficulties and having limited time to spend on studying. The difficult situation of this group of students in Italy is even more evident if compared with the Northern European countries where, thanks to policies aimed to favour study enrolment and completion of students with children, they are between 15% and 33% of the HE population.

The share of students with migrant origins enrolled in HE is especially low in Italy (14%) in comparison with the other EHEA countries (37.8% on average). Access to university is influenced by school track selection mechanisms brought about at the secondary school level, which push migrant students who want to continue studying to opt for non-academic paths (Mantovani, 2018; Romito, 2016). Moreover, even though second generation immigrants have higher attainment (26.7%) than native-born with a native background (19.1%), research highlights that their employment rates are lower (66.7% against 68.6%) (Eurostat, 2016). Although the information on university students with migrant background in Italy is not systematically collected, data from preliminary research indicate that in 2014 the share of students with migrant origin from secondary school who enrolled in HE was significantly lower compared to that of their native background peers (Lagomarsino & Ravecca, 2014; Paba & Bertozzi, 2017). This data reflects an interesting cultural paradox of Italian university policies. While HE institutions are increasingly emphasising the value of internationalisation and ingoing mobility of students from abroad, they apparently discount the international group of first and second generation immigrant learners, who are a consistent and more stable part of the students' population (Bertozzi, 2018; Teichler, 2015).

Finally, in 2018 students with a disability or learning difficulties enrolled in HE in Italy were 14% of the HE population (Eurostudent, 2018a). This data is similar to those from other HE institutions in Europe, which indicate an average rate of 18% (Eurostudent, 2018b). However, not all students with a disability or learning difficulties want to disclose their condition, so data available can underestimate the real share of impairments among students. Investigation shows that students, especially those with a less severe condition, are often afraid of being viewed as unclever and labelled with the stigma which is still associated with disability in many HE institutions (Grimes et al., 2019; Marshak et al., 2010; May & Stone, 2010). The most reported disorders are those affecting the mental as well as sensory and perceptual areas, followed by chronic physical pathologies. About 15% of students report feeling negatively conditioned in their studies as a result of their condition. Moreover, most of them (62%) feel little or not at all supported by the HE institutions. This is especially true for students whose condition has a strong impact on their ability to attend HE.

9 The Limits of Good Practices

Beyond the challenges connected to the widening of participation to HE of specific social, cultural or age groups, previous experiences from universities engaged in promoting diversity programmes show that focusing just on increasing the enrolment rates of vulnerable students is not enough to achieve the goal of improving the inclusiveness of the overall academic environment (Archer et al., 2005; Ball, 2016). Although an open doors policy is valuable, increasing the retention rate of vulnerable students is also pivotal to warrant that they would be able to successfully manage and complete their educational path. Educational gaps are the by-product of the wider socio-economic circumstances that affect the students' context. Therefore, the objective of attaining more fair and open equitable conditions in HE is strictly linked to the investment provided by EU and national governments in the public system of education as a whole. What many vulnerable groups of students have in common is a lack of confidence (often inherited from the family environment) in the way instruction can boost cultural capital and, consequently, multiply personal and professional opportunities, defying feelings of worthlessness and self-fulfilling prophecies of failure. However expensive could be the effort of providing support to vulnerable students, we have to bear in mind that costs of exclusion need also to be calculated in terms of negative implications the drop-out phenomenon has both at the socioeconomic and personal level, as it simultaneously hinders the ability to produce national wealth as well as individual wellbeing and self-esteem (Altbach, 2009; Deem & Brehony, 2005).

This entails calling into question the common view of vulnerable students as subjects suffering from some deficit that they should overcome. Seeing students as in some way "defective" is the main reason for their difficulties in the academic environment. While it diverts attention from barriers they face in all aspects of HE settings and organisation, it also prevents identifying the real causes of exclusionary pressures that impede vulnerable students to access and succeed in the academic path. Therefore, the adoption of inclusive policies in HE cannot be based merely on special programs addressed to meet the needs of specific students' groups, but requires embracing an overall strategy for inclusion involving the entire university body and warranting that policies have a real effect on the way disadvantaged students are perceived and treated (Brennan & Naidoo, 2008; Gidley et al., 2010). Furthermore, it implies that unambiguous statements about inclusion are incorporated in universities' strategic plans, ensuring adequate investment in project management activities that provide clear directions about the process to be implemented at all institutional and community levels. Such process links to all relevant practices aimed at achieving more equitable conditions not just for the target students, but for all learners, encompassing a number of possible improvements concerning the way limited enrolment rules are managed, curricula shaped, teaching and learning strategies developed, and access to services provided. If inclusion involves challenging the way education reproduces socioeconomic and cultural inequalities, enabling the access of specific groups must be associated with systematic questioning of the values universities implicitly or overtly adopt in pursuing their everyday practices.

Underprivileged students are vulnerable especially because they don't own the same cultural capital as their peers. They miss vital information about what HE implies and how they can have access to it. Moreover, even when access can be secured, the risks and costs of participation of vulnerable learners to HE are greater compared to the other students. Even small critical situations can produce a deep impact on their ability to deal with the requirements of the university career, as they face a system not designed to accommodate their needs but, on the contrary, conceived having in mind typical young, male and white students belonging to the upper and middle class (Read et al., 2003; Wylie, 2005). Consequently, the urge to widen participation in order to support economic growth and sustainability of universities is insufficient to guarantee the entrenchment of the inclusive process into HE institutions, unless it will be connected to a clear-cut aspiration and commitment towards achieving social justice for all learners.

10   Good Practices in Italy: A Few Examples

Good practices addressed to ease the HE access, retention, and completion of vulnerable students in Italy are traditionally based on a model of inclusion that essentially focuses on learners with disabilities (Dovigo, 2016). Special schools were abolished in Italy in the late Seventies, paving the way to the admission of disabled students to HE. The law that acknowledged disabled students' right to access HE has been in place since 2000. As a consequence, support services for students with a disability are available in every Italian university today. However, the process of actually considering them as ordinary members of the academic environment is far from being fully achieved. The inclusion in HE of other vulnerable groups in terms of socioeconomic conditions, gender, learning difficulties, ethnic background and so on, is even more complex, as provisions are connected to specific programs that each institution fosters on the basis of the strategic plan adopted. As a consequence, with the exception of services addressed to students with a disability, the way inclusive policies concerning vulnerable students are designed and implemented widely varies from one university to another, depending on available resources and local interests, as well as the institutional sensitivity to issues raised by students' pressure groups that advocate for more provisions.

Below we summarise some examples of good practices currently managed by Italian universities. They are representative of the programmes academic institutions nowadays promote to encourage the participation of vulnerable students to HE.[1]

- Educational counselling (University of Turin): the activity aims to sustain students with a disability and learning difficulties over their study path by offering individual guidance and designing personalised learning programmes. The educational counselling provides students individual support by laying out pedagogical plans (individual education plan, personalised teaching plan), as well as by helping them identify study methods that work.
- Peer tutoring services (University of Padua): the student tutors support students with disabilities over their study path by helping them to get classes, reserve places in the classroom, retrieve course materials (if the student was unable to attend classes due to health reasons), and mediate with teachers to individualise exam contents and procedures.
- "Learn to learn" group support (University of Naples): the support service is aimed at students who, despite having the skills needed to potentially deal with the university demands, are late in doing exams or unable to obtain good results due to emotional or relational factors. The service offers nine weekly meetings and involves a follow-up meeting after some months. The counselling activity helps students examine the specific problems faced and identify suitable strategies for improving academic performance.
- Two cards for transsexual or transgender students (University of Bologna): while in the process to obtain legal reassignment of sex (including the

modification of identity documents), transsexual or transgender students can be uncomfortable with the contrast between their name and appearance, for example when they are called out during exams. Consequently, the university provides students two cards, one with the original name, the other with the new name.
- Asylum seekers to university project (University of Pavia): since 2015 the university gives 15 asylum-seekers the opportunity to attend a first or second level course of study with total exemption from university fees for the legal duration of the course. Moreover, for the same period asylum-seekers are offered free housing at the university residences, study assistance, free access to all university canteens and sports facilities, as well as paid training internships promoted by the various university departments.
- Tackling gender disparities (University of Trento): the project offers basic training at the bachelor level on gender issues to provide knowledge of contemporary discourses on gender. It also promotes specific post-graduate education courses, tackles gender inequalities, analyses critical issues for a gendered redefinition of the disciplines, and promotes awards and/or scholarships on equal opportunities and gender studies.
- Trust counsellor (University of Turin): following the issue of the code of conduct against sexual harassment and regulation for prevention and protection of workers against mobbing, the university created the trust counsellor service. The counsellor listens to and protects people who have reported to be a victim of harassment and/or mobbing and provides information and training about the prevention of different forms of violence.
- Parenting support (University of Trento): started up as a pilot project in 2014/15, the project aims both to strengthen already existing services (such as the university nursery school) and to introduce specific measures in support of parenthood for the student population with children, by designing a system of services and benefits in connection to the economic situation of parenting students.
- Baby card project (University of Cagliari): the project aims at preventing the study dropout of parent students and those who become so during the course of university studies. The baby card entitles pregnant and female students with children up to 10 years-old to get access to dedicated services, as reserved parking spaces at the university site, facilitations in reserving the time for taking exams, free access to course materials provided through e-learning, privileged admittance to the counters of the student administration and university offices, and access to the university's "pink rooms", suitable for mothers and children and equipped with a baby changing table, relaxation chairs and children's furniture.

11 Conclusions

The good practices we presented above are aimed to widen the participation of vulnerable students to HE, focusing on specific needs and groups. Even though since their implementation these practices have proven to be effective and sustainable over time, they also pose some specific questions, as universities attempt to further expand their ability to support projects about equity and inclusion of vulnerable learners.

Firstly, as we observed, structural factors related to the socio-economic conditions and, above all, the family cultural capital of students have a deep impact on their ability to enrol, and especially, complete the university pathway, as the level of resiliency of vulnerable learners tends to be lower in comparison with other students. Consequently, the effect of good practices on vulnerable students can be reduced by the influence of those factors.

Secondly, investigation shows that good practices are not easily transferable from one academic context to the other. Even though they demonstrated to be effective in a specific environment, different conditions at the local level often preclude from using a "copy and paste" approach when university administrations try to adopt practices that successfully worked elsewhere. Hence, adaptations are usually required to meet the specific requirements of each university setting in terms of norms, organisation, culture, and targeted population.

However, such challenges should not prevent from promoting good practices aimed at improving inclusion in EU universities. To this, mutual understanding and collaboration between academic institutions are pivotal to ensure that vulnerable students will achieve more equitable access, retention, and completion of HE in the next years.

Acknowledgement

This document has been produced as a part of the project "ACCESS4ALL – Laboratory for Policies and Practices of Social Development in Higher Education" (Ref. 2015-1-ES01-KA203-015970) co-funded by the European Union (Erasmus+ Programme).

Note

1 A more detailed description of HE good practices can be found on the ACCESS4ALL website (https://access4allproject.eu/bestpractices).

References

Aina, C. (2013). Parental background and university dropout in Italy. *Higher Education, 65*(4), 437–456.

Aina, C., Baici, E., & Casalone, G. (2011). Time to degree: Students' abilities, university characteristics or something else? Evidence from Italy. *Education Economics, 19*(3), 311–325.

Altbach, P. G., Reisberg, L., & Rumbley, L. E. (2009). *Trends in global higher education: Tracking an academic revolution*. UNESCO.

Archer, L. (2007). Diversity, equality and higher education: A critical reflection on the ab/uses of equity discourse within widening participation. *Teaching in higher Education, 12*(5–6), 635–653.

Archer, L., Hutchings, M., & Ross, A. (2005). *Higher education and social class: Issues of exclusion and inclusion*. Routledge.

ANVUR. (2016). *Rapporto sullo stato del sistema universitario e della ricerca 2016*. National Agency for the Evaluation of the University and Research System.

ANVUR. (2018). *Rapporto sullo stato del sistema universitario e della ricerca 2018*. National Agency for the Evaluation of the University and Research System.

Azzolini, D., & Barone, C. (2013). Do they progress or do they lag behind? Educational attainment of immigrants' children in Italy: The role played by generational status, country of origin and social class. *Research in Social Stratification and Mobility, 31*, 82–96.

Ball, S. J. (2016). Education, justice and democracy: The struggle over ignorance and opportunity. In A. Montgomery & I. Kehoe (Eds.), *Reimagining the purpose of schools and educational organisations* (pp. 189–205). Springer International Publishing.

Ballarino, G., & Panichella, N. (2016). Social stratification, secondary school tracking and university enrolment in Italy. *Contemporary Social Science, 11*(2–3), 169–182.

Ballarino, G., & Perotti, L. (2012). The Bologna process in Italy. *European Journal of Education, 47*(3), 348–363.

Bertozzi, R. (2018). University students with migrant background in Italy. Which factors affect opportunities? *Italian Journal of Sociology of Education, 10*(1), 23–42.

Booth, T., & Ainscow, M. (2011). *Index for inclusion: Developing learning and participation in schools*. Centre for Studies on Inclusive Education.

Bowl, M., & Bathmaker, A. M. (2016). 'Non-traditional' students and diversity in higher education. In *Routledge handbook of the sociology of higher education* (p. 1720). Routledge.

Bowman, N. A. (2011). Promoting participation in a diverse democracy: A meta-analysis of college diversity experiences and civic engagement. *Review of Educational Research, 81*, 29–68.

Bratti, M., Broccolini, C., & Staffolani, S. (2010). Higher education reform, student time allocation and academic performance in Italy: Evidence from a Faculty of Economics. *Rivista italiana degli economisti, 15*(2), 275–304.

Brennan, J., & Naidoo, R. (2008). Higher education and the achievement (and/or prevention) of equity and social justice. *Higher Education, 56*(3), 287–302.

Cammelli, A., & Gasperoni, G. (2015). *16th Almalaurea report on Italian university graduates' profile. Opportunities and challenges for higher education in Italy* (No. 74). AlmaLaurea Working Papers series.

Checchi, D., Fiorio, C. V., & Leonardi, M. (2013). Intergenerational persistence in educational attainment in Italy. *Economic Letters, 118*(1), 229–232.

Chun, E. B., & Feagin, J. R. (2019). *Rethinking diversity frameworks in higher education.* Routledge.

Coertjens, L., Brahm, T., Trautwein, C., & Lindblom-Ylänne, S. (2017). Students' transition into higher education from an international perspective. *Higher Education, 73*(3), 357–369.

Codling, A., & Meek, V. L. (2006). Twelve propositions on diversity in higher education. *Higher Education Management and Policy*, 1–24.

Contini, D., Cugnata, F., & Scagni, A. (2018). Social selection in higher education. Enrolment, dropout and timely degree attainment in Italy. *Higher Education, 75*(5), 785–808.

Contini, D., & Scagni, A. (2013). Social-origin inequalities in educational careers in Italy. *Determined to Succeed? Performance versus Choice in Educational Attainment.*

Crozier, G., Reay, D., Clayton, J., Colliander, L., & Grinstead, J. (2008). Different strokes for different folks: Diverse students in diverse institutions–experiences of higher education. *Research Papers in Education, 23*(2), 167–177.

Dakka, F. (2015). Differentiation without diversity: The political economy of higher education transformation. In *The Palgrave international handbook of higher education policy and governance* (pp. 323–341). Palgrave Macmillan.

Deem, R., & Brehony, K. J. (2005). Management as ideology: The case of 'new managerialism'in higher education. *Oxford Review of Education, 31*(2), 217–235.

Di Pietro, G. (2012). The Bologna process and widening participation in university education: New evidence from Italy. *Empirica, 39*(3), 357–374.

Dovigo, F. (2016). Linking theory to practice in inclusive education. In F. Dovigo (Ed.) *Special educational needs and inclusive practices. An international perspective* (pp. 33–62). Sense Publishers.

Espenshade, T. J., & Radford, A. W. (2013). *No longer separate, not yet equal: Race and class in elite college admission and campus life.* Princeton University Press.

European Commission. (2019). *Education and training monitor 2019 Italy report.* Author. https://ec.europa.eu/education/resources-and-tools/document-library/education-and-training-monitor-2019-italy-report_en

European Commission/EACEA/Eurydice. (2018a). *National student fee and support systems in European higher education – 2018/19. Eurydice – Facts and figures.* Publications Office of the European Union. https://eacea.ec.europa.eu/national-policies/eurydice/sites/eurydice/files/fee_support_2018_19_report_en.pdf

European Commission/EACEA/Eurydice. (2018b). *The structure of the European education systems 2018/19: Schematic diagrams. Eurydice facts and figures.* Publications Office of the European Union. https://eacea.ec.europa.eu/national-policies/eurydice/sites/eurydice/files/fee_support_2018_19_report_en.pdf

Eurostat. (2019a). *Tertiary educational attainment by sex, age group 30–34.* https://ec.europa.eu/eurostat/web/products-datasets/-/t2020_41&lang=en

Eurostat. (2019b). *Early leavers from education and training.* https://ec.europa.eu/eurostat/documents/2995521/9751510/3-26042019-AP-EN.pdf/49c38a50-52b5-4f97-95f7-483a570fbb36

Eurostudent. (2018a). *Ottava indagine Eurostudent. Le condizioni di vita e di studio degli studenti universitari 2016–2018.* Associazione Cimea.

Eurostudent. (2018b). *Social and economic conditions of student life in Europe: EUROSTUDENT VI 2016–2018: Synopsis of indicators.* W. Bertelsmann Verlag.

Fabricius, A., & Preisler, B. (Eds.). (2015). *Transcultural interaction and linguistic diversity in higher education: The student experience.* Springer.

Gidley, J. M., Hampson, G. P., Wheeler, L., & Bereded-Samuel, E. (2010). From access to success: An integrated approach to quality higher education informed by social inclusion theory and practice. *Higher Education Policy, 23*(1), 123–147.

Grimes, S., Southgate, E., Scevak, J., & Buchanan, R. (2019). University student perspectives on institutional non-disclosure of disability and learning challenges: Reasons for staying invisible. *International Journal of Inclusive Education, 23*(6), 639–655.

Guri-Rosenblit, S., & Sebková Teichler, U. (2007). Massification and diversity of higher education systems: Interplay of complex dimensions. *Higher Education Policy, 20*, 373–389.

Haigh, M. (2014). From internationalisation to education for global citizenship: A multi-layered history. *Higher Education Quarterly, 68*(1), 6–27.

Hazelkorn, E. (2015). *Rankings and the reshaping of higher education: The battle for world-class excellence.* Springer.

Huisman, J., & van Vught, F. (2009). Diversity in European higher education. In *Mapping the higher education landscape. Towards a European classification of higher education.* Springer.

Hurtado, S., & Deangelo, L. (2012). Linking diversity and civic-minded practices with student outcomes. *Liberal Education, 98*(2), 14–23.

Kottmann, A., Antonowicz, D., Boudard, E., Coates, H., Cremonini, L., Decataldo, A., … Reale, E. (2015a). *Dropout and completion in higher education in Europe. Annex 3: Country case studies Europe policy briefings Australia, USA.*

Kottmann, A., Cremonini, L., Kolster, R., Westerheijden, D. F., & Vossensteyn, J. J. (2015b). *Dropout and completion in higher education in Europe: Annex 2: Short country reports*. Publications Office of the European Union.

Istat. (2016). *Italia in cifre 2016*. Author. https://www.istat.it/it/files/2016/12/ItaliaCifre2016.pdf

Istat. (2018a). *Rapporto sulla conoscenza 2018*. Author. https://www.istat.it/storage/rapporti-tematici/conoscenza2018/Rapportoconoscenza2018.pdf

Istat. (2018b). *Popolazione al 1° gennaio di 19 anni*. Author. http://dati.istat.it/

Istat. (2018c). *Rapporto BES 2018. Il benessere equo e sostenibile in Italia*. Author. https://www.istat.it/it/files//2018/12/Bes_2018.pdf

Istat. (2019a). *Incidenza dei giovani Neet di 15–29 anni (non occupati e non in istruzione)*. Author. http://dati.istat.it/Index.aspx?DataSetCode=DCCV_NEET

Istat. (2019b). *Noi Italia. 100 statistiche per capire il Paese in cui viviamo 2019*. Author. http://noi-italia.istat.it

Lagomarsino, F., & Ravecca A. (2014). *Il passo seguente. I giovani di origine straniera all'università*. Franco Angeli.

Maiolo, M. E., Cortini, M., & Zuffo, R. G. (2013). Education or employment? The challenging choice of today's youth. *Procedia-Social and Behavioral Sciences, 84*, 298–302.

Mantovani, D., Gasperoni, G., & Albertini, M. (2018). Higher education beliefs and intentions among immigrant-origin students in Italy. *Ethnicities, 18*(4), 603–626.

Marshak, L., Van Wieren, T., Ferrell, D. R., Swiss, L., & Dugan, C. (2010). Exploring barriers to college student use of disability services and accommodations. *Journal of Postsecondary Education and Disability, 22*(3), 151–165.

May, A. L., & Stone, C. A. (2010). Stereotypes of individuals with learning difficulties: Views of college students with and without disabilities. *Journal of Learning Disabilities, 43*(6), 483–499.

MIUR. (2017). *Gli immatricolati nell'a.a. 2016/2017 il passaggio dalla scuola all'università dei diplomati nel 2016*. Author. http://www.istruzione.it/allegati/2016/Immatricolazioni201 5-16.pdf

Mok, K. H., & Neubauer, D. (2016). Higher education governance in crisis: A critical reflection on the massification of higher education, graduate employment and social mobility. *Journal of Education and Work, 29*(1, 1–12.

OECD. (2018). *Education at a glance 2018: OECD indicators*. Author.

OECD. (2019). *Education at a glance 2019: OECD indicators*. Author.

Paba, S., & Bertozzi, R. (2017). What happens to students with a migrant background in the transition to higher education? Evidence from Italy. *Rassegna Italiana di Sociologia, 2*, 315–352.

Read, B., Archer, L., & Leathwood, C. (2003). Challenging cultures: Student conceptions of "belonging" and power at a post-1992 university. *Studies in Higher Education, 28*(3), 261–277.

Romito, M. (2016). I consigli orientativi agli studenti di origine straniera nella scuola secon- daria di primo grado. Un caso a parte? *Rivista Italiana di Sociologia, 57*(1), 31–54.

Teichler, U. (2008). Diversification? Trends and explanations of the shape and size of higher education. *Higher Education, 56*(3), 349–379.

Teichler, U. (2015). The impact of temporary study abroad. *Eurosla Monographs Series, 4*, 15–32. http://www.eurosla.org/monographs/EM04/Teichler.pdf

Trow, M. (1973). *Problems in the transition from Elite to mass higher education*. Carnegie Commission on Higher Education. Berkeley Press.

Trow, M. (2006). Reflections on the transition from elite to mass to universal access: Forms and phases of higher education in modern societies since WWII. In J. J. Forest & P. G. Altbach (Eds.), *International handbook of higher education* (pp. 243–280). Springer.

Triventi, M. (2014). Does working during higher education affect students' academic progression? *Economics of Education Review, 41*, 1–13.

Triventi, M., Panichella, N., Ballarino, G., Barone, C., & Bernardi, F. (2016). Education as a positional good: Implications for social inequalities in educational attainment in Italy. *Research in Social Stratification and Mobility, 43*, 39–52.

Turri, M. (2016). The difficult transition of the Italian university system: Growth, underfunding and reforms. *Journal of Further and Higher Education, 40*(1), 83–106.

Van Vught, F. (Ed.). (2009). Mapping the higher education landscape. In *Towards a European classification of higher education*. Springer.

Vergolini, L., & Vlach, E. (2017). Family background and educational path of Italian graduates. *Higher Education, 73*(2), 245–259.

Wilcox, P., Winn, S., & Fyvie-Gauld, M. (2005). 'It was nothing to do with the university, it was just the people': The role of social support in the first-year experience of higher education. *Studies in Higher Education, 30*(6), 707–722.

Wylie, J. R. (2005). Non-traditional student attrition in higher education: A theoretical model of separation, disengagement then dropout. In *Australian association for research in education 2005 conference papers*.

Younger, K., Gascoine, L., Menzies, V., & Torgerson, C. (2019). A systematic review of evidence on the effectiveness of interventions and strategies for widening participation in higher education. *Journal of Further and Higher Education, 43*(6), 742–773.

Zotti, R. (2015). *Should I stay or should I go? Dropping out from university: An empirical analysis of students' performances*. Working Paper 70. AlmaLaurea Inter-University Consortium.

CHAPTER 5

Good Practices and Experiences for Inclusion in Portugal

Miguel Jerónimo and Fernanda Paula Pinheiro

Abstract

The implementation in Portugal of the Bologna process brought new challenges to Higher Education, namely in the necessary guarantee of access and success of students. By providing a greater spectrum of opportunities for young people and adults to raise their humanistic training, scientific knowledge and their academic qualifications, HEI have incorporated the heterogeneity and multiculturality of our societies. The academic community in its whole has suffered a radical change. The students, with their individual differences and specific needs, have acquired greater visibility and importance in the definition of institutional strategies and in the adoption of more flexible and adapted teaching/learning models and practices. Policies for inclusion have been the answer to this major shift. The Polytechnic of Leiria is one of the Portuguese HEI that has been deeply committed, to the principles of inclusion, actively seeking to contribute to the training and empowerment of its students, regardless of their specificities. Promoting educational success and building a more sustainable society is the guiding matrix for its action. To this end, it develops multiple actions and programs designed to facilitate the inclusion of students with some type of specific need and/or in a situation of social, psychological or economic vulnerability. The self-assessment process, triggered within the scope of the ACCESS4ALL Project, led by the Universidad Autònoma de Barcelona, allowed the identification of critical points and the potential for improvement resulting from the valorisation of diversity, as a teaching and learning resource

Keywords

higher education – inclusion – special needs students – self-assessment tool – innovation – diversity

1 Introduction

The higher education system in Portugal, according to the Bologna process, was introduced in the Basic Law on Education by Law No. 49/2005 of 30 August and regulated by Decree-Law 74/2006 of 24 March (DGES, 2015). This system has been fully implemented by public and private universities and polytechnics, since 2009/2010, and since then structured into three cycles. The bachelor's and master's degrees are conferred by universities and polytechnics. The bachelor's degrees have a duration of between six to eight semesters corresponding respectively to 180 or 240 ECTS (European Credit Transfer System), and master's degrees which include 90 to 120 credits have a duration of between three and four semesters.

After the 1st cycle of studies, the access to the course of study leading to a master's degree depends on a student's separate application that meets the regulations set by the legal and statutorily competent body of the higher education institution to which the student intends to apply which include, inter alia "Rules on admission to the course of study, in particular the academic and curricular conditions; the rules of application; the criteria for selection and ranking; and the securing process and promotion" (Article 26 – Decree-Law No. 74/2006 of 24 March).

Some universities also provide integrated master's degrees, with 300 to 360 credits and a duration of between ten to twelve semesters. In these cases, a degree corresponds to the first six semesters – 180 credits, after which the student receives a mobility diploma. Although it does not allow them to practice the profession, it can facilitate their transfer to another institution of higher education in order to complete the integrated master's degree (Veiga, 2015). Exceptionally, in the case of integrated courses of study leading to a master's degree, access and entry to the cycle of studies leading to the degree is ruled by the applicable law. The completion of the 3rd cycle of studies, PhD, is confined to universities. In the 2nd and 3rd cycles the public defence of a dissertation, project work or internship report is necessary.

Alongside these three study cycles, the Professional Higher Technical Courses (CTESP), which correspond to a higher education short cycle and are non-degree awarding were created in 2014. These courses, corresponding to 120 ECTS and which have a two-year duration, are only offered by the polytechnic higher education institutions (Decree-Law No. 43/2014 of 18 March).

"The Polytechnic of Leiria aims to be an institution for all. It values higher education which includes everyone, regardless of their specific characteristics and works to adjust its action so as to allow for the participation of all" (Mangas et al., 2017). Strategically positioned in a Region of multiple social,

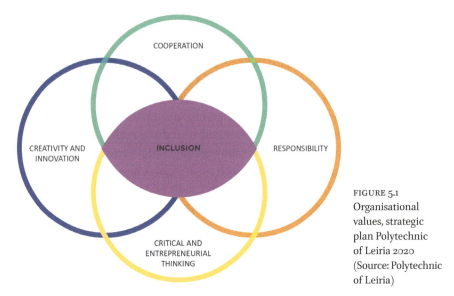

FIGURE 5.1 Organisational values, strategic plan Polytechnic of Leiria 2020 (Source: Polytechnic of Leiria)

environmental, economic and cultural particularities, the Polytechnic of Leiria assumes inclusion as one of the primary values of its action. Not only on the level of internal dynamics, but also in its relationship with the national and international community, other important values such as "cooperation", "innovation" and "critical and entrepreneurial thinking" (Strategic Plan, 2020) are considered.

There is a set of experiences and actions (evidence of good practices) that seek to ensure inclusion in the whole Academy and transform the Polytechnic of Leiria into an institution for all, regardless of the particularities of each one who studies and/or works there.

Promoting inclusion is an everyday mission. Reality imposes a constant requirement: inclusion has to be built! As the system generates multiple mechanisms that create inequality, injustice and discrimination, institutions set the strategic pace in the fight against exclusion, particularly those who are concerned with educational matters such as Higher Education Institutions, within the scope of their training functions, scientific research and knowledge and innovation sharing. This fight not only ensures equal rights and opportunities, but also access to (higher) education and promotion of educational success.

HEIs will not be able to overcome inequalities by themselves but they can and should be a relevant part of the solution, as examples of equity and diversity. Multiple examples of good inclusion practices generated in and with the Polytechnic of Leiria can be shared, and all with a common denominator: the students.

In an increasingly multicultural and heterogeneous society, of which the academic communities are a strong reflection, and in which individual differences have more and more visibility and power, integrating the principles of inclusive education into the agenda of all leaders and stakeholders poses major challenges and opportunities for sharing, cooperation and negotiation. The latter help "overcome barriers that limit the presence, participation and achievement of learners; respond to the diversity of the needs of each and every one, with a focus on those who have traditionally been excluded from learning opportunities (in A guide for ensuring inclusion and equity in inclusion, UNESCO). Selected good practices in the area of equity and inclusion will be presented and discussed next. They are a result of many years of initiatives among the academic community.

2   Good Practices from Portugal: Polytechnic of Leiria

2.1   FASE® – *Social Student Support Fund*

FASE® has been designed to complement the various existing formats of direct social support (scholarships and emergency aid) by providing its student collaborators a monthly grant, in cash or in kind. The main purpose is to promote equal opportunities in educational success, regarding the social responsibility of the Institution. Attaining this goal presupposes:
- supporting students in serious financial need who are committed to finishing their courses;
- combatting early school leaving; promoting school success;
- contributing to the consolidation of the educational path and strengthening academic and professional qualifications of students;
- encouraging participation in working life, under conditions that ensure the simultaneous development of academic activities;
- promoting academic and social integration and also strengthening the link between the Polytechnic of Leiria and its students.

2.2   *Production of Support Materials and the Use of Different Support Resources for Blind Students*

Production of support materials and use of the different support products for blind students (CRID – Center for Digital Inclusion). Initially the teachers send materials of their curricular units. Later they are adapted through specific software and printed in Braille and high relief. Once they are ready, the materials are distributed to students so that they are in the possession of all the documents required for lessons in equity with their peers.

The project started in 2015. There is no timetable with a predictable duration in the long run. We believe that this is a kind of strategy that makes sense to be carried out with no end in sight.

2.3 Supporting Higher Education Students with Specific Learning Difficulties: Dyslexia, Dysorthographia, Dysgraphia

Psychological assessment: at first, it is essential that students go through a process of (re)psychological evaluation to assess the existing difficulties in reading and writing. This step is performed in a psychology consultation in the Polytechnic of Leiria's Student Support Service (SSS). Depending on the results of this evaluation, intervention strategies to be carried out are outlined and it is also suggested that the student request the 'student with a Special Educational Needs status'.

Psychopedagogical intervention: Due to the students' demonstration of interest and depending on availability and the specific needs of each one, it is possible to create small support groups including counselling sessions (SSS) and re-education and pedagogical interventions (iACT – Inclusion and Accessibility in Action Research Unit: Polytechnic of Leiria). If the conditions that are necessary to create groups are not met, the intervention remains available individually, in psychology consultations and/or tutorials on re-education strategies for difficulties in reading and writing.

2.4 Supporting Group for Higher Education Students with Specific Learning Difficulties: Dyslexia, Dysorthographia, Dysgraphia

Before entering the group, it is essential to assess the student's profile in reading and writing. This step is performed in a psychology consultation at IPLeiria's SSS (Student Support Service). Depending on the results of this evaluation, intervention strategies to be carried out are outlined and applied in the group. The psychopedagogical intervention is implemented by iACT (Inclusion & Accessibility in Action Research Unit: Polytechnic of Leiria) while the development of soft skills, which are considered essential are addressed by the Student Support Service.

2.5 Financial Literacy Educational Programme

The enormous increase, diversity and complexity of financial products and services make the task of evaluating and comparing costs, benefits and risks associated to each product or service difficult. It should also be noted that higher education students have to deal with economic crises, which often culminates in school dropout because of the lack of skills to manage financial resources. Additionally, in the near future with the entry into the labour market, these students will make their first medium term financial choices, such as house or car loans and savings. Thus, we can assume the special relevance of financial education in the context of higher education. To understand the financial literacy level of students at the Polytechnic of Leiria, we applied an inquiry that addressed issues such as: understanding basic financial concepts (such as spread and EURIBOR); understanding the effects of economic-financial variables on savings and credit; the way the students plan expenditures and incomes; selection criteria to choose financial products and services. To improve financial knowledge, we promote practical seminars for students which occur at several campus of the Polytechnic of Leiria. These seminars are addressed to the academic community, with particular emphasis on students with support grants. We also hold conferences with financial specialists. The program is specially targeted to students with grants support, but anyone in the academic community can participate.

3 Institution Self-Assessment

The aim of the project ACCESS4ALL is to promote the social and educational inclusion of the above mentioned groups as well as the non-traditional students into higher education, thus satisfying the priorities of the Erasmus+ Programme and clearly approaching one of its main characteristics "to promote equality and inclusion, providing easier access to students from disadvantaged backgrounds and with less opportunities in comparison to their peers" (ERASMUS+ European Programme, 2015).

The implementation of this major objective implies, among other specific objectives, the identification of guidelines to be implemented by Higher Education Institutions, in order to promote initiatives aimed at encouraging the access, attendance and successful conclusion of under-represented students in Higher Education.

For this purpose, an ACCESS4ALL Self-Assessment Tool has been developed, called "Mapping of dimensions of the ACCESS4ALL Higher Education Institutions" that aims to assess not only the HEI values and principles, but also the organisational characteristics for promoting innovation and inclusion. This tool will be tested by consortium member partners [Autonomous University of Barcelona (Spain), Polytechnic of Leiria (Portugal), University of Bergamo (Italy), University of Bucharest (Romania), University of Bristol (United Kingdom) and University Jyvaskyla (Finland)] and by the stakeholders involved, and after it is adjusted it will be applied in any European or International Higher Education Institution.

The application of the self-assessment tool to key actors of the Polytechnic of Leiria's organisational structure allowed to obtain a profile in terms of inclusion, considering the two main dimensions under analysis: institutional factors (which include "HEI organisational maturity", "Institutional innovation" and "Knowledge sharing"). And the inclusion factors themselves (which include "Inclusion shared understanding", "Policies for inclusion" and "Actions for inclusion").

It is important to emphasise that the resulting self-diagnosis representation may generate a structured reflection on the current situation of inclusion in the institution, because it is based on the perceptions of a group of internal actors at a given moment for this purpose. Therefore, the A4A self-assessment tool has been developed for those Higher Education Institutions (HEIs) willing to explore and improve their innovative and inclusion policies.

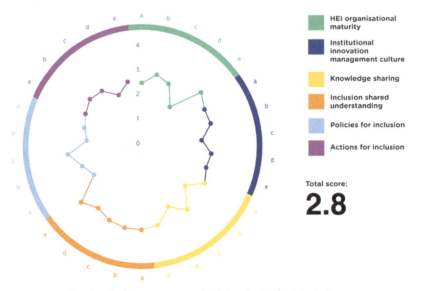

FIGURE 5.2   Results of self-assessment at the Polytechnic of Leiria, A4A, 2017

Positioning of the Polytechnic of Leiria (Dimension Score: 1–2, 2–3, 3–4, 4+), as an inclusive institution is discussed in the following sections.

3.1   *HEI Organisational Maturity*

The overall score of this dimension is 2.7. The higher education institution should incorporate procedures and mechanisms that allow to review and update the institutional project for inclusion in its internal operating regulations. A certain level of autonomy of the organic units in the definition of their action projects should be safeguarded. Consequently, the institution should ensure an accountability system.

3.2   *Institutional Innovation Management Culture*

The overall score of this dimension is 2.8. The information generated by the existing monitoring systems should be used to plan and anticipate the changes that may affect the institution. Therefore, the Higher Education Institution should have strategic plans that also affect the decisions of the curricular area. Those responsible for leading the change should share their decisions through widely accepted communication systems and strategies. In light of this, strategies should be planned in order to minimise possible resistance to change.

3.3 Knowledge Sharing

The overall score of this dimension is 2.9. Collaborative work between professionals needs to be promoted as an effective tool in resolving issues that can be shared. Thus, the Higher Education Institution should ensure support for collaboration between different professional profiles and experiences by providing simplifying technological tools, as well as other resources, spaces and time. It is about encouraging meetings and promoting knowledge sharing between the different members of the organisation, both formally and informally. On the other hand, the Higher Education Institution should collaborate with its counterparts, at a local and national level, in order to help improve the conditions of access, attendance and academic success of the vulnerable groups.

3.4 Inclusion Shared Understanding

The overall score of this dimension is 3.3. At this level it is intended to ensure the involvement of all stakeholders (teachers, students, technical and administrative staff and other employees from the educational community, internal and external) to improve and increase inclusion in the higher education institution. The institution shall promote actions aimed at the involvement and commitment of all stakeholders in the effective promotion of inclusion. These actions should enable the active and participative performance of all actors in the different institutional areas, enabling access to information and the good use of resources and services available at an institutional level, as well as a better interaction between the different actors in the strengthening of an inclusion culture.

3.5 Policies for Inclusion

The overall score of this dimension is 2.6. In order to improve and promote more appropriate inclusion policies, higher education institutions should activate strategies to improve the participation of all stakeholders in the design and implementation of inclusion policies. After the academic community has achieved knowledge and understanding of the inclusion policies, academic leaders should actively involve all stakeholders in the implementation of these policies. This means that all stakeholders may participate in training programs and transfer this knowledge to the practice of their daily activity.

3.6 Actions for Inclusion

The overall score of this dimension is 2.7. It is desirable to plan and develop student support programs within a broad framework of an improvement plan for access, attendance and success of students in higher education. Student support programs and services should consider not only the diversity of roles, functions and responsibilities of the different sectors involved in the academic community (teachers, students and technical and administrative staff and services), but also the different strategies and guidance and mentoring actions at a global level of the HEI and specifically of the organic unit (school, faculty or center).

The results in the previous graphic indicate that in terms of factors related to inclusion, one of the strengths of the Polytechnic of Leiria is the existence of a clear and shared idea about inclusion (and its understanding).

On the other hand, one of its weaknesses focused on the field of inclusion policies, as measured by the self-assessment tool. At this critical point, the Polytechnic of Leiria plays a role in involving and mobilising all actors in the organisational and institutional dynamics, in order to foster a proactive behaviour in the implementation of inclusion-promoting policies, which recognise formal support for diversity, considering it a resource for learning and participation.

This dimension ensures that inclusion is transversal to all the HEI's action plans. Policies encourage the participation of students and teachers while they are part of the institutions, as well as encourage relationships with the community.

Faced with the current challenges of society, the role of educational institutions and HEIs in particular, (re)construction of communities and the development of inclusive values is increasing, and it is imperative to recognise that inclusion in education is one of the central aspects of inclusion in society.

FIGURE 5.3
Ecosystem of inclusion at the Polytechnic of Leiria (Source: Polytechnic of Leiria)

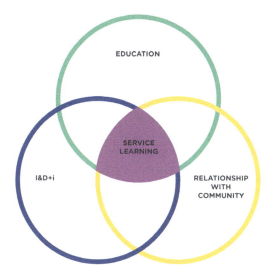

FIGURE 5.4
Academic community engagement matrix (Source: Polytechnic of Leiria)

The self-assessment tool made it possible to trace a positive situation of the proficiency of the Polytechnic of Leiria in the promotion of inclusion. However, it also pointed out the dimensions which are necessary to improve. The social and educational inclusion of all students in the Polytechnic of Leiria's ecosystem is and will continue to be a priority issue of action/mission, in order to guarantee a more equitable, inclusive and sustainable field.

The Polytechnic of Leiria intends to continue to follow the path that creates an educational environment that promotes inclusion, through the pillars of education/training and research, and also in the relationship with the surrounding community, according to a logic while working in collaboration with all stakeholders.

4 Conclusions

The Polytechnic of Leiria is completely committed to and also contributing to the social and personal integration of all its students, regardless of the singularities that characterise each one of them and/reducing the architectural obstacles on the *campi*. For this, the guiding plan for strategic initiatives are to:
1. Consolidate innovative and differentiating solutions for students with special educational needs in a more permanent way;
2. Develop projects and activities in the area of inclusion, accessibility and citizenship;
3. Create web space to share the institution's services, projects and activities in the areas of inclusion and citizenship.

The increasing number of students with Special Educational Needs (ENEE) in recent years at the Polytechnic of Leiria posed challenges to the entire academic community, while giving more visibility to the specific needs of this group. However, it also included references to situations of the social and/or economic disadvantage of international students from South America and China, among others. Those references included those entering higher education in adulthood through alternative access routes, with careers and family responsibilities, but who are committed to the requirement of lifelong learning in terms of employability.

In short, the heterogeneity and specificity of students in the universe of higher education encourages the awareness that the paradigm of education has changed (UNESCO, 2017), that is, it is necessary to know the barriers that each student may have in access to learning, in order to improve the quality of the education system, so that the barriers can be eliminated, taking each and every one to the limit of their potentialities.

In 2019 the Presidency of Polytechnic of Leiria decided to find a systematic, organised and sustainable way of receiving, monitoring and ensuring that students with special educational needs (SSEN) entered, remained and completed their academic training at the university level. With the support of an external advisor, in this case, from the Padre António Vieira Institute (IPAV), the Polytechnic of Leiria decided to start the "100% Inclusive!": a Program, whose synthetic definition is that of a pilot project, of social innovation for the integral inclusion of SSEN. The main ongoing actions of this project are to:

1. create conditions that allow real-time perception of the universe of students with special educational needs in the Polytechnic of Leiria and its characteristics;
2. adopt the "Inclusive Simplex" to reduce by 30% the time required between the application for status and its awarding;
3. make "Welcome Kits" available to all new students of the Polytechnic of Leiria and to the students with special educational needs, as well as provide a Teacher Support Manual for the teachers who have students with special educational needs;
4. create the function of Case Manager of students with special educational needs, who will monitor them from their entry to their conclusion of studies at the Polytechnic of Leiria;
5. elaborate and carry out the Individual Inclusion Plan for any student with special educational needs, which contains all the information related to that student, as well as the work developed during their follow-up;
6. elaborate a code of ethics and deontology that comprises a set of basic principles, by which the Case Manager and the Case Management Team should govern their action;

7. create an "Hours Credit Card", which supports the learning of each student with special educational needs;
8. create a "100% IN® Inclusive Model Residence", adapted to the students with special educational needs;
9. implement the "100% IN® Inclusive IPL Marathon (Hack For Good)";
10. create the "Buddies 100% IN®" project to support students with special educational needs through the FASE® Program.

Acknowledgement

This document has been produced as a part of the project "ACCESS4ALL – Laboratory for Policies and Practices of Social Development in Higher Education" (Ref. 2015-1-ES01-KA203-015970) co-funded by the European Union (Erasmus+ Programme).

References

Agência Nacional Erasmus+ (2015). http://www.erasmusmais.pt/comunicacao/noticias/223- erasmus-2012-2013-factos-numeros-tendencias.html

Ainscow, M. (2009). Tornar a Educação Inclusiva: como esta tarefa deve ser conceituada? In O. Fávero, W. Ferreira, T. Ireland, & D. Barreiros (Eds.), *Tornar a educação inclusiva/organizado*. UNESCO. http://bibliotecadigital.puc-campinas.edu.br/services/e-books/184683por.pdf

Decreto-Lei no. 43/2014, de 18 de março. (2014). *Cria e regula os cursos técnicos superiores profissionais*. Diário da República No. 54, 1a Série (pp. 2074–2081).

Decreto-Lei no 74/2006, de 24 de março. (2006). Regime jurídico dos graus académicos e diplomas do ensino superior. Diário da República No. 60, Série I-A (24-03-2006) (pp. 2242–2257).

DGES (Direção Geral de Ensino Superior). (2015). *Ensino Superior; Processo de Bolonha*. http://www.dges.mctes.pt

Mangas, N., et al. (2017). *Strategic plan 2020 polytechnic of Leiria*. Edition Instituto Politécnico de Leiria. Leiria, Legal Deposit 424 656/17. https://www.ipleiria.pt/wp-content/uploads/2017/05/Plano-Estrategico-2020_en_spreads.pdf

UNESCO. (2017). *A guide for ensuring inclusion and equity in education*. Author. http://unesdoc.unesco.org/images/0024/002482/248254e.pdf

Veiga, A. (2015). Análise do Sistema de ensino após o processo de Bolonha. In M. Rodrigues & M. Heitor (Eds.), *40 Anos de Políticas de Ciência e de Ensino Superior*. Almedina.

CHAPTER 6

Good Practices and Experiences for Inclusion in Higher Education in Romania

Elena Marin, Miaela Stîngu and Romiță Iucu

Abstract

Romanian universities are focusing more on the social aspects in tertiary education by implementing different support mechanisms in order to overcome considerable challenges, such as the high number and population diversity of disadvantaged groups (people from rural areas, individuals with a Roma background, people with low incomes, people coming from orphanages, etc.). Related to the support mechanism developed and implemented across Romania, we tried, in this chapter, to present several good practices available at national level when it comes to the equity and inclusion. Such examples are targeting, different aspects such as financial aids for students that may encounter problems during their studies. This aid has an impact on long term basis, because the students that benefited from this aid tend not to drop out their courses. Moreover, this chapter includes the results of University of Bucharest's self-assessment tool. The results from this self-assessment tool suggests some possible actions to improve our university innovative and inclusion capacity, especially in the field of "Policies for inclusion" or "HEI organisational maturity".

Keywords

equity – inclusion – disadvantaged groups – strategic plan for inclusion – self-assessment tool – Romania

1   Introduction

In Romania, after 1990, the universities were the first kind of institution to start the reforms for democratisation of education. Therefore, every university in

Romania has its own internal policies regarding admission, exams and conditions for graduation.

The academic year starts in the first week of October. As Romanian higher education (HE) institutions are autonomous, they may decide on the academic schedule. Each year is divided into two semesters. Each semester lasts approximately 18 weeks.

In 2017/2018, the national system of higher education comprised 93 institutions of higher education. State universities represent 59% of the higher education institutions and 73% of the total faculties.

The legal framework for the implementation of the Bologna Process in Romania was introduced between 2004 and 2006 and the structure of the Higher Education system follows the structure presented as in Figure 6.1.

FIGURE 6.1   Romania's higher education system

Regarding the number of European Credit Transfer System (ECTS) in Romania, the 1st cycle (Bachelor) includes a minimum of 180 and a maximum of 240 ECTS and is finalised with the level 6 of European Qualifications Framework; more specifically, one year of Bachelor day studies corresponds to 60 ECTS, while a BA programme typically takes 3–4 years to complete, depending on the field and area of specialisation. The length of Engineering, Law and Theology studies is 4 years. The Pharmacy faculty lasts 5-years and is the equivalent of 300 transferable study credits (ECTS equivalent), whereas the Medicine, Dentistry, Veterinary Medicine programmes, which last 6 years, are equivalent to 360 ECTS.

The 2nd cycle (Master's) includes a minimum of 90 and a maximum of 120 transferable study credits and takes 1–2 years to complete. In order to access the 3rd cycle (PhD level), 300 ECTS are needed.

During the 3rd cycle (PhD) some Doctoral Schools use ECTS only for the first year of advanced studies, to demonstrate accumulated credits for taught part of the PhD (involving class attendance). Some Doctoral Schools use, on the other hand, ECTS for the full programme of doctoral candidates (workload referring to taught courses and preliminary research papers). Doctoral studies in theory include 240 ECTS, whereas advanced studies in Doctoral Schools include 60 ECTS.

The number of students enrolled in the higher education at bachelor level decreased significantly between 2011–2016 (from 539.9 thousand to 405.6 thousand). In the academic year 2016/2017, 531,586 people were registered in the higher education institutions in Romania. Of the total number of people enrolled in higher education in 2016/2017, 76.3% were pursuing undergraduate degree programs, 19.5% master's degree programs, 3.6% doctoral degree programs, and 0.03% postgraduate programs (postdoctoral programs, in-depth and postgraduate programs, postgraduate specialisation programs). At the end of 2016/2017 academic year, 80,035 graduated at bachelor level, 35,807 graduated at master level, 1888 graduated at doctoral and post-doctoral level (INS, 2016–2018).

According to the Law of national education (1/2011),[1] higher education in public universities is free for a number of students with daily attendance, allocated yearly by the Government, and tuition is financed from the state budget, for public universities. A person may benefit from financing from the budget for a single graduation, respectively, master's degree and PhD programme.

Tuition fees exemptions are established by the Law of national education (Art. 205) for candidates coming from foster care (at least one place per university) and those coming from environments with high socioeconomic risk or socially marginalised – Roma people, high school graduates in the rural environment or cities with less than 10,000 inhabitants (number to be decided by each university senate).

To sum up, the conditions for benefiting from free higher education are: to be admitted on the subsidized positions on a merit base, to be a full time student, to be a first-time student (a student can benefit of gratuity for only one cycle), to be at socioeconomic risk (limited places). The gratuity is maintained over the entire course of the studies and does not change on a yearly basis (on a merit base or other criteria).

The remaining positions in public universities are available by paying the tuition fee decided upon by the university Senate. The payment of tuition fees applies a percentage of full-time students, and all the half-time and distance students. All students enrolled in private universities have to pay a fee.

In Romania, a minority of full-time students (less than half) are paying tuition fees in publicly funded higher education institutions. The fees amount between 100 and 1000 euro/year, with social studies having the lowest rates and art students (film) having the highest.

The Law of national education stipulates that grants for students in public universities, in every stage of the education cycle (undergraduate, master, PhD) are decided upon and financed from the state budget. Universities may supplement the scholarship fund from own extra-budgetary funds.

The Romanian support system is based on grants and combines need-based and merit-based grants which we will explain in later sub-chapter.

Students benefit also from other forms of financial support, mentioned in the National Law of Education:
– subsidies for accommodation and boarding;
– free health care and psychological assistance at the university medical centers and psychologists', or state medical centers and hospitals;
– 50% reduction for local public transport, domestic transport by road, railway and ship. Students from foster care have free transportation;
– free access to museums, concerts, theatre performances, opera, movies and other cultural and sports events organised by public institutions, within the limit of the budgets of the respective institutions;
– free camps for candidates coming from environments with high socioeconomic risk or socially marginalised.

2   A Policy Perspective on the Social Dimension of Higher Education in Romania

The social aspect is a key component amongst the country targets. Visible steps have been made in the last 20 years, starting with policy papers that triggered some changes in society.

Among the most important phases achieved so far are:
– Setting the Commission for Prevention and Fight against Poverty in 1998 who prepared a "Strategy for the Prevention of and Fight against Poverty", which, although it was not adopted by the government, represented the first strategic document to lay down the principles of social policies.
– Setting up of an Anti-Poverty and Promotion of Social Inclusion Commission (CASPIS), which operated between 2001 and 2006. The aim of this commission as to conduct key research in order to strengthen the fight against poverty.
– Signing in 2005 of a Joint Social Inclusion Memorandum by the Government and the European Commission that aimed to identify the key challenges faced by Romania in promoting social.
– In 2006 a Government Decision (no. 1217/2006) was passed that contained a national mechanism for promoting social inclusion.

All citizens have equal opportunities	The basic needs of every citizen are met	Differences between individuals are respected	All people feel valued and can live in dignity
Everyone deserves the opportunity to participate fully in the economic, social, political, and cultural life of their society and to enjoy the benefits of doing so. Equal opportunities mean that individual circumstances beyond their control do not determine people's quality of life.	Along with respect for and protection of fundamental human rights, one of the main preconditions for a decent quality of life is meeting citizens' basic needs for housing, food, sanitation, and security as well as for basic community services such as education, healthcare, and social services. These key elements enable people to live in dignity, to have control over their lives, and to actively participate in the life of their communities. The responsibility for developing their own social integration capacities and for being actively involved in handling difficult situations rests with every individual as well as with his or her family, and public authorities.	Each individual is unique. Individual differences can be along the lines of race, gender, ethnicity, socioeconomic status, age, sexual orientation, and beliefs (religious and otherwise) as well as physical, cognitive, or social abilities. The concept of diversity goes beyond tolerance; it encompasses acceptance and respect. Valuing diversity in a positive and nurturing way increases the chance that everyone will reach their potential and that communities will pro-actively use this potential.	All human beings are born free and equal in dignity and rights (Article 1 of the UN Declaration of Human Rights). When a person feels valued and lives in dignity, they are more likely to be in control of their lives and to participate in and become an active member of society.

FIGURE 6.2   Main aspects presented in the National Strategy on Social Inclusion and Poverty Reduction 2015–2020

- Approval of the Social Assistance Reform Strategy in 2011. A series of key objectives that have acted as guiding principles for the government in the past few years.
- Passing of Law no. 292/2011 on social assistance, defining homelessness and actual measures to be taken by local public authorities, establishing the complementarity between social benefits and social services, and strengthening the principles of social solidarity and collaboration between local public authorities in the social assistance sector.
- Adoption of a new strategy National Strategy on Social Inclusion and Poverty Reduction 2015–2020, who stated that the Government of Romania will ensure that all citizens to be provided with an equal opportunity to participate in society, to feel valued and appreciated, to live in dignity and that their basic needs to be met and their differences respected.

The National Strategy on Social Inclusion and Poverty Reduction 2015–2020 (Tesliuc et al., 2015) is the main official document that provides a reference point of the progresses made. The main aspects mentioned in the strategy are summarised in Figure 6.2.

3 An Institutional Perspective on the Social Dimension of Higher Education in Romania

As stated before, higher institutions in Romania have a high level of autonomy. Therefore, every four years, every university elaborates an institutional strategy focusing on different aspects. One of the aspects that many universities tackle in their strategies is the social dimension. We will shortly analyse the strategies of four universities in Romania, that represent the main areas of Romania.

3.1 *University of Bucharest (UB)*

University of Bucharest is the largest university in Romania with 19 faculties, 29 bachelor domains, 208 master programs, 21 doctoral schools with a total of around 31500 students at all levels. The University of Bucharest has a notable initiative, that of attempting to accede to the elite international universities through a visible presence in world rankings. It is a feasible objective which involves efforts from all staff and students, but that is commensurate with the size, quality and the aspirations of the university. In 2016 the University of Bucharest remains in the 701+ series of the best world universities, according to QS University Rankings, the most popular global ranking for universities and among the most important 500 universities in the world, according to QS Ranking of Universities by Subject. In Universities of Bucharest according to the Strategic Plan developed in 2019 an important stress is put on the non-discriminatory access and social inclusion of all students, which coagulates the democratic values that the UB places in the center of its education processes. Treating all students with equal respect, fairness and denial are the core values within the UB alongside with cultivating tolerance and accepting difference and diversity, promoting intercultural and inter-ethnic understanding.

3.2 The West University of Timisoara (UVT)

Over the last 12 years, the University has responded to changes in national educational policy, to demographic shifts, to a radically different economy and marketplace requirements, to emerging local and regional needs, and to new technologies. The University equips individuals with skills needed for effective contribution to society. This work is currently done through eleven faculties that provide a wide range of undergraduate and graduate programs. In respect to the social dimension, the West University of Timisoara aims at increasing social equity in the UVT, both by adapting the educational spaces and those related to the needs of students with special needs, as well as by supporting vulnerable groups, both to access tertiary education and to successfully complete their studies.

3.3 *Babeș-Bolyai University (UBB)*

Babeș-Bolyai University is the oldest university in Romania and it offers study programmes that aim at increasing career opportunities. UBB has 242 undergraduate study programmes, of which 147 undergraduate programmes are in Romanian, 70 in Hungarian, 10 in German, 14 in English and 1 in French. Babes-Bolyai University is involved in international programmes which offer UBB students the opportunity to study abroad at one of the partner universities and gives foreign students the chance to study at UBB. Babes-Bolyai University collaborates through mobility programmes with many universities from Europe, North America and South America, Africa, Australia and New Zealand.

Regarding the social dimension, the UBB Strategic Plan mentions the importance of stimulating democratic values, the social inclusion of all students, and tries to promote the policies on equal opportunities. The measures taken aim at: strengthening the university's status as the main factor of culture and social and humanistic education and respecting the cultural and axiological differences existing in the academic, social and economic environments. The university incorporates and promotes the following main values, such as freedom of thought and expression; search and promotion of truth; integrity, fairness, social responsibility, respect for diversity and intercultural cooperation.

3.4 *Alexandru Ioan Cuza University of Iași (UIAC)*

Alexandru Ioan Cuza University of Iași is the oldest higher education institution in Romania. Since 1860, the university has been carrying on a tradition of excellence and innovation in the fields of education and research. With over 24,000 students and 717 academic staff, the university enjoys high prestige at national and international level and cooperates with 504 universities world-wide. Alexandru Ioan Cuza University is a member of some of the most important university networks and associations: the Coimbra Group, EUA – European University Association, Utrecht Network, International Association of Universities, University Agency of Francophonie and the Network of Francophone Universities (RUFAC). These partnerships offer us the opportunity to experience changes, to have student and teacher mobilities and joint academic, research and strategy programmes. The UIAC Strategic plan mentions the principle of fairness in education. The university guarantees a fair system in terms of admission, participation and completion of studies for all students.

4   Examples of Good Practices and Experiences for Inclusion in Higher Education

While analysing the good practices available at national level when it comes to the equity and inclusion, we considered necessary to identify target groups in order to better underline the necessity of a clearer strategic plan for inclusion. Therefore, we identified 7 categories such as: orphan students by both parents; students with financial problems; students with medical problems; students with visual impairment and dyslexia; Roma students; students with remarkable learning outcome, with excellent research and professional activities, social activities, cultural and organisational activities; students/citizens from tertiary UE states which want to study in Romanian. Starting from the seven categories identified above we look into the practices of two of the most important university at national level, the University of Bucharest (UB) and West University of Timisoara (WUT). After a closer examination eight examples of activities that aim at supporting disadvantaged students were chosen to be presented as good practices.

4.1   *Scholarships*
4.1.1   Social Aid Scholarships (UB and WUT)
The aim of this scholarship is to ensure financial support for students coming from social disadvantaged background so that they could pay for their accommodation and other expenditure. It also has an impact on long term because the students that benefited from this aid tend not to drop out of their course. They will receive an amount of 80 euro (300 ron) with the condition that the student has fulfilled his/her student's duties (attended university courses). The social aid scholarships are allocated based on the average monthly net income.

4.1.2   Occasional Social Aid Scholarship (UB and WUT)

This scholarship helps ensure students social and financial support for occasional problems that students encounter during their studies and it also has an impact on long term because the students that benefited from this aid tend not to drop out their course. This type of scholarship provides students that encounter different types of social and financial difficulties: students orphaned by both parents', coming from orphanages or foster care; students whose family haven't obtained in the last three months an average income per month/per family member less than 75% of the minimum national wage. Maternity grant is assured to student or students whose wife has no income and consists it of a scholarship for childbirth and motherhood and a grant to purchase clothing newborn baby students may be granted the scholarships in case of death of student's family member

4.1.3   Excellency Scholarships (UB and WUT)

The aim of this scholarship is to motivate students to learn and be involved in academic activities. Students with a good activity towards all the years in University, research and professional activities, social activities, cultural and organisational activities are granted a scholarship of 120 euro. These scholarships had a positive impact on students making them more implicated in university's activities, more mature and motivated. This impact has been measured through the number of files that fulfil the criteria each year. In the selection criteria are not mentioned race, age, or ethnicity.

4.1.4   Special Scholarships for Olympics (Only for the 1st at Bachelor's Degree) (UB and WUT)

All students that have won different school competitions have the right to be accepted at any national university they apply for and they are exempted from paying the admission tax and university fees. to assure the access of good students at a decent living in a big city and to continue to motivate them to learn and assure them their appreciation. West University of Timisoara grant annually a different amount of scholarships for students in the 1st year of Bachelor's Degree which in their 12th grade have been on one of the first three students at a national Olympic or had participated at any international phase of Olympics, from the funds of university.

4.2   *Programs/Projects*

4.2.1   You vs. Stereotype (UB)

The purpose of the project is to deliver real information about the vulnerable groups. The project was made so psychology and educational sciences students can be aware of the vulnerable group existence. The reason for this project is that for a psychologist and a specialist in educational sciences the key words should be objectivism, tolerance. Students need not only to be aware, but to find a way to help them, to find a way to leave behind all the stereotypes these people are surrounded by. So, the transferability to target groups (students) was possible through workshops, debate, live library. It was a small project with just 15 participants, but at the end of the project a small group of people at the Faculty of Psychology and Educational Sciences knew more about vulnerable groups, met vulnerable groups' people and for a whole week had the attention on what it really means a vulnerable group in Romania. The project was evaluated as a success, the feedback was a positive one, therefore it will be resumed every year.

4.2.2   Preparatory Year for Learning Romanian Language (WUT)
The aim of this program is to help foreign students integrate in Romania's system of HE and to have access at different opportunities of study. It also helps them learn Romanian language and makes easier their social skills for the future. This program is addressed to students from tertiary UE states which want to study in Romanian for their Bachelor's degree or MA, students/citizens from countries that belong UE. This preparatory year from West University of Timisoara is mandatory for foreign students that wish to follow study programmes in Romanian language. During a year they manage to learn the part of Romanian language that is useful for their next choice of faculty. This preparatory year can be adopted by a wider scale of universities which have the possibility to share their budget in this kind of activity and have demands from foreign students. Of course, this activity can be scaled down to smaller institutions like high schools maybe, that can offer this kind of activity. There is a wide range of transferability. This preparatory year can also be a part of an enterprise or a factory because people from foreign countries are coming much more in Romania and they need to have a job, or actually they are coming for a particular kind of job.

4.3   *Centers or Laboratories*
4.3.1   Assistive Technology Lab (UB)
The aim of this project is to encourage blind people's access to higher education programmes and increase the chances of graduation among students with visual impairments. It also aims at ensuring that blind students will have access to study conditions similar to those of sighted students by using equipment and assistive creation that are available in six centers. The equipment consists of:
– Machine ZY-FUSE – an excellent educational tool for playing graphic information in the form of tactile images;
– Computer equipped with the following additional software: JAWS 6.0, ABBYY Fine Reader;

- VictorReader device – allows listening audio books in Daisy format;
- Audio books in Daisy format;
- Konica Minolta bizhub 215 multifunctional, with a great print speed and an excellent resolution.

The actors involved were university teachers and students. This project is going to be implementing in other centers, such as public libraries can provide access to a relative large number of people, not just those involved in university studies.

4.3.2 Pedagogical Integration and Support Center (WUT)

Pedagogical Integration and Support Center has as mission the development of an inclusive ambiance, centered on performance where people with disabilities bring their contribution to creating a culture of tolerance, diversity and active participation by allowing and promoting a university environment based on the principles of equal opportunities in education, assisting students with special requirements, development and innovation in the field of special education and optimising practices in integrating this students in an equal environment.

This center can be adopted by a wider scale of universities which have the possibility to share their budget in this kind of activity. It is known that cannot be asked from a smaller university or a poor one to grant this kind of center but every university should appreciate and help its special students and help them benefit the process of HE. Of course, this activity can be scaled down to smaller institutions like high schools maybe, that can offer this kind of center. This center brought West University of Timisoara closer to the students with disabilities and helped them to receive the special education they need, also integrating them, making the place more accessible and helping teachers to create new ways of evaluation and teaching depending on the type and degree of deficiency the students have. The positive impact on people helped the target group to be more confident. There are not any documents to show the evolution of the center, but by counting the students with disabilities in West University of Timisoara we can figure it out it was a success.

5 The Institutional Strategic Plan of Inclusion at the University of Bucharest

The mission of the University of Bucharest is to be the most important higher education institution in Romania through the high standards of the academic endeavor guaranteed on all departments. The main goal of the University of Bucharest is to obtain the highest quality of educational services and of research activity possible, by adopting international-grade competitive standards and by manifesting a continuous interest in the assurance of quality, interdisciplinary collaboration and leadership, as well as in the excellence of the activities of the professors and of the employees.

The University of Bucharest models its educational process based on the needs of the society of knowledge, in which the formation of competences and abilities plays an essential role. Renewal and reformation are constitutive processes.

In order to apply efficient methods in this process, the University of Bucharest makes its strategies and objectives public, debates them and applies them in such a way so that members of the academic community can feel encouraged to contribute with their own ideas and initiatives. The University of Bucharest promotes an ethical climate of trust and communication on all levels, anticipates changes and elaborates on pro-active plans.

The University of Bucharest advances four fundamental principles of research and academic education:
- fundamental and applied research which reflects the engagement of the whole academic community for deepening and extending knowledge in the fields of natural sciences, social sciences and humanistic sciences;
- critical thinking, which allows the free expression of the diversity of the intellectual styles and of the methods of research specific to each research field existing in the University of Bucharest;
- To provide a highly qualitative education system which coagulate the democratic values of the University of Bucharest by placing, at the center of its educational processes, the student and its individual particularities.
- the engagement of the public, through which the University of Bucharest legitimises itself towards the society and through which it expresses its desire to find solutions based on knowledge for the current issues the country is facing.

In order to achieve the indicators presented above the University of Bucharest, through the Department of Counseling and Career Guidance is implementing some actions that are, currently aiming at providing:
- career counselling;
- vocational orientation;
- information regarding the UB study domains;
- counselling and psychological evaluation;
- capability evaluation;
- it develops programmes which are of interest for the students related to the business field and with the labor market;
- it organised career events, trainings and workshops, events where students interact directly with specialists in various fields, professional development opportunities (internships, volunteering, company visits, part-time jobs, short-term jobs) in partnership with private companies and institutions in various fields;
- it develops the alternative lodging programme and social integration programmes;

– it represents the University in fairs and educational, career-related events. Also, the center provides assistance through psychological counselling we get involved in finding solutions to overcome problematic situations which can affect a student's experience as a whole, starting from the entrance examination to graduation, by taking into account:
– getting through emotional difficulties
– support for self-knowledge
– the evaluation of values, interests and professional abilities
– stress management during exam sessions
– In this framework, a group of key agents took part of the seminar about promoting inclusion in Higher Education and uses the A4A self-assessment tool to explore and improve our innovative and inclusive policies.

In a nutshell, the A4A self-assessment tool covers six broad factors organised into two main dimensions: (A) Institutional related factors (HEI organisational maturity, Institutional innovation management culture, Knowledge sharing) and (B) Inclusion related factors (Inclusion shared understanding, Policies for inclusion, Actions for inclusion).

Figure 6.3 shows the result of this self-assessment filled in by the University of Bucharest staff members.

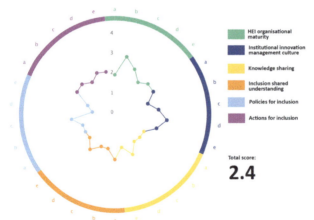

FIGURE 6.3
A4A profile of the University of Bucharest

Regarding each dimension evaluated, the tool is suggesting some possible actions to improve our innovative and inclusion capacity (see Table 6.1). As we can see, our weaker dimensions are "Policies for inclusion" with a total of 1.2 points and "HEI organisational maturity" with 2.2 points.

5.1 Aspiration

Based on the A4A diagnosis and the Pyramid for inclusion model, the main goal of the A4A strategic plan for improving inclusion in the University of Bucharest

INCLUSION IN HIGHER EDUCATION IN ROMANIA 129

TABLE 6.1 A4A self-assessment tool diagnosis and suggestions at the University of Bucharest

Dimension and Score (from 1 to 4)	
HEI organisational maturity (Dimension score: 2.2)	Depending on the changes and demands of the environment, procedures and mechanisms that allow the institution to review and update the institutional project should be incorporated into the internal operating regulations. In this project, the different units, departments or faculties should enjoy some autonomy to determine their own plans of action. As a direct consequence of this autonomy, the institution must self-provide a system of accountability.
Institutional innovation management culture (Dimension score: 2.6)	Harnessing the information generated by existing monitoring systems should serve to plan and anticipate the changes that affect HEI. The HEI must have strategic plans that will also affect the decisions of the curriculum field. The different leaders of change must share decisions through widely agreed systems and communication strategies. For this, strategies can be designed to be articulate to minimise possible resistance to change.
Knowledge sharing (Dimension score: 2.2)	It is necessary to promote collaborative work among professionals as an effective tool to solve problems that can be shared. For this reason, the organisation must provide support the collaboration between professionals of different profiles and with various experiences, providing technological tools that facilitate it, as well as other resources, spaces and times. It is a matter of favouring meetings and promoting the sharing of knowledge among the different members of the organisation, both in a formal and informal way. On the other hand, the HEI needs to work together with other institutions of its environment – local and national – around improving the care of vulnerable groups.

(*cont.*)

TABLE 6.1 A4A self-assessment tool diagnosis and suggestions at the University of Bucharest (cont.)

Dimension and Score (from 1 to 4)

Inclusion shared understanding
(Dimension score: 3)

To guarantee the implication of all the agents (teachers, students, administrative staff, etc.) for the improvement and increasing of the inclusion in the institution. The institution has to promote actions addressed to the implication and compromise of all the agent towards inclusion. These actions have to facilitate all the agents' active and participative action in the different institutional areas, facilitating the access to information and the good use of all the available resources and services, as well as the better interaction among them towards the strengthening of an inclusive culture.

Policies for inclusion
(Dimension score: 1.2)

HEI are called to adopt measures to improve or to promote more suitable policies for the HEI. In this sense they should put in place awareness' strategies. Considering that the basic stage represents a very initial phase in the policies for inclusion process, in order to progress to more development, stage the HEI managers should communicate the policies to all the academic community, make them aware of these policies and help them to be more responsive to these policies. Strategies as: plans for dissemination, flows of communication are possible.

Actions for inclusion
(Dimension score: 2.6)

It is desirable to design and develop student support programs within the broad framework of a plan for improving admission, permanence, and discharge of students at the university. Programs and services to support the student must consider the diversity of roles, functions and responsibilities of the different sectors involved in the university community (teachers, students and administration staff and services), but also the different strategies and orientation actions and tutorials have to be incardinated, global of the university as well as specific of faculty and center.

will be to provide a highly qualitative education system which coagulate the democratic values of the University of Bucharest by placing, at the center of its educational processes, the student and its individual particularities.

This main goal will be achieved through the following objectives:

O1: Making the university more accountable of the importance of developing a more inclusive university

O2: Implementing and assessing the internal institutional policies that aim to develop a more inclusive university.

O3: Implementing a set of support mechanisms in order to sustain the development of a more inclusive university.

5.2 *Monitoring and Evaluation*

Table 6.2 shows the main elements configuring our A4A strategic plan, including actions, key agents, and achievement indicators.

6 Conclusion

As part of the European Higher Education Area (EHEA), Romania has committed to respect the 2015 Yerevan Communique agreements related to widening participation in higher education and support institutions that provide relevant learning activities in appropriate contexts for different types of learners, including lifelong learning. Higher education institutions have agreed to enhance the social dimension of higher education, improve gender balance and widen opportunities for access and completion, including international mobility, for students from disadvantaged backgrounds (Yerevan Communique, 2015).

As a result, Romanian universities paid more attention to social aspects in regard to policy and financial allocations that indicate a greater focus on the issue of equity in tertiary education. As presented in the case studies from previous pages' Romanian higher education tried to implement different support mechanisms in order to overcome considerable challenges, such as the high number and population diversity of disadvantaged groups (people from rural areas, individuals with a Roma background, people with low incomes, people coming from orphanages, etc.).

Still, the difficulties students face nowadays are constantly changing so higher education institutions have to keep up with these changes and to start acting proactively in order to ensure that "access to, participation in and outcomes of tertiary education are based only on individuals' innate ability and study effort. They ensure that the achievement of education potential at tertiary level is not the result of personal and social circumstances, including of

TABLE 6.2 A4A strategic plan at the University of Bucharest

Main objective: To provide a highly qualitative education system which coagulate the democratic values of the University of Bucharest by placing, at the center of its educational processes, the student and its individual particularities.

O1: Making the university more accountable of the importance of developing a more inclusive university

Action/Activity	General indicators	Methodology/ Techniques/ Proceedings	Timing (years) 1 2 3 4	Responsible person	Budget (month and in future years) n n+1 n+2 n+3 n+4
1.1. Creating a space for discussions through group meetings open to the entire university community in order to support the development of a more inclusive university	Creating a specific set of indicators and instruments to improve knowledge about inclusion and its current situation through a periodical dissemination process	Group meetings	X X X X X X X X X X	Vice-rectorates of students, Academic staff, Administrative staff and Communication and promotion Deaneries	
1.2. Developing campaigns in order to disseminate the latest initiatives take in order to support the university to became more inclusive		Campaigns on specific aspects to promote inclusion	X X X X X X X X X X	Vice-rector for communication and promotion Deaneries	

(cont.)

TABLE 6.2   A4A strategic plan at the University of Bucharest (cont.)

O1: Making the university more accountable of the importance of developing a more inclusive university

Action/Activity	General indicators	Methodology/ Techniques/ Proceedings	Timing (years)				Responsible person	Budget (month and in future years)				
			1	2	3	4		n	n+1	n+2	n+3	n+4
1.3. Providing training aimed at students, teachers and research staff, administration and services staff and institutional decision-makers.		Create and disseminate training materials on university inclusion	X	X X	X X X	X X X	Vice-rectorates for Academic Programming, Quality, Innovation, and Strategic Projects					

(cont.)

TABLE 6.2 A4A strategic plan at the University of Bucharest (cont.)

O2: Implementing and assessing the internal institutional policies that aim to develop a more inclusive university.

Action/Activity	General indicators	Methodology/ Techniques/ Proceedings	Timing (years)				Responsible person	Budget (month and in future years)				
			1	2	3	4		n	n+1	n+2	n+3	n+4
2.1. Review and update the Strategic Plan of the UB	Updating the Strategic Plan at the UB level through a more specific set of actions related to inclusion that will be developed by the Department of Counseling and Career Guidance	Establish follow-up and control mechanisms related to internal institutional policies that aim to develop a more inclusive university	X	X			Rector and government team					
				X	X	X						
2.2. Empowering the Department of Counseling and Career Guidance to promote educational equity		To locate services and programs for inclusion within the framework of the governance structure of the university and of a single organisational unit	X	X			Rector and government team					
				X	X	X						

(cont.)

TABLE 6.2 A4A strategic plan at the University of Bucharest (cont.)

O2: Implementing and assessing the internal institutional policies that aim to develop a more inclusive university.

Action/Activity	General indicators	Methodology/ Techniques/ Proceedings	Timing (years)				Responsible person	Budget (month and in future years)				
			1	2	3	4		n	n+1	n+2	n+3	n+4
2.3. Strengthening the Career counseling and guidance; the Psychological counseling and the Career opportunities of all students		Complete guidance and mentoring programs with actions aimed at all discriminated groups and individuals			X	X	Rector and government team					
		Specialise services and programs according to required guidance needs				X						

(cont.)

TABLE 6.2 A4A strategic plan at the University of Bucharest (cont.)

O3: Implementing a set of support mechanisms in order to sustain the development of a more inclusive university.

Action/Activity	General indicators	Methodology/ Techniques/ Proceedings	Timing (years)				Responsible person	Budget (month and in future years)				
			1	2	3	4		n	n+1	n+2	n+3	n+4
3.1. Implementation of mechanisms for participation and accountability regarding the development of a more inclusive university	Promotion of the use of services and resources for inclusion	To guarantee methodologies and systems of teaching, learning and evaluation with an inclusive approach	X	X			Vice-rectorate of Students, Administration staff, Teaching and Research staff and Academic Planning					
			X	X	X							
			X	X	X	X						
							Deanships and university degree Coordinators					

(cont.)

TABLE 6.2   A4A strategic plan at the University of Bucharest (cont.)

O3: Implementing a set of support mechanisms in order to sustain the development of a more inclusive university.

Action/Activity	General indicators	Methodology/ Techniques/ Proceedings	Timing (years) 1 2 3 4	Responsible person	Budget (month and in future years) n n+1 n+2 n+3 n+4
3. 2 Establishing a research center on inclusion that will help guarantee accessibility to materials, teaching spaces, information of accessibility, technologies, security and protection, mobility and transport		Guide human, material and functional resources to inclusion		Vice-rectorate of Students Research staff	

factors such as socio-economic status, gender, ethnic origin, immigrant status, place of residence, age, or disability" (OECD, 2008, p. 14).

Acknowledgement

This document has been produced as a part of the project "ACCESS4ALL – Laboratory for Policies and Practices of Social Development in Higher Education" (Ref. 2015-1-ES01-KA203-015970) co-funded by the European Union (Erasmus+ Programme).

Note

1   Law of National Education 1/2011, https://edu.ro/sites/default/files/_fi%C8%99iere/Legislatie/2019/Legea%20nr%201%20Educatiei%20Nationale%20actualizata%202019.pdf

References

Education Ministry. (2018). *Report on the state of the national higher education system in Romania for the academic year/Raportul asupra stării sistemului național de învățământ superior din România pentru anul universitar 2017–2018*. https://www.edu.ro/sites/default/files/Raport%20privind%20starea%20%C3%AEnv%C4%83%C8%9B%C4%83m%C3%A2ntului%20superior%20din%20Rom%C3%A2nia_%202017%20-2018.pdf

Law of National Education 1/2011. https://edu.ro/sites/default/files/_fi%C8%99iere/Legislatie/2019/Legea%20nr%201%20Educatiei%20Nationale%20actualizata%202019.pdf

OECD. (2008). *Tertiary education for the knowledge society* (Vol. 2). Author.

Strategic Plan of the Al. Ioan Cuza University. (2016–2020). https://www.uaic.ro/wp-content/uploads/2016/10/Planul-strategic-30.09.2016.pdf

Strategic Plan of the Babeș-Bolyai University. (2016–2020). https://www.ubbcluj.ro/ro/despre/prezentare/files/strategii/plan_strategic_2016_2020.pdf

Strategic Plan of the University of Bucharest. (2016–2020). https://www.unibuc.ro/wp-content/uploads/2018/12/Plan-Strategic-2016-2020.pdf

Strategic Plan of the West university of Timişoara. (2016–2020). https://www.uvt.ro/files/912ddaf702d70a706882b6fdc9a9bdbce369fe60/

Tesliuc, E., Grigoras, V., & Stanculescu, M. (2015). *Background study for the National Strategy on Social Inclusion and Poverty Reduction, 2015–2020*. World Bank.

Yerevan Communiqué. (2015). http://www.ehea.info/media.ehea.info/file/2015_Yerevan/70/7/YerevanCommuniqueFinal_613707.pdf Accessed at: https://www.uvt.ro/files/912ddaf702d70a706882b6fdc9a9bdbce369fe60/

CHAPTER 7

Good Practices and Experiences for Inclusion in Spain

Cecilia Inés Suárez

Abstract

The achievement of inclusion and equity in higher education systems is understood as a process rather than a final situation: building inclusive education requires planning, implementation and evaluation of a wide range of strategies. In Spain, the Salamanca Declaration (CRUE, 2018a) has highlighted the role of universities not only as agents of transformation of the economic and social system but also regarding their critical contribution when it comes to achieving educational inclusion. This chapter is aimed to identify good practices that make a clear contribution to the inclusion in the Spanish higher education system. First, we present the main features of the Spanish higher education system and the theoretical model developed for this study, drawn into four axes of inequality in higher education. Next, we analyse eight selected good practices from six Spanish Universities related to four topics: Gender, Disability, Refugees and Sexual and Gender Diversity. For each topic and good practice, we provide information regarding the Spanish legal framework, general data from current research and information obtained from the university's website. Finally, we indicate the importance of continuing to carry out research, actions and strategies in the field of higher education aimed at an increasingly inclusive university system in Spain.

Keywords

higher education – equity – inclusion – diversity – good practices – Spain – gender – disability – refugees – sexual and gender diversity

1   **Introduction**

Equity and inclusion are crucial for achieving success in the social dimension of higher education in Europe. The idea of a student body that reflects a society's diversity – as a sign of all citizens having access to higher education – as well as the goal that students successfully graduate despite the difficulties associated with social and/or economic inequalities reflects the European Commission's interest in building a system of higher education based on equity, inclusion and high quality standards. This aspiration was already reflected in the Bologna Declaration (1999) and, more specifically, in each of the various declarations of the European Higher Education Area (EHEA). In these, the member states highlighted the fundamental role of universities in ensuring conditions for the completion of higher education studies, especially for those students who are in a situation of vulnerability and specifically taking into account the principles of equity and inclusion (Prague, 2001; Berlin, 2003; London, 2007; Leuven and Louvain-la-Neuve, 2009; Budapest and Vienna, 2010; Bucharest, 2012; Yerevan, 2015). More recently, in the Yerevan Communiqué (2015), the ministers participating in the EHEA strengthened their commitment to the social dimension so that, by 2020, the European Higher Education Area might contribute effectively to the development of inclusive societies. Based on these commitments and guidelines, the member countries introduced new legislation, designed new plans and programmes, and/or adapted university structures, among other measures.

The achievement of inclusion, equity and, in general, the building of inclusive higher education systems is understood as a process rather than a final situation. As such, the development of this process requires not only the commitment of the stakeholders involved in higher education, but also the planning, implementation and evaluation of various strategies that provide relevant and suitable responses to the needs that arise in each social moment. This becomes even more meaningful if we consider that it is a question of overcoming sociohistorically constructed social inequalities related to gender, ethnic or racial origin, disability and economic status. These include those inequalities that affect the educational and academic trajectories of people in situations of vulnerability in higher education. The attainment of inclusive and quality institutions responds, in the same way, to the *modernisation* of European higher education (Eurydice, 2014), since it has to provide training in competencies that allow all students to participate as citizens and workers in today's society.

The Spanish higher education system has not been oblivious to these provisions. The Salamanca Declaration (2018), which emerged from the Fourth International Meeting of Rectors of the Conference of Rectors of Spanish

Universities (CRUE),[1] has highlighted the role of universities as agents of transformation of the economic and social system. This declaration also mentions that although universities reflect social inequalities, they can also contribute to addressing them by exemplifying equity and diversity in educational institutions. At the same time, this task cannot be carried out exclusively by higher education institutions: it is clear that universities cannot solve structural social inequalities on their own, but that they must instead collaborate with each other and with all sectors of society (the government and politicians, the private sector, local communities, non-governmental organisations, and the media, among others).

Within this framework, this chapter identifies a set of good practices that are carried out within the setting of Spanish universities and are related to some aspect of achieving inclusion, equity and diversity. The concept of good practices is not exempt from certain controversies within the educational field; here, however, it is understood as a set of initiatives and strategies that stand out due to their contribution to a university that is more inclusive, respectful of diversity and oriented towards achieving success in the social dimension in higher education. In the categories of initiatives and strategies, both plans and programmes have been considered as well as intra- and interinstitutional actions, seeking to account for the diversity and significance of the actions that are being developed in the Spanish context.

With this goal in mind, this chapter is organised into three sections. The first focuses on presenting both general data on the Spanish higher education system, in order to contextualise its main characteristics, as well as the analysis model developed for this study – which is in turn organised into four axes of inequality in higher education.

The next section describes and analyses the good practices selected from a bibliographic and archival search of Spanish universities' databases and websites. To complement each of these sections, legislative information and data on the Spanish context have been included, based on official reports and recent research.

Finally, by way of conclusion, the main contributions made in this study are summarised, indicating the importance of continuing to carry out research, actions and strategies in the field of higher education aimed at an increasingly inclusive university system.

2   The Spanish Higher Education System

Data published by the Spanish Ministry of Science, Innovation and Universities for the 2017–2018 academic year indicates that:

- The higher education system in Spain comprises 84 universities (82 of which are active), of which 50 are publicly owned and 32 are privately owned.
- Spanish universities are distributed as follows: 235 campuses (universities with in-person attendance) and 113 institutional headquarters (distance-learning universities and other special universities).
- The autonomous Community of Madrid and Catalonia have the largest number of universities (14 and 12 respectively) in comparison with the other autonomous communities, although Andalusia has the highest concentration of publicly owned universities (comprising a total of 10 of the 11 universities that operate in Andalusia).
- The offering of bachelor's degrees in public universities increased from 2464 in the 2012–2013 academic year to 2864 in the 2017–2018 academic year. This trend can be seen in each of the five main disciplinary branches (social and legal sciences, engineering and architecture, arts and humanities, health sciences, and natural sciences).
- In the 2017–2018 academic year, a total of 1,289,233 students enrolled on bachelor's degree courses and 1911 enrolled in first and second cycles (Ministerio de Ciencia, Innovación y Universidades, 2019).

In relation to inclusion, it is worth highlighting the *inclusive education approach* defined by the Ministry of Education, Culture and Sports, which aims to guarantee, at all levels, an educational action that results in the maximum development of the students at the same time as the cohesion of the members of the community. Among its principles, the following stand out, linked directly to the achievement of inclusion and equity:

- Diversity is a positive element that enriches the educational community and contributes to interdependence and social cohesion.
- The search for equity and excellence must take all students into account.
- Educational attention is directed at improving the learning of all students and must be adapted to individual characteristics.
- Inclusion implies identifying and minimising learning difficulties and participation, while maximising the resources of educational attention in both processes.

In higher education, Organic Law 6/2001 on Universities established in its 24th Additional Provision that "Universities shall guarantee equal opportunities for students and other members of the university community who have disabilities, prohibiting any form of discrimination and establishing measures of positive action aimed at ensuring their full and effective participation in the University field" (p. 53). It should be noted that certain aspects of this law were modified in 2007 by Organic Law 4/2007 on Universities (BOE no. 89, 2007).

We highlight in later sections of this chapter only what is relevant in inclusion issues, such as the creation of gender equality units.

Another important provision regarding inclusion in higher education is Royal Decree 412/2014, which mandates (Article 5) that admission to official university studies should respect the principles of equality, non-discrimination, merit and ability; and devotes Chapter IV to defining the regulations for access to undergraduate studies for students over 25 years old, access to higher education through the accreditation of work or professional experience, access for people over 45 years old and people with disabilities. Chapter V of the decree, on the other hand, establishes specific criteria for the allocation of places in public universities to: those over 25 years old, those over 45 years old and those over 40 years old who are able to prove they have work or professional experience, as well as students with disabilities, among others.

From this starting point, the analysis model used for this chapter considers good practices in relation to the following four criteria that may generate situations of inequality in higher education: gender, disability, refugee status, and sexual and gender diversity.

These are also common issues in the European context (Eurydice, 2014, 2018), to which can be added other factors that may condition inclusion and participation in higher education, such as those related to socioeconomic

TABLE 7.1   Inequality axes used in the analysis model[2]

Axis of inequality	Definition
Gender	Female participation in higher education (as students, researchers or teachers), over- or underrepresentation of women in certain study courses and university settings (Eurydice, 2011).
Disability	People who have a disability that makes it difficult for them to participate in higher education.
Refugees	People from third countries who have attained this status in Spain according to the current legislative framework.
Sexual and gender diversity	Recognition and valuing of different identities and gender orientations. However, situations of discrimination, inequality and/or violence in higher education can be observed.

status, age, the need to work and study, and ethnic or racial origin. It should be made clear then that gender status and sexual identity, for example, are not factors of inequality per se but do lead to blatant inequality in higher education when associated with other factors (such as discrimination, poverty or harassment).

The application of this model has initiatives and strategies to be identified, as presented in Table 7.2.

The good practices selected in this study also share some common features: they are initiatives that are integrated into the institutional structures

TABLE 7.2   Good practices in inclusion analysed in Spain

Axis of inequality	Name	University (autonomous community)
Gender	Centre Dolors Piera	University of Lleida (UDL) (Catalonia)
	Protocol for action against sexual harassment and harassment for reasons of sex, sexual orientation, gender identity or gender expression	Universitat Autònoma de Barcelona (Autonomous University of Barcelona, UAB) (Catalonia)
Disability	Unit for the Integration of People with Disabilities	Universitat de València (University of Valencia, UV) (Valencian Community)
	Support Programme for Teaching and Research Staff (PDI) and Administrative and Service Staff (PAS)	Universitat de València (University of Valencia, UV) (Valencian Community)
Refugees	Office for Reception of Refugees (UCMrefugees)	Complutense University of Madrid (UCM) (Madrid)
	Support programme for refugees and those coming from conflict zones	University of Barcelona (UB) (Catalonia)
Sexual and gender diversity	Office for Sexual Diversity and Gender Identity	Complutense University of Madrid (UCM) (Madrid)
	Strategic Plan for the Promotion of Respect, Diversity and LGBT+ Equality	University of Zaragoza (UDZ) (Aragon)

themselves (which provides for their permanence over time), they have a budget allocation that allows them to function, and they include planning of medium- to long-term activities. All of these features contribute to the sustainability of the good practices. Along similar lines, they also demonstrate the responsibility that universities have in addressing global inclusion in Spanish higher education. Finally, the fact that these are publicly owned universities reinforces the idea of their fundamental commitment to the creation of a fairer and more equitable society.

3   Good Practices for Promoting Inclusion in the Spanish Higher Education System

3.1 *Good Practices from a Gender Perspective*

According to data in the report La Universidad española en cifras 2016/2017 (The Spanish University in Figures 2016/2017) (CRUE, 2018b), 54% of undergraduate students in Spain are women. However, the same report contains some data related to gender equity issues: student preferences focus on the areas of education and health and welfare and decrease in relation to the areas of engineering, architecture and information and communications technology; the presence and evolution of female university lecturers are insufficient and the hiring of female *associate* lecturers has increased, revealing that it is women who have taken on teaching responsibilities with less job security and lower salaries. In this regard, the First Summit of Female Rectors of Spanish Public Universities defined a total of 20 priorities in the area of gender equality, including the following: consolidation of the gender perspective in curricula; the reduction of the gender gap in the fields of STEM, healthcare and education; the widespread implementation of training in equality and gender throughout the university community; the introduction of positive action measures to promote the presence of women in researcher and lead project manager positions; and the establishment of a university policy of zero tolerance towards sexist violence.

At the state level, the 12th Additional Provision of Organic Law 4/2007 on Universities (BOE no. 89, 2007, which modifies Organic Law 6/2001) established that universities must have units within their organisational structures that are responsible for developing functions related to the principle of equality between women and men. These gender equality units have the general objective of promoting and driving equal opportunities between women and men via the education system and of helping prevent gender violence through education. Among their other functions, the units are responsible for the preparation of technical studies and reports on gender equality policies in education and they develop activities in cooperation with other administrations and entities to raise awareness and promote full equality between women and men. There are a total of 46 units in the whole of Spain (see Table 7.3).

In the case of Catalonia, the *Women and Science* section of the Secretariat of Research Universities (SUR) webpage is worth mentioning. The page provides access to all the equality units of Catalonia's universities.

In addition to these units, some universities have developed their own actions to address gender issues. In this regard, the example of the Centre Dolors Piera at the University of Lleida (UDL) deserves mention. The Centre was founded in 2006 following an agreement between the Interdisciplinary Seminar on Women's Studies and the University for the use of the bibliographic and archival collection at the Women's Studies and Documentation Centre. It should be noted that, by 2003, the University of Lleida had already approved in its statutes the promotion of education in values as an integral part of the learning process and for the transmission of the values of justice, equality, responsibility, solidarity, participation and full citizenship.

The Centre intends to promote the gender perspective across disciplines in the UDL, embracing the areas of management, teaching and research. Examples of actions carried out include providing guidance in the design of teaching sessions and questionnaires from a gender perspective and actions to promote the use of non-sexist language, such as the review and correction of inclusive language. Also worthy of mention is that it not only offers its services to the university community itself, but also to external institutions and individuals, such as advising on rights in matters of conciliation and gender violence and the preparation of diagnoses, reports and specific sessions on equality plans.

In creating an organisation free of sexism and gender violence, the *Protocol of Action Against Sexual Harassment and Harassment for Reasons of Sex, Sexual Orientation, Gender Identity or Gender Expression, and Sexist Violence*, approved by the Governing Board of the Universitat Autònoma de Barcelona in 2018 is also worthy of mention. This protocol is one of the actions of the *UAB free of gender violence* project developed by the UAB Observatory for Equality and which has been active since 2013. The protocol establishes the creation of a Technical Advisory Commission, at the request of the UAB Foundation, to respond to applications for intervention, follow-up and rulings on the resolution of situations of sexual harassment and/or harassment for reasons of sex, sexual orientation, gender identity or expression and/or situations of sexist violence.

At a more global level, the aforementioned project contemplates the development of actions and resources in the areas of awareness, prevention,

TABLE 7.3   Gender equality units in Spanish universities

Autonomous community	University
Andalusia	University of Cadiz
	University of Huelva
	University of Málaga
	Pablo de Olavide University (Seville)
	University of Seville
	University of Granada
	University of Almería
	University of Jaén
	University of Córdoba
Aragon	University of Zaragoza
Asturias (Principality of)	University of Oviedo
Balearic Islands	University of the Balearic Islands
Basque Country	University of the Basque Country
Canary Islands	University of La Laguna
	University of Las Palmas de Gran Canaria
Cantabria	University of Cantabria
Castile and León	University of Burgos
	University of Salamanca
	University of Valladolid
	University of León
Castile–La Mancha	University of Castilla–La Mancha
Catalonia	Universitat Autònoma de Barcelona
	University of Barcelona
	University of Girona
	University of Lleida
	Universitat Politècnica de Catalunya (Polytechnic University of Catalonia)
	Pompeu Fabra University
	Universitat Rovira i Virgili (Tarragona)
Extremadura	University of Extremadura
Galicia	University of A Coruña
	University of Santiago de Compostela
	University of Vigo
La Rioja	University of La Rioja

(*cont.*)

TABLE 7.3   Gender equality units in Spanish universities (cont.)

Autonomous community	University
Madrid (Community of)	Autonomous University of Madrid
	Universidad Carlos III (Charles III University)
	Complutense University of Madrid
	Polytechnic University of Madrid
Murcia (Region of)	University of Murcia
	Polytechnic University of Cartagena
National Distance Education University (UNED)	Office for Equality
Navarre (Chartered Community of)	Public University of Navarre
Valencia (Community of)	University of Alacant
	Universitat de València (University of Valencia)
	Miguel Hernández University
	Universitat Jaume I
	Universitat Politècnica de València (Polytechnic University of Valencia)

SOURCE: BASED ON INFORMATION FROM HTTP://WWW.EDUCACIONYFP.GOB.ES/EN/MC/ IGUALDAD/UNIDADMEFP/IGUALDADUNIVERSIDADES.HTML (ACCESSED 26 OCTOBER 2020), MINISTRY OF EDUCATION AND VOCATIONAL TRAINING

attention and coordination aimed at addressing situations of gender violence that may arise on campus. This initiative is all the more significant given that 62% of the students have knowledge of or have experienced situations of violence against women in the Spanish university context, but only 13% have identified them as such (Valls, Puigvert, Melgar, & Garcia-Yeste, 2016).

3.2   *Good Practices in Disability Support*

Teaching students with disabilities or those with "special educational needs" has been one of the primary criteria for defining what is understood as inclusion in education (Ainscow & Miles, 2008). From this perspective, an institution is inclusive to the extent to which it implements actions that achieve, above all, the removal of architectural barriers in order to contribute to student accessibility. However, this approach has been extended to consider that inclusion in education is not only a question of physical accessibility, but rather a process to ensure the construction of an institution that welcomes all students.

In the case of Spain, there are two main events that define a change in disability support in universities: (a) recognition of this situation in Organic Law

6/2001 on Universities and (b) the recommendation made to universities by the Spanish Committee of Representatives of Persons with Disabilities that they should include specific provisions on disability support in the process of drafting their statutes in 2002 (Ministerio de Educación. Secretaría General de Universidades, 2011). In view of these precedents, university initiatives have looked at the development of structures, service programmes (tutorial sessions, job placement, sports, and information), grants and scholarships (for example, for transport), and the prioritisation of enrolment, among other aspects.

Data published in the Third University and Disability Study (Fundación Universia, 2016) revealed the presence of a total of 17,634 university students with disabilities in the 2015–2016 academic year (1.7% of all students in the 55 public and private universities taking part in the study). This data makes more sense when analysed in relation to higher education. There is a decreasing trend for higher levels of university studies to show lower proportions of students with disabilities. Thus, while undergraduate students with disabilities accounted for 1.8%, postgraduate and master's students accounted for 1.2%, and those studying for a doctorate accounted for 0.9% (Fundación Universia, 2016, p. 89).

In this respect, two significant initiatives developed by the Universitat de València should be noted:
– the Unit for the Integration of People with Disabilities and
– the Support Programme for Teaching and Research Staff (PDI in Spanish) and Administrative and Service Staff (PAS in Spanish).

The Unit for Integration arose with the goal of promoting equal opportunities and non-discrimination in the university environment, specifically based on programmes aimed at students, teaching staff and service personnel.

Of these programmes, the one called "Awareness, Training and Volunteering" is worth mentioning. This involves collaborative actions inside and outside the University to promote a positive attitude towards the inclusion of people with disabilities. It should be noted that, in 2017, a total of 394 voluntary actions were carried out. These were the most numerous (52%) compared to 206 awareness and training actions and 164 dissemination and information actions (Universitat de València, 2017, p. 17).

The figure of the volunteer is key in this programme since they are the ones who provide support in assisting students who have disabilities and who need this grant in order to integrate into university life. Some of the specific actions carried out by volunteers involve adapting material, providing information, opening new dossiers and providing academic support.

The same Unit carried out a significant experiment with the Support Programme for Teaching and Research Staff (PDI) and Administrative and Service

Staff (PAS) within the framework of the *Regulations on Measures for the Integration of Teaching and Research Staff with Disabilities*, approved by the Governing Council on 31 October 2007 and replaced by a new regulation approved on 28 March 2013.

The *Regulations on Measures* are aimed at all teaching and research staff, whether public employees or those with a work contract, who have a recognised disability, with the goal of facilitating their integration into the Universitat de València. For this purpose, the following lines of action are proposed: (a) financial aid for the development of the teaching and research function and (b) aid for teaching support.

In the first case, financial aid would be provided to compensate for additional expenses incurred by teachers with disabilities. These grants would be made on a competitive basis to those involved in teaching and research with a degree of disability of 33% or more.

In the case of aid for teaching support, a series of measures are contemplated to facilitate the provision of classes to teachers who have some degree of disability:

– From the point of view of mobility: accessible classrooms will be assigned, always on the same campus.
– Teaching schedules compatible with rehabilitation processes and/or specific medical treatments will be assigned, when proven to be necessary.
– A reduced teaching schedule may be requested in cases where a degree of disability greater than 33% is identified.

According to data in the *Report on Activities of the Unit for People with Disabilities* (Universitat de València, 2017) the number of applications has increased since the introduction of the service in 2008. In 2017, a total of 60 applications were received out of 83 teaching and research staff. It should be noted that not all users use the service to request the financial aid that is offered but instead, on occasion, to request other types of support (advice, documentation formalities, among others). It is also noteworthy that women use this service more than men do (54% compared to 46% of men in the same university collective).

3.3 Good Practices in Relation to Refugees

The Convention Relating to the Status of Refugees (United Nations, 1951) established access to education as one of the fundamental aspects of refugee rights and welfare (Chapter IV, p. 6). The 2016 New York Declaration for Refugees and Migrants signed by the member states of the United Nations reaffirmed their commitment to address the issues associated with the continuity of education of migrant and refugee students. The refugee crisis taking place in Europe is

TABLE 7.4   Universities participating in the Refugees Welcome Map

Autonomous community	University
Andalusia	University of Seville
	University of Almería
Catalonia	University of Barcelona
	University of Lleida
Madrid (Community of)	Complutense University of Madrid
	Camilo José Cela University
	Universidad Carlos III of Madrid
Galicia	University of A Coruña
	University of Santiago de Compostela
Valencian Community	University of Alacant

SOURCE: BASED ON "REFUGEES WELCOME MAP", EUROPEAN UNIVERSITY ASSOCIATION, HTTPS://EUA.EU/101-PROJECTS/541-REFUGEES-WELCOME-MAP.HTML (ACCESSED 27 JANUARY 2020)

also reflected in higher education: only 1% of the young refugee population enters university (UNHCR, 2016).

Included among the seven recommendations made by UNESCO (2019) for guaranteeing the right to education of all people are (a) protecting the right to education of migrants and displaced persons and (b) including migrants and displaced persons in national education systems.

The recognition of this issue in the Spanish context has encouraged the participation of universities in various initiatives and has led to various strategies at the institutional level.

In this regard, a total of 10 Spanish universities (nine publicly owned and one privately owned) participate in the Refugees Welcome network of the European University Association as part of higher education policy.[3]

This network, which brings together universities from all over Europe, proposes to document the commitment of higher education institutions to providing support to refugee students and is designed to be a space for exchange and collaboration between institutions.

At the state level in Spain, the universities that make up the CRUE agreed in their 2015 General Assembly on a series of joint measures, which include:
– facilitating access to refugee students who are university students in their country of origin;

- facilitating collaboration between Spanish universities and refugees who are university lecturers in their country of origin; and
- promoting volunteer actions among students, in collaboration with other administrations and agents, especially in those disciplines most directly related to the problem (CRUE, 2015).

This agreement does not exclude actions that each university may undertake to address this set of problems. Some institutions have therefore undertaken specific actions, four of which we highlight in this section: two from public universities and two from private ones.

In the first case, the Complutense University of Madrid (UCM) has an *Office for the Reception of Refugees (UCMrefugees) within the Area of Sociocultural Diversity (as delegated by the Rector for Diversity and the Environment), which aims to promote coexistence, inclusion and mutual understanding among all members of the university community. This office provides* personalised attention, has developed a reception plan, and also offers training and collaboration services with entities outside the UCM.

The UCM Refugee Reception Plan includes among its services the possibility of accessing financial aid (up to 100%) for tuition, academic guidance or the possibility of accommodation in a UCM hall of residence. The plan provides for access to bachelor's, master's or doctoral students who have started or completed university studies in their country of origin or who wish to do so in Spain.

On the other hand, the Self-Help Guide for Refugees from Syria was designed specifically to work on the possible psychological consequences affecting those who have been forced to migrate by war. The content of the guide is organised into three blocks that aim to help the students understand possible reactions to their situation as refugees as well as some strategies to deal with these reactions when they affect the students' everyday lives (in the "What is Happening to Me? Most Common Reactions" chapter); a section for families offering guidance on how to accompany the refugee student process and detect whether they need professional help (in "How Can I Help My Children?"); and a list of some of the resources available to the students (in "Other Resources").

At the level of public universities, the Support Programme for Refugees and People from Conflict Areas of the University of Barcelona (UB) is also worthy of mention. It is coordinated by the Solidarity Foundation of the University of Barcelona and was designed with the objective of facilitating access to higher education for people from this collective.

The programme has two main areas of action: (a) academic support and social integration and (b) networking and cooperation. In these areas, accompaniment and support actions of an academic, educational and social type, enrolment scholarships, and language courses (Catalan and Spanish) have been developed, as well as legal and psychological assistance and support for integration into the labour market, among others.

Within this programme there is also a course called Transition to Bachelor's Degrees and Training in Human Rights and the Culture of Peace, which began in the 2016–2017 academic year and from which a total of 14 students from Syria and Afghanistan graduated. This course is carried out in collaboration with Barcelona City Council and has a duration of 500 hours of content related to the intensive study of Catalan and Spanish, an introduction to university life and topics related to Human Rights and the Culture of Peace. Scholarships offered within the framework of this programme include not only accommodation and maintenance but also legal, psychological and social assistance, as well as academic guidance.

Regarding the actions of cooperation and networking, the Mare Nostrum Project is worthy of note (with funding from the Catalonian Development Cooperation Fund) designed with the aim of incorporating the multidimensional perspective of refugees in local entities, as players contributing to the construction of peace.[4]

- Noteworthy details of the actions developed by this programme include:
- There are 28 people studying within the framework of the programme. Moreover, the enrolment of 15 more people in the University's transition course is planned for the 2019–2020 academic year.
- It developed an intrauniversity network (with its own groups and departments) and an interuniversity network (with other universities such as the Universitat Politècnica de Catalunya).
- It includes collaboration with social entities, municipalities and other civil society organisations, among others (University of Barcelona, 2018, p. 18–31).

It should also be noted that this programme has been included as good practice in the inHERE project (Higher Education Supporting Refugees in Europe)[5] and the RESCUE project (Refugees Education Support in MENA Countries),[6] and has received other distinctions for work related to the reception and integration of refugees.

As for the initiatives of privately-owned universities, there is the 2017 scholarship programme sponsored by the Universitat Oberta de Catalunya (Open University of Catalonia, UOC) for refugee students or asylum seekers who were in refugee camps in Greece waiting to be relocated elsewhere in Europe. Twenty-five refugees from 19 to 34 years old (24 of them from Syria and one from Afghanistan) took part in this first call for scholarships and the UOC offered them training to learn Catalan and English at the University's Centre for Modern Languages. Participants in the programme also received the assistance and psychosocial support of 25 mentors, responsible for orienting and guiding the process during the training. Although the recipients were living in another territory, this initiative exemplifies the type of actions undertaken.

Finally, the privately-owned Camilo José Cela University (UCJC), in conjunction with Santander Bank, has designed the Integra Project, aimed at facilitating access to university for international students from countries in conflict, so they can begin or resume their university studies. In October 2016, a total of 10 young refugees from Syria, Iraq, Ukraine and Afghanistan began participating in this programme by studying various degrees at the UCJC, although they first had to complete a training phase in language competencies, emotional intelligence tools, democratic and constitutional values, and learning communication and expression skills and strategies. This initiative was also recognised with the 2018 European Citizens' Prize.[7]

3.4 Good Practices in Sexual and Gender Diversity

The situations of discrimination and/or violence experienced by students and which are associated with sexual orientation, gender identity and expression, or variations in sex may also have an impact on these students' opportunities in higher education and employment, among other areas (IGLYO, 2018). Similarly, the meta-analysis by Penna Tosso (2015) concluded that there are high levels of homophobia in higher education. More specifically in the Spanish case, Pichardo Galán and Puche Cabezas (2019) point out the persistence of epistemological, physical, bureaucratic and symbolic barriers for students who have experienced gender and sex-related discrimination and violence in Spanish universities, despite progress in legislation. In relation to these, they point to the "domino effect" resulting from the first law on transsexuality at the regional level. This law, passed in 2009 by the Chartered Community of Navarre, although subsequently repealed by another one, was the stimulus for each of the 17 autonomous communities to approve their own legislation on gender diversity in the 2009–2018 period. It should be noted that the authors' analysis shows that these laws contain explicit provisions and recommendations for embracing this diversity in the university environment.

Standing out in this regard are the Guide for Incorporating Sexual and Gender Diversity in Catalan Universities on the Basis of Law 11/2014, published by the Government of Catalonia in 2018 (with versions in Spanish and English, in addition to Catalan). The guidelines establish four areas of action: *university community, discrimination and harassment, teaching, and research*. Within each of these, there are specific actions with the overall objective of creating a university community free from homophobia, transphobia and biphobia and with a willingness to address sexual and gender diversity.

Regarding institutional strategies, in 2016 the Complutense University of Madrid (UCM) created the Office for Sexual Diversity and Gender Identity. This office, the first of its kind in a public university, is part of the UCM Diversity and Inclusion Support Unit and provides care for students, teaching and administrative staff, whether in groups or individually, in person or remotely. Services include information, advice and mediation in cases of conflict or harassment due to homophobia or transphobia. In the 2016–2017 academic year, assistance was provided to 52 people, 32 in person and 20 remotely (via telephone, e-mail and social networks). Similarly, various awareness and visibility as well as training and research activities have been developed for the different university faculties (UCM, 2016–2017).

The Strategic Plan for the Promotion of Respect, Diversity and LGBT+ Equality presented by the University of Zaragoza in 2018 was produced with the purpose of increasing sensitivity to this issue, empowering the LGBTQ+collective within the scope of this university and contributing to the understanding of diversity as a positive feature of the university community.

Among the actions discussed in this plan are:
– guaranteeing respect for and protection of the right to equality and non-discrimination on the basis of sexual orientation of all students, teaching staff and anybody providing services in the university environment;
– promoting informative and training actions for the teaching staff about the LGBTQ+ reality in order to help them to detect, prevent and protect acts of discrimination or harassment; and
– continuing to assist and support – within their scope of action – students, teaching staff or administration and services staff who may be subject to discrimination on the basis of sexual orientation within the educational community (University of Zaragoza, 2018, p. 1).

Similarly, other universities have chosen to incorporate actions related to sexual and gender diversity as part of the gender equality units, gender equality plans and/or other structures and initiatives to support equality and diversity, such as protocols designed to prevent harassment and sexist violence.

Finally, this section also takes into account the significant initiatives for incorporating sexual diversity in the university curriculum in that the implementation of training courses for students has led to positive effects in reducing the extent of homophobia in higher education (Penna Tosso, 2015). Pichardo Galán and Puche Cabezas (2019) point out that the University of Málaga was one of the pioneers in actions related to sexual diversity in the Spanish context, by including a course called Community of Lesbians, Gays, Transsexuals and

Bisexuals in their University Master's in Social and Community Research and Intervention programme. The course includes content in across three axes – *identity, social networks,* and *the LGBTQ+community and collective* – from a psychosocial perspective that aims to focus the analysis on aspects such as the needs of this collective, its social and community welfare, social support, empowerment and discrimination (University of Málaga, 2019–2020).

5   Conclusions

Higher education is a public social good and a duty of the State (UNESCO/IESALC, 2008) and, although it is not part of compulsory education, the possibilities of access and participation for all students must therefore be guaranteed. Universities, as an integral part of the higher education system, have a fundamental role in achieving success in the social dimension. In an overall sense, the strategies and measures implemented – both at the national level in the form of plans and policies and at the institutional level in the form of specific actions or programmes for improving access and the retention of all students – is related to the construction of a more inclusive society, as it impacts more broadly on the inclusive higher education agenda.

In this chapter, we have reviewed a set of good practices aimed at achieving the social dimension in higher education in Spain. They exemplify the efforts that are being made for building a university – and by extension a society – that not only recognises diversity as a fundamental value, but also becomes involved in the social problems that affect it and that necessarily lead to the designing of new structures and training programmes and the allocation of resources so that the process of building inclusion takes shape. It is clear that there are still challenges and areas that need to be analysed. In this sense, it would be useful to continue to undertake studies to investigate university practices at the classroom level focused on the teaching-learning process with an inclusive orientation or practices focused on the inclusion of ethnic or racial minorities in the context of Spanish universities.

Finally, and as already noted, the achievement of educational inclusion in higher education is a process that evolves over time; although it certainly comes with its own difficulties it is also a process in which achievements and progress are recognised. For this very reason, we must continue to work towards inclusion, based on common agreements between various social sectors – whether they be those that are responsible for formulating and implementing policies, educational agents, teachers and directors, or students – and society as a whole.

Acknowledgment

This document has been produced as part of the project "ACCESS4ALL – Laboratory for Policies and Practices of Social Development in Higher Education" (Ref. 2015-1-ES01-KA203-015970) co-funded by the European Union (Erasmus+ Programme).

Notes

1 The Conference of Rectors Spanish Universities is a non-profit association that has been operating since 1994 and brings together 76 Spanish universities (50 private and 26 public) (http://www.crue.org/SitePages/Inicio.aspx).
2 The definitions presented are approximations in relation to the objective of this presentation. Although it is not our purpose to carry out an exhaustive analysis of each of these axes in this chapter, for further details see Gairín and Suárez (2014).
3 See https://eua.eu/101-projects/541-refugees-welcome-map.html
4 For further information, see http://www.solidaritat.ub.edu/la-fundaci-solidaritat-ub-coordina-el-projecte-mare-nostrum-de-suport-i-consolidaci-de-la-solidaritat-local-envers-les-persones-refugiades/
5 For further information, see https://www.inhereproject.eu/es/resultados/catalogo-de-buenas-practicas
6 For further information, see https://www.rescuerefugees.eu/best-practices/access-to-education/
7 For further information, see https://www.ucjc.edu/2018/09/proyecto-integra-la-ucjc-recibe-premio-parlamento-europeo-2018/

References

Ainscow, M., & Miles, S. (2008). Por una educación para todos que sea inclusiva ¿Hacia dónde vamos ahora? *Perspectivas, 145*(1), 17–44.
CRUE. (2015). *Comunicado Refugiados*. Author. https://www.crue.org/Documentos%20compartidos/Comunicados/Comunicado_Refugiados.pdf
CRUE. (2018a). *Declaración de Salamanca.* Author.
CRUE. (2018b). *La Universidad Española en Cifras – 2016/2017.* Author.
European Commission/EACEA/Eurydice. (2011). *Modernisation of Higher Education in Europe: Funding and the social dimension.* EU Education, Audiovisual and Culture Executive Agency.
European Commission/EACEA/Eurydice. (2014). *Modernisation of higher education in Europe 2014: Access, retention and employability.* EU Education, Audiovisual and Culture Executive Agency.

European Commission/EACEA/Eurydice. (2018). *The European Higher Education Area in 2018: Bologna process implementation report.* Publications Office of the European Union.

Fundación Universia. (2016). *Universidad y Discapacidad. III Estudio sobre el grado de inclusión del sistema universitario español respecto de la realidad de la discapacidad.* Fundación Universia.

Generalitat de Cataluña. (2018). *Guía para la incorporación de la diversidad sexual y de género a partir de la Ley 11/2014.* Generalitat de Cataluña.

IGLYO – International Lesbian, Gay, Bisexual, Transgender, Queer and Intersex Youth & Student Organisation. (2018). *LGBTQI inclusive education report.* Author.

Jefatura del Estado. (2007). *Ley Orgánica 4/2007, de 12 de abril, por la que se modifica la Ley Orgánica 6/2001, de 21 de diciembre, de Universidades.* Author.

Jefatura del Estado. (2001). *Ley Orgánica 6/2001, de 21 de diciembre, de Universidades.* Author.

Ministerio de Ciencia, Innovación y Universidades. (2019). *Datos y Cifras del Sistema Universitario Español. Publicación 2018–2019.* Author.

Ministerio de Educación, Cultura y Deporte. (2014). *Real Decreto 412/2014 de 6 de junio, por el que se establece la normativa básica de los procedimientos de admisión a las enseñanzas universitarias oficiales de Grado.* Author.

Ministerio de Educación y Formación Profesional. *Unidades de Igualdad de Género en Universidades.* Author. https://www.educacionyfp.gob.es/educacion/mc/igualdad/presentacion/igualdaduniversidades.html

Ministerio de Educación. Secretaría General de Universidades. (2011). *Las políticas sobre la discapacidad en el sistema universitario español.* Author.

Naciones Unidas. (1951). *Convención sobre el Estatuto de los Refugiados.* Author.

Naciones Unidas. (2016). *Declaración de Nueva York para los Refugiados y los Migrantes.* Author.

Penna Tosso, M. (2015). Homofobia en las aulas universitarias. Un metaanálisis. *REDU, 13*(1), 181–202.

Pichardo Galán, J. I., & Puche Cabezas, L. (2019). Universidad y diversidad sexogenérica: barreras, innovaciones y retos de futuro. *Methaodos. Revista de Ciencias Sociales, 7*(1), 10–26.

UNESCO. (2019). *Informe de Seguimiento de la Educación en el Mundo 2019 – Migración, desplazamiento y educación: construyendo puentes, no muros.* Author.

UNESCO/IESALC. (2008). *Declaración Final de la Conferencia Regional de la Educación Superior en América Latina y el Caribe. Conferencia Regional de Educación Superior.* Author. http://www.iesalc.unesco.org.ve/docs/wrt/declaracioncres_espanol.pdf

Universitat Autònoma de Barcelona. (2018). *Protocolo de actuación contra el acoso sexual y el acoso por razón de sexo, de orientación sexual, de identidad de género o de expresión de género.* Author.

Universidad de Barcelona. (2018). *Memoria de Actividades Programa UB de apoyo a personas refugiadas*. Author.

Universidad Complutense de Madrid. (2016–2017). *Memoria de actividades de la Unidad de Apoyo a la Diversidad e Inclusión*. Author.

Universidad Complutense de Madrid. (n.d.-a). *Guía de Autoayuda para Refugiados procedentes de Siria*. Author. https://www.ucm.es/clinicadepsicologia/noticias/guia-de-autoayuda-a-los-refugiados-procedentes-de-siria

Universidad Complutense de Madrid. (n.d.-b). *Plan de Acogida a Personas Refugiadas*. Author. https://www.ucm.es/plan-de-acogida

Universitat de Lleida, Centre Dolors Piera. (n.d.). http://www.cdp.udl.cat/home/index.php/ca/

Universidad de Málaga. (2019–2020). *Guía docente Asignatura Comunidad de Lesbianas, Gays, Transexuales y Bisexuales*. Author.

Universitat de Valencia. (2013). *Reglamento de Medidas para la Integración del Personal Docente e Investigador con Discapacidad*. Author.

Universitat de Valencia. (2017). *Memoria de actividades de la Unidad para la Personas con Discapacidad*. Author.

Universidad de Zaragoza. (2018). *Proyecto ADIM Advancing in LGBT Diversity Management in the Public and Private Sector que servirá de apoyo al Plan Estratégico para el fomento del respeto, la diversidad y la igualdad LGBT+ de la Universidad de Zaragoza*. Author.

Valls, R., Puigvert, L., Melgar, P., & Garcia-Yeste, C. (2016). Breaking the silence at Spanish universities: Findings from the first study of violence against women on campuses in Spain. *Violence Against Women*, 22(13), 1519–1539. https://doi.org/10.1177/1077801215627511

CHAPTER 8

Policies and Strategies on Widening Access and Experiences of Inclusive Practices in Higher Education in England

Lisa Lucas and Sue Timmis

Abstract

This chapter outlines some of the widening participation policies to increase equity and access to higher education in England that were introduced since the 1990s and provides a critical perspective on the extent of their success. The governing bodies set up to monitor and evaluate these developments are introduced alongside the 'Access Agreements' that must be produced by all English universities to demonstrate steps they are taking to widen participation. The challenges for universities are identified and the framework of 'strategising as a process' as well as the A4A 'Pyramid Inclusion Model' are utilised to consider how universities can respond in ways that can maximise the involvement of different stakeholders. Some of the good practices that have been successful at the University of Bristol are introduced and these form the basis of increasing access for under-represented groups but also building more inclusive communities within the institution. The good practices discussed include, Access to Bristol, The Foundation Year in Arts and Humanities, Peer Mentoring and Be More Empowered for Success. It is argued that there is work still to be done but with a range of stakeholders involved in such initiatives and forms of distributed leadership then meaningful change is possible.

Keywords

widening participation – diversity – inclusive cultures – strategising – Pyramid Inclusion Model – distributed leadership

1 Introduction

Increasing access to higher education, particularly for under-represented groups is an important part of government policy on higher education in England and across the UK. There have been a range of policies introduced from the 1990s onwards alongside changes in government bodies responsible for enacting and monitoring change and improvement on increasing equity of access to higher education. The aim of this chapter is to outline the context of policy change in higher education in England and to discuss in detail the experiences of one university in England in developing strategic plans for ensuring fair access and participation for students from under-represented backgrounds. These experiences are discussed in relation to the ACCESS4ALL toolkit and in particular, the A4A Pyramid for Inclusion and the complexities of developing, enacting and evaluating strategies and policies for inclusive practices. A range of 'good practices' explored as part of the A4A project will be discussed to demonstrate the complexities and challenges of addressing inequities in higher education as well as successes.

2 Higher Education Policy and Widening Access

This chapter is being written as a new Conservative government has been elected to power in the UK with a mandate to ensure Brexit (British exit from the European Union) takes place. Brexit has potentially catastrophic implications for the UK economy and for the higher education sector. Details on the policy agenda for higher education have not yet been announced though there would be an expectation that much of the agenda put forward by the previous Conservative administrations will continue. The policy context, particularly relating to access to higher education will be discussed alongside the continuing challenges faced.

The UK has around 160 higher education institutions and is ostensibly publicly funded although increasingly it relies on private finance, particularly student fees (albeit that this is underwritten by the UK government). Since the introduction of tuition fees following the Teaching and Higher Education Act 1998, these have steadily increased and following the Browne Review in 2010, fees were raised to £9,000 a year starting from 2012 in England. The cost of tuition for one year in England is now £9,250 (2019/20). However, the post-18 review of Education and funding known as the 'Augur review' carried out in 2019 recommended that fees be reduced to £7,500 per year, though no action has yet been taken on this by the previous or newly elected Conservative governments. The other countries in the United Kingdom have different approaches to fees policy, with Wales more recently following the English example of raising fees and lower fees charged in Northern Ireland. In contrast, there continues to be no fees charged in Scotland. In England, there was a bursary component to help with student maintenance, but this has been replaced by loans for both fees and maintenance (relative to parental income), which means that students in England leave university with large debts from loans estimated to be between £30,000–£60,000. Given these high levels of debt, there has been concern that the increasing costs of higher education might deter applicants and so there is much concern about ensuring a 40% participation rate and particularly debates on how to ensure more participants from under-represented groups.

Widening participation into higher education of under-represented groups was a significant aim of New Labour governments from 1997–2010 and assumed a high priority with significant policy programmes, funded organisations and activities. Widening participation was a key aspect of the 2003 White Paper 'The Future of Higher Education', which led to the 2004 Higher Education Act. The Act introduced student fees, extended student bursaries and set up a new Office for Fair Access (OFFA). Substantial funding was made available for new initiatives, including the Higher Education Funding Council for England's (HEFCE) Aim Higher Programme, which operated with 42 area partnerships (142 universities and 800 schools) across England to encourage and support the participation of students from lower socio-economic backgrounds. There have been questions about the success of changes in participation rates (Harrison, 2011) and of the underlying discourses of widening participation focused on "diversity" and "choice" (Archer, 2007). Harrison (2011) concluded that whilst there had been modest improvement in widening participation of those from state funded schools and from lower socio-economic backgrounds, this improvement had not been seen at the Russell Group, the prestigious group of top UK universities, thus continuing a system that produces "entrenched privilege" (p. 464). McCaig (2016) further argues, that there may be differential effects across different universities such that due to increased marketisation, the less prestigious universities (often referred to as the post-1992 university sector) have their finances reduced further and as a result are less able to support the much larger number of under-represented groups that would attend these universities.

The Coalition Government 2010–2015 (Conservative and Liberal Democrats) and the subsequent Conservative Governments made strident policy changes in relation to Higher Education. The White Paper 'Students at the heart of the system' (2011) saw student fees increase to £9,000 per annum (payable after graduation when a salary of £21,000 is reached), substantial bursaries for students from low socio-economic groups, increased funding for the Office For Fair Access (OFFA) and increased emphasis on institutional access agreements – where institutions set out their strategies to widen participation. Much of what might be seen as the gains for those students from lower socio-economic groups in the availability of grants and bursaries was taken away. These were replaced at the institutional level where modest bursaries could be awarded and some element of fee waiver.

OFFA's Strategic plan 2015–2020 highlighted key under-represented and disadvantaged groups, which included: students from low socio-economic backgrounds and disadvantaged neighbourhoods, disabled students, students from some minority ethnic groups and care leavers (i.e. those who have been in the care of local authorities). Only some minority ethnic groups were included as some are successful in gaining entry and achieving success in higher education. OFFA highlighted improvements that have been made in increasing access to higher education for students from low socio-economic backgrounds and emphasises the 60% increase in participation of 18 years olds, resulting in 18% participation in 2014. There is, however, recognition of continuing inequities, with students from more advantaged backgrounds being two and a half times more likely to enter HE and seven times more likely to enter universities with the highest entry requirements, pointing to the 'entrenched privilege' mentioned above. This also holds for Black, Asian and Minority Ethnic (BAME) students whose participation increased to 20.2% in 2013/14 but who continue to be not well represented in highly selective institutions. The Government aimed to double the percentage of people from disadvantaged backgrounds entering higher education by 2020, compared to 2009, and increase the number of Black, Asian and Ethnic Minority (BAME)[1] students going into higher education by 20% by 2020.

In 2017 the Higher Education Research Act set out the proposal to establish the 'Office for Students' (OfS), which happened in April 2018. The OfS is the single body to regulate higher education in England to replace HEFCE and OFFA and includes responsibilities therefore, for ensuring fair access to higher education in England. The OfS Annual review in 2019 set out the details of what is seen as a 'slow but steady' improvement in equality of access and participation in higher education for students from under-represented groups and highlighted the ongoing complex challenges still faced. However, it was recognised that continuing inequities existed for students in relation to social class background, ethnicity as well as students with disabilities. It was also emphasised that the number of mature students had halved since 2012 alongside a reducing numbers of part-time students after the introduction of higher fees in England. There was also recognition of the continuing entrenched and persistent inequality of access to the elite universities, the 'Russell group' or high tariff universities (i.e. those demanding high grades for access to their programmes of study). The University of Bristol belongs to this category of institution and so it an interesting case study of the strategies and struggles to increase access for those from under-represented groups. In order to understand these challenges within universities, some of the initiatives taking place at the University of Bristol will be discussed later in this chapter but first a discussion of the complexities of how to ensure successful strategies, including some of the ideas and tools developed as part of the A4A project.

3 Strategy as a Process for Change – A4A Pyramid for Inclusion

The A4A toolkit was devised to enable institutions to consider, plan and evaluate their strategies, plans and ideas for ensuring fair access to higher education and to enable students to be successful in their studies. It was developed with representatives from universities across six European countries and represents a flexible toolkit that could be utilised in different universities and different national contexts. The ethos of the toolkit was to think of the need for flexibility and also to consider the complexities of widening participation strategies, which are not fixed but take place within a changing policy landscape both at the international, national and local university context and in relation to wider institutional strategies. They must be seen as a process taking place in these changing and complex environments. Developing strategy, therefore, is not about developing a fixed set of ideas but must be responsive to changing contexts and involve the dynamic interaction of multiple stakeholders. The idea, therefore, is to see strategising as a process rather than focus simply on the content of strategy documents and plans, although these can be important for clarifying aims and providing the focus for conversations and interactions between stakeholders. The development of the A4A 'Pyramid Inclusion Model' aimed to capture the dynamic process of strategy-in-action within specific organisations and through the dynamic interaction and leadership of a range of stakeholders.

The concept of 'strategising' or understanding strategy as a process is important for considering not just the influence of the environment but also the active agency of individual organisations (Frolich et al., 2013). Furthermore, Adserias et al. (2017) argue that a 'full-range' style of leadership is required and also a recognition of the importance of 'grass-roots leadership' at different levels of the organisation and call for a better understanding of how "institutional leaders might best align the efforts of faculty, staff and students to advance the diversity agenda" (p. 328). Similar arguments are made by Frolich et al. (2013), in their concept of 'strategising', which has been influential in the development of the A4A 'Pyramid Inclusion Model'. They emphasise the "the complex and multi-level processes with strong intra-organisational bottom up and horizontal process, involving a broad group of intra-organisational members" (p. 85). These ideas were influential in informing the A4A 'Pyramid Inclusion Model', which aimed to depart from the idea of having a fixed set of strategies and instead encourage reflection and planning through a dynamic interaction of stakeholders located within specific environmental and cultural organisations. These ideas are also important in thinking about the realities of institutional life and the importance of new ideas and innovations at different levels of the institution and involving a range of actors from Vice Chancellors and Senior Leaders to central support services, including 'Student Access and Participation' teams, academics and programme leaders as well as students themselves. As will become clear in the discussion of the initiatives and strategies at the University of Bristol, the active agency of all of these potential stakeholders are important in driving change forward and ensuring progress in fair access and student success.

4 Fair Access, Diversity and Student Success at the University of Bristol

The OFFA and now the OfS is the responsible body overseeing entry to higher education of students from under-represented backgrounds. This includes ensuring that universities develop an 'access agreement', which sets out their strategies and plans for creating diversity of participation in their universities, particularly at elite institutions which are historically less diverse and admit students from more wealthy and advantaged backgrounds. The following sections will discuss the evidence and approach taken at one English university and detail some of the good practices that were developed and that have been documented as part of the A4A project.[2] It is important to emphasise that these are seen as 'good' practices and not 'best' practice, which for the reasons outlined above should be seen always in context of the national and local policy context. The good practices identified at the University of Bristol were developed as part of an ongoing programme of policies and activities to widen access to more diverse groups and also ensure successful participation and outcomes for students from all backgrounds. However, this is a changing context and the dynamics policies and 'strategising' processes are necessary to ensure continuing progress.

The University of Bristol is a highly selective, research-intensive, elite university. It is a 'high tariff' institution requiring very high entry grades for admission. It enrols a relatively low proportion of undergraduate students from under-represented and disadvantaged groups. In particular, as with other highly selective institutions, there are low proportions of students from low socio-economic backgrounds and BAME students. The University is very keen to achieve a more diverse student community and has had long-term plans in place to achieve this, which are detailed in the yearly Access Agreements. A main focus of access agreements is the development of strategies to encourage undergraduate applications from low-performing schools. The majority of the university's undergraduates are from predominantly more privileged backgrounds with a high proportion from private schools, though the percentage of students from state schools has been increasing. Bristol is unusual in that, in spite of being a prosperous city, the child poverty rate in the city is high and can be as high as 44% in the economically disadvantaged area of South Bristol. In addition, BAME pupils and those with English as an alternative language underperform at all levels of education. The main thrust of access/widening participation strategies is, therefore, on supporting those from such deprived communities to consider higher education, ideally at an elite university such as Bristol.

The University of Bristol engages in a wide variety of policies and practices in order to increase participation of under-represented groups. As part of the Access Agreement and the strategy to widen participation, the University of Bristol invests in access measures to include; financial support for students from low income backgrounds and a comprehensive programme of activities to support outreach, retention and progression of students from under-represented groups. For the academic year 2019–2020, the university will spend £3.6 million pounds on outreach activities, £2.2 million pounds on student success and progression activities and £9.2 million pounds on a student finance package. This makes a total investment of £15 million. The student recruitment team plan a wide range of outreach activities, including, Open Days, School and College Events, HE talks and workshops and Summer Schools. There is also a Widening Participation Student Support team and a dedicated advisor for Mature and Part-time students, a recent initiative to support BAME students within the university called Be More Empowered (BME) for Success Programme, as well as a range of Disability Services for students requiring help with disabilities. The University of Bristol has initiated a range of policies and practices and these will be discussed with particular focus on four key strategies relating to both access to the university and successful student progression at the university.

5   Good Practices – Ensuring Fair Access to Higher Education

The University of Bristol has been at the forefront of some innovative activity in widening access and diversity at the institution and has initiated new ideas such as the Bristol Scholars Scheme to allow local students from across Bristol schools who come from under-represented groups but demonstrate high ability to access programmes.[3] These students are given additional support from the university to help achieve their study goals. The University of Bristol has also received an award for the Sanctuary Scholarships offered to refugees and asylum seekers. There have been 37 scholarships awarded since 2016 and they provide fee waivers and bursaries to help support refugee and asylum seekers to attend the university without facing financial barriers. In addition, along with many other UK universities, there are contextual offers made to students from under-represented groups to allow them to access university, whilst taking into account the challenges faced. An offer of two grades less than the norm can be made to students who come from lower performing schools, areas where access to higher education is traditionally lower, students who are care-experienced and those who have taken part in the universities many outreach programmes. The university has a range of outreach programmes, including summer schools and taster days. However, in this section the range of opportunities available through 'Access to Bristol' will be discussed and also the innovative Foundation Year in Arts and Humanities as examples of good practices.

6   Access to Bristol

Access to Bristol began in 2005 and provides local students with an opportunity to attend the university. The scheme is designed as a curriculum enrichment opportunity for students taking A-levels or equivalent qualifications. Students attend a series of sessions, including a variety of subjects within Sciences, Social Science and Arts and Humanities. Each session is designed to give students an idea of what it is like to study at the University, working with academics and current students who can offer advice and guidance about higher education and their chosen area of study. There is no qualification obtained at the end of the scheme, but the aim is to enable students to attain higher grades that will give them the entry requirements for university. A ceremony is held at the University of Bristol to acknowledge? those who have successfully completed the Access to Bristol sessions. In 2015/16 Access to Bristol contained 23 subject streams (7 of which took place twice through the year), each of which required 6 two-hour academic taster sessions delivered by academic staff. In 2015/16 a total of 628 students completed the Access to Bristol programme. Students came from 68 different state schools/colleges across the local area. In 2019/20 there are now 29 subject streams representing the large range of areas of study at the university.

> In the five-year period from 2013–2014 to 2017–2018 applications to the University from Access to Bristol participants increased by nearly 200 per cent (155 to 458). For 2017 entry we received 458 applications to the University from Access to Bristol students, against a progress measure of 171, with 135 progressing to our degree programmes against a progress measure of 46. This intake of 135 students is more than double that of the previous year (64). Such figures suggest that the guaranteed offer, academic content of the programme, support through the application process and financial support package is proving effective. As such we will retain the guaranteed offer and provide a transition year fee waiver and bursary for such students in 2019–2020. (University of Bristol Access and Participation Plan 2019–2020)

Access to Bristol has grown significantly in scale since it began in 2005 and now operates two cohorts of participants every year. The model of taster sessions offered within Access to Bristol can also be done at a more ad hoc, local level such as other initiatives like 'Insight into Bristol' and also offering tailored talks for local schools.

Students who are successful on the programme are guaranteed an interview and a place at the university so long as they meet the entrance requirements. This would involve eligibility for a contextual offer of two grades less than the normal offer and also access to a Bristol bursary. The financial support available is a fee waiver in the first year (£9,250 currently) and also a bursary of £3,855 for each year of study.

The Access to Bristol scheme has resulted in a much larger diversity of students at Bristol from under-represented groups. However, the schemes success is measured not only by the number of students who take up a place at Bristol but also the many who might go on to university places elsewhere in the UK.[4]

6.1 Foundation Year in Arts and Humanities

The Foundation Year in Arts and Humanities is aimed at participants aged 17 or over 70 – or any age in between – and who come from any ethnic, educational, professional or social background. It is concerned not with what students have done in the past, or their prior attainments, but in what they have the potential to achieve in the future. The Foundation Year aims to equip them with the knowledge and skills to bridge their potential future study at undergraduate level. Throughout the course students are introduced to a range of study skills that are essential for studying the arts and humanities at undergraduate level. Students also receive a broad introduction to each of the subjects covered by the course and how these have developed over time. By examining specifically what it means to be human, now and in the past, students look back over 2,500 years examining how the society we inhabit and the culture we share has been shaped by ideas, historical events, and works of art. The course is one year full-time and involves two days per week at the university, including six hours of contact time and a minimum of 10 hours independent study. The course involves compulsory and optional units. Students are introduced to a wide range of assessment on different courses including; exams, essays, presentations and portfolio of work. Applicants who complete the course satisfactorily are guaranteed a place on an undergraduate degree within the University Faculty of Arts and Humanities. Participants who achieve an overall average of at least 40% will have passed the course and will receive a Certificate in the Arts and Humanities. However, in order to progress onto an undergraduate programme, a higher level of achievement is required as follows:

– An overall average of 60% or above;
– An overall average of 50% or above and at least one unit mark of 60% or above;
– An overall average of 40% or above, subject to a progression review meeting.

The first cohort of students began in 2013 and in 2013/14, 24 students (89%) successfully completed the year. 20 are now in full-time undergraduate education: 19 at Bristol; 1 at Leeds. 2 also went on to study part-time elsewhere. From the 2014/15 cohort, 17 are studying at Bristol, and three have taken up places elsewhere, including at University College London and Kings College London. Students are achieving highly on the Bristol degrees, with some getting marks in the 70s and 80s on their first-year units. The programme has been successful in recruiting diverse, talented and motivated students. There is an intake of between 25 and 30 students per year. Of 27 people on the course in 2014/15, 90% did not have A-Level qualifications. 72% were mature, 34% were local, 38% from low participation neighbourhoods, 20% had a disability and 20%

were from BAME groups. 78% of students had a household income of under £25k.

> 101 students commenced the FYAH programme 2013–2016, of whom 83 per cent had a successful outcome and 75 per cent went on to a degree programme. 66 students went on to 21 separate degree programmes in Bristol and 10 to degrees at other institutions. Of these students, 7 have now graduated (2 with a First and 5 with a 2.i) and 2 have continued to postgraduate study. Of the 66 students who continued to a degree at Bristol, 4 have withdrawn or discontinued (6 per cent). Of the 17 students who did not complete FYAH, 3 have subsequently gone on to study elsewhere. (University of Bristol Access and Participation Plan 2019–2020)

Since 2019 the programme has been extended to include Social Sciences and has been renamed the Foundation in Arts and Social Sciences (CertHE) and includes courses from across the Arts and Social Sciences Faculties. This has allowed for a significant expansion of the programme. It is important to highlight that the innovation of this programme was initiated by academics in the Arts Faculties at the university who were keen to see change. Full details of the development of the programme can be found in publications by these academics (McLellan et al., 2016). Their experiences also resulted in the publication of a book, which deal with the important question of fair access to universities and 'Who is the University For' (Sperlinger et al., 2018).

These two initiatives therefore demonstrate the range of stakeholders in developing innovative practice. 'Access to Bristol' is a university wide scheme, initiated from leadership in the student recruitment office but also involves academics who run the courses and external stakeholders such as schools and teachers. The Foundation in Arts and Social Sciences was initiated by academics but was also supported by leaders within the university as well as academics teaching on the programme. This demonstrates, therefore the importance of dynamic interactions of key stakeholders and multiples agents in driving change within the university.

7   Good Practices – Ensuring Support and Positive Experiences

The University of Bristol Access and Participation Plan (formerly Access Agreement) is concerned not simply with extending access and diversifying the student body at the university but also ensuring that all students from any background can have a positive experience and be successful in their studies.

A range of initiatives have been put in place to help support students and also for students to help each other. Many of these initiatives are university wide rather than focusing on specific groups of students.

There are a range of terms used to understand the idea of widening participation of under-represented groups to higher education and in recent years there has been a move away from a focus solely on access to considering the development of more inclusive cultures within higher education, as indicated by Wray (2013) who states:

> One way of looking at these definitions is to suggest that the focus has moved away from identifying specific sub-groups of students and towards the structure, processes and practices within the institution which create barriers to equitable experiences. (p. 5)

It is possible, therefore, to think about inclusion as a nested process as presented in Figure 8.1.

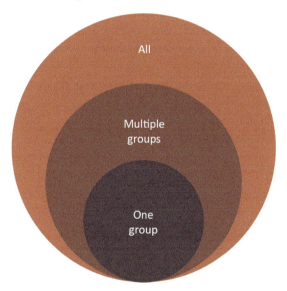

FIGURE 8.1   Inclusion as a nested process (adapted from Wray, 2013)

Some of the initiatives discussed in this section are aimed at all students but can be seen as potentially helping particular groups at the same time. However, more recently, the university has put in place targeted support for certain groups, for example establishing a mature students' support network and the BME (Be More Empowered) programme for Black, Asian and Minority Ethnic students', which was started in the academic year 2018/19 and which is discussed below after outlining the well-established peer mentoring and peer assisted study schemes.

7.1   *Peer Mentoring*

Peer support is recognised as important for all students, but in particular, for under-represented students. It is not just the transition to higher education but participating in the day to day academic and social life of university that can be more challenging and limit a sense of belonging (Timmis & Munoz-Chereau, 2019). Such students are often positioned as 'other' from their first day at university where they are required to 'fit in' to the existing institutional and peer cultures (Crozier, Reay, & Clayton, 2010). Thomas (2017) argued that the most critical aspect of retention and success in higher education was encouraging meaningful interactions between staff and students in order to foster 'a culture of belonging' (p. 17). Peer mentoring is one mechanism that universities can adopt to support peer to peer interactions and help students develop a sense of belonging within university settings.

As an example of this, the long-established peer mentoring scheme at the University of Bristol aims to provide academic and pastoral support for students in their transition to university. The objectives of peer mentoring are as follows:
– To foster a positive and inclusive atmosphere, improve their experience and encourage a sense of belonging;
– To match mentors to new students from the time of students' first arrival at the University and throughout the first year;
– To provide personal and professional development opportunities for students acting as peer mentors.

New first year students are invited to take part in the scheme through a written communication, which includes a copy of the guide once they have received their letter offering them a place. Under-represented students are targeted with a further, follow up email to encourage these students in particular to take this up, although the scheme is open to everyone. Students wishing to take part and work with a mentor are asked to complete a short online form in early September. A welcome event is then held to introduce the scheme and for students to ask questions. Mentors (those providing the support) and who are all postgraduates and Mentees (those receiving support) are then matched. Mentors receive training and some have had specific training in particular areas, for example disabilities such as Aspergers syndrome and then work with students with particular needs. The aim is to match mentors and mentees in September each year so that new first year students can receive support even before they arrive.

The scheme began in 2006 with a small pilot in the faculty of Social Sciences and Law. Since then it has expanded every year and in 2013/14 the scheme was extended to all first year students in the university. In 2015/16 1503 first year undergraduate students opted to have a peer mentor. This is 28% of the first-year population. At least 338 (24%) were international students. From non-traditional groups of those who were known to be UK students (58%), the scheme worked with 181 students from ethnic minorities (11% increase), 114 students from low participation neighbourhoods, 45 students with a disability (18% decrease), and 28 mature students (although there were 62 mature students overall). In addition, although not an agreed University widening participation (non-traditional student) indicator, students with no parental history of HE have also been identified. 247 students with no parental history of HE participated in the programme (69% increase). These students may require additional support in their transition to the University of Bristol due to having no parental experience of HE to draw on.

The success of the scheme and increasing numbers of participants points to the importance and value of interactions with peers in developing a sense of belonging to the university and this is also the case with the peer assisted study scheme is now discussed.

7.2 Peer Assisted Study Sessions

The Peer Assisted Study Sessions or PASS is part of Study Support in the Student portal on the University website which provides academic and pastoral support for students in their transition to university and during their degree programme. The PASS objectives are:
- To help students make the academic transition to university level and style of study.
- Working as a PASS leader also aims to provide personal and professional development opportunities for students.

Peer assisted study sessions are timetabled weekly, subject-based student-led forums for first-year students, where questions relating to course material and studying. The sessions are led by PASS leaders. These are students from later years of the programme in the university, who are trained to act as PASS leaders.

Benefits of the scheme are advertised as:
- a safe place to ask questions
- gain a deeper understanding of the course material
- make new friends on your course
- get practical advice and improve your study skills
- build confidence in your subject area

– meet students from later years on your course and learn from their experiences

Sessions appear on student timetables. It has been scaled up from a small initial pilot in one school in one faculty in 2006 to a university-wide scheme for all first year student and numbers have increased year on year. In 2019/20, the scheme is offered in 24 subjects. Examples of topics include; Course content, exam skills, revision skills, essay planning, adapting to independent study, academic writing, referencing, time management, presentation skills, note-taking and critical reading.

The PASS scheme is evaluated every year through an annual survey in May, once the academic support sessions have ended. The 2016 evaluation data showed that 92% of PASS attendees who had responded to the surveys said that peer support had improved their student experience to some extent. The more contact the students had with PASS leaders, the greater benefit they reported for their student experience. It is not only first years who benefit from taking part in the peer support programme. 100% of PASS leaders said that being a peer supporter had improved their own student experience.

In addition, the support team have consulted and worked with PASS leaders and attendees to develop improvements over time. PASS attendees and leaders are invited to contribute the development of the scheme. All PASS leaders and attendees are consulted about how to develop the scheme further, including through the annual evaluation of the programme. The scheme is specifically designed to help students in demystifying university cultures, academic language and practices and gives targeted support for academic studying.

Interviews conducted with the leaders of the scheme showed that it was relatively easy to set up but the training of PASS leaders and the integration with academic departments was a critical part of the process. Some of the quotes from students who have benefitted from the programme include:

> As a mature student it is harder to make contact with other students. PASS helped with the feeling of disconnection as well as study skill confidence.

> It was so refreshing to talk to and be guided by the PASS mentor team … [they] imparted their knowledge of Uni life … helped us settle in, alleviated our fears and humanised our experience. Signposting us with their experiences and expert knowledge.

> PASS is good for knowing that you're in the same boat as other people in what you find challenging/stressful – meaning that I was more confident

to speak up in seminars etc because I realised I wasn't the only one who won't have fully understood!

7.3 *Be More Empowered (BME) for Success Programme*

The University of Bristol is one of the Russell Group Universities with the fewest number of BAME undergraduate students (particularly home Black students). This programme was set up in 2018, following the publication of a 2017 report commissioned by the University to investigate the experiences of BAME undergraduate students and the extent to which claims of an attainment gap were well founded and what could be done to address such a gap. The report was based on a mixed methods study, which clearly demonstrated that there was a significant attainment gap evident for students from BAME communities. 'In 2015/16 31% of white students graduating achieved a first-class degree, compared to 20% of BAME students. Likewise, proportionately more BAME students (14%) who graduated achieved a 2:2 classification than white students (7%)' (Phillips et al., 2017, p. 6). The report also identified barriers for BAME students and made recommendations on how to dismantle them. A whole university action plan was established which is reviewed annually. The Be More Empowered (BME) for Success programme was set up a one of the key mechanisms in the plan for addressing these issues.

The programme is aimed at BAME undergraduates includes a number of different strands and is supported by a co-ordinator and a dedicated team of people (Student inclusion team). One its core functions is setting up and enabling a team of twenty-four trained students who are employed to help make a difference to the experiences of BAME students. They are called BME Success Advocates and they have received training and are supported by the Student Inclusion Team to ensure that the views that they put forward are representative of the views of Undergraduate BAME students at Bristol, rather than individual views. They are divided into three sub teams, which have different foci and undertake a series of projects, as shown below:

The Review team: comprising 12 advocates, where the aim is to support the University through School or Faculty level initiatives around learning and teaching in order to make it more inclusive and engaging for BAME students. Projects have included BAME in STEM subjects and exploring a mentoring scheme.

The Belonging team: comprising 6 advocates, which aims to develop a greater sense of belonging and positive student experience for BAME students through initiatives that promote visible role models, social equality or wellbeing. Projects here include a support group for Black men called the Black Men talk group, open to men who self-identify as male and Black (African, Caribbean or

Mixed heritage) and a similar group called Black Men Black Women talk group which is open to both women and men who self-identify as male or female and Black (African, Caribbean or Mixed heritage). This team has also established the Black and Minority Ethnic Powerlist, which aims to improve links between students and the wider Bristol community, and to provide students with more visible role models to inspire them in their own careers, activities and engagement with the city.

The Events team: comprising 6 advocates who organise informative and engaging events for students, throughout the academic year in partnership with Schools, Faculties and Bristol Students Union. These have included talks from key BAME figures in the creative industries and a Black History Month programme organised by the student BME programme advocates in collaboration with the Bristol Students' Union events team.

A guide for staff on BAME inclusion has also been produced which outlines practical tips and advice on improving teaching when working with diverse student groups – in the classroom, advice on designing inclusive assessments and in day-to-day interactions. A number of awareness raising measures are also in place. These include a mailing list and regular monthly newsletter. A dedicated area of the university website, a series of student blogs which are included as content on the website, a student facing 'Be More Empowered for Success' programme brochure and a poster campaign around the campus has also been undertaken.

Whilst the initiative is still in its infancy, the diverse mechanisms and emphasis on student-led teams and projects appear to be making an impact by offering both visibility and positive measures to support belonging and student agency. These initiatives are also clearly linked to university strategy and plans and offer some imaginative ideas for both social and cultural change within a traditional university. It is hoped that these activities can begin change the culture and lack of representation at the university, particularly for those from BAME communities, as this quote demonstrates:

> Not only are we navigating our way through the cultural rollercoaster of the university arena, but doing so without subject narratives, lecturers or pastoral carers that we can relate to. This is why initiatives such as BME Success is such an important step in improving the overall experience for BME students that choose Bristol university. With such amazing strides made through the actions of individual students, such as Chante Joseph's BME Power List and Yannick Yalipende' Black Men Talk, to improve and uphold the achievements of students of Colour, it is now time for the uni-

versity to advance and question where they wish to stand on the Eurocentric culture of supposedly multicultural universities. (Sodiq-Ajala, n.d.)

8   Conclusion

A range of initiatives and strategies at one university in England have been discussed and shown to demonstrate how important national policy making and context is for understanding how universities shape their institutional strategies and ideas for fair access and both inclusive and targeted student support. It has also been shown that it is critical to have a range of stakeholders involved in such initiatives and the importance of distributed leadership at all levels of the institution in order to effect real change. In the examples of good practice given, stakeholders, including students and academics as well as administrative leaders were important not just in devising new policies and initiatives but also enabling them to happen and achieve success, There is much work still to be done in ensuring that levels of inequality in UK higher education are addressed but it is important to understand the complex mechanisms by which successful change can happen and to learn from good practices where they exist.

Acknowledgement

This document has been produced as a part of the project "ACCESS4ALL – Laboratory for Policies and Practices of Social Development in Higher Education" (Ref. 2015-1-ES01-KA203-015970) co-funded by the European Union (Erasmus+ Programme).

Notes

1. We are using the most current term for this group, BAME (Black, Asian and Minority Ethnic students) but some authors or documents still refer to this group as BME (Black and Minority Ethnic students).
2. Full details of the good practices at all six of the partner universities are available on the project website (https://access4allproject.eu).
3. See http://www.bristol.ac.uk/study/outreach/post-16/scholars/
4. Full details of the scheme can be found on the university website (http://www.bristol.ac.uk/study/outreach/post-16/access/).

References

Adserias, R. P., Charleston, L. J., & Jackson, J. F. L. (2017). What style of leadership is best suited to direct organizational change to fuel institutional diversity in higher education? *Race, Ethnicity and Education, 20*(3), 315–331.

Archer, L. (2007). Diversity, Equality and higher education: A critical reflection on the ab/uses of equity discourse within widening participation. *Teaching in Higher Education, 12*(5–6), 635–653.

BIS. (2011, July). *Students at the heart of the system*. TSO.

Crozier, G., Reay, D., & Clayton, J. (2010). The socio-cultural and learning experiences of working class students in higher education. In M. David (Ed.), *Improving learning by widening participation in higher education* (pp. 62–74). Routledge.

DfES. (2003) *The future of higher education: White paper*. HMSO.

Frølich, N., & Huisman, J. (2013). A re-interpretation of institutional transformations in European higher education: Strategising pluralistic organisations in multiplex environments. *Higher Education, 65*, 79–93.

Harrison, N. (2011). Have the changes introduced by the 2004 higher education act made higher education admissions in England wider and fairer? *Journal of Education Policy, 26*(3), 449–468.

McCaig, C. (2016). The retreat from widening participation? The national scholarship programme and new access agreements in English higher education. *Studies in Higher Education, 41*(2), 215–230.

McLellan, J., Pettigrew, R., & Sperlinger, T. (2016). Remaking the elite university: An experiment in widening participation in the UK. *Power and Education, 8*(1), 54–72.

OFFA. (2016). *Strategic plan 2015–2020*. https://www.offa.org.uk/wp-content/uploads/2015/03/OFFA-Strategic-Plan-2015-2020.pdf

Phillips, A., Rana-Deshmukh, A., & Joseph, C. (2017). *The BME attainment gap. University of Bristol and University of Bristol students' union joint report*. http://www.bristol.ac.uk/media-library/sites/sraa/Website%20bme-attainment-gap-report.pdf

Sodiq-Ajala, K. (n.d.). BME success advocate – Belonging team [Blog]. https://www.bristol.ac.uk/directory/student-inclusion-services/student-inclusion-team/bame/

Sperlinger, T., Pettigrew, R., & McLellan, J. (2018). *Who are universities for? Re-making higher education*. Bristol University Press.

Thomas, L. (2012). *Building student engagement and belonging in higher education at a time of change: Final report from the what works?* Student Retention and Success Programme, York, UK.

Timmis, S., & Muñoz-Chereau, B. (2019). Under-represented students' university trajectories: Building alternative identities and forms of capital through digital improvisations. *Teaching in Higher Education*. doi:10.1080/13562517.2019.1696295

Wray, M. (2013). *Developing an inclusive culture in higher education: Final report.* Higher Education Academy.

PART 3

Promoting Strategic Change for Inclusion in Higher Education

∵

CHAPTER 9

Developing Strategic Change Moving towards Inclusion of Underrepresented Students in Higher Education

Fabio Dovigo

Abstract

In the last twenty years, the goal of developing the social dimension of Higher Education has been part of the wider effort many universities around the world have undertaken to improve and diversify tertiary education through strategic change. However, the recent shift towards a global, highly competitive and market-oriented university system has put growing pressure on academic centres concerning the expansion and differentiation of the research and teaching offered. New forms of organisation have been generated to address these demands, leading to rapid merging or splitting of academic departments, as well as to the establishment of new providers. This process affects the diversity of each university with regard to specific knowledge profiles; teaching, learning and problem-solving styles; and, more generally, the institutional mission, governance and inner culture. The diversification of the student population is an important component at this level, as the success of education programmes offered in most of Higher Education is linked to the ability to provide teaching activities that address learners from diverse backgrounds. The chapter examines what are the consequences of the modernisation and change of the tertiary education sector for the implementation of programmes aimed to foster the inclusion of underprivileged students in Higher Education.

Keywords

widening participation – strategic change – organisation – inclusion – diversity – underrepresented students – social dimension – equality – equity – quality

1 Between Equity and Excellence

In the last twenty years, the goal of developing the social dimension of higher education (HE) has been part of the wider effort many universities around the world have undertaken to improve and diversify tertiary education through strategic change. As structures that aim to serve research and teaching purposes, universities have long been differentiated into unitary or binary systems, depending on the direction each country took in defining an integrated or, conversely, separated organisation of activities. However, the recent shift towards an international HE system characterised by a highly competitive and market-oriented approach has put growing pressure on academic centres concerning the expansion and differentiation of the research and teaching offered (Locke, 2014; Olssen, 2016). As a result, new forms of organisation have been generated to address these growing demands, leading to rapid merging (or splitting) of academic departments, as well as to the establishment of new HE providers. The traditional partitions between academic roles and intervention areas have become less defined, giving rise to hybrid and diversified forms of 'coopetition', both within single institutions and across national and international relationships (Muijs & Rumyantseva, 2014). The emerging global phenomenon of the multiplication and massification of HE organisations has thus led to the creation of large multi-disciplinary and multi-purpose universities (or 'multiversities'), in which research-intensive institutions growing at the global level tend to replace universities based on the conventional unitary/binary model (Becher & Trowler, 2001; Marginson, 2017).

This process is reflected at the level of vertical HE stratification, which relates to graduates' quality, reputation and prospective status. However, it also affects the horizontal diversity of each university with regard to specific knowledge profiles; teaching, learning and problem-solving styles; and, more generally, the institutional mission, governance and inner culture (Teichler, 2008). The diversification of the student population is an important component at this horizontal level, as the success of education programmes offered in most of HE is linked to the ability to provide teaching activities that address learners from diverse backgrounds, in terms of age, gender, abilities, culture, and so on (Crosier & Parveva, 2013). However, with a few exceptions (such as, for example, the good practices in UK universities described in this volume), most HE institutions in Europe are not inclined to see student diversity as an integral part of their organisational identity (Reichert, 2009; Riddell & Weedon, 2014). On the contrary, they generally assume it to be an inevitable consequence of the modernisation of the tertiary education sector, which can be addressed through the provision of special services, as long as they do not interfere with core academic business. As a consequence, while the increasing participation in HE of underrepresented students is regularly mentioned in strategic plans and other statutory university documents as a highly important objective, institutional policies and practices in this regard usually remain limited and scattered (ESU, 2019a, 2019b; EUA, 2019; Usher, 2015).

This lack of interest concerning the inclusion of disadvantaged students in European tertiary education is remarkable, especially in comparison with the intense debate that has surrounded this topic for decades in the United States. Whereas in Europe the discourse has centred on the concept of widening participation as a way of including students from lower social, economic or cultural backgrounds, in the USA the emphasis has traditionally been on diversity in terms of underrepresentation in HE of students (and teachers) from ethnic and racial minorities (Berrey, 2011; Gurin et al., 2020; Hurtado, 2007; Jayakumar, 2008). These two perspectives also mirror a different approach to this issue. For example, American colleges tend to solve the problem of taking up students from ethnic minorities by adopting a quota system that reserves a share of places for students from those groups (Allen, 2005; Baez, 2003). European universities, on the other hand, have more limited scope in managing the enrolment of students, as national governments still have significant influence on determining how the student selection process is run. More specifically, universities have some room to set quantitative targets by introducing limited enrolment procedures, but are not allowed to differentiate qualitatively with regard to the admission of students (European Commission/Eurydice, 2014; Eurostudent, 2019).

The question is also embedded in the current polarisation that universities are facing worldwide concerning the relationship between excellence and equity (Reay et al., 2005; Shaw, 2009). As we noted above, the tertiary education sector is dealing with global competitive pressure that often translates into a quest for 'excellence'. In this sense, excellence is interpreted as a ranking mechanism that aims to increase the stratification of the HE system by differentiating high-quality from average or low-quality universities. Accordingly, the massification of HE tends to reproduce the well-established pattern already in place at the secondary school level, where attending liberal arts schools instead of professional or vocational institutes determines the path students will take with regard to future HE enrolment, employment and, more generally, life options (Triventi, 2013; Vignoles & Murray, 2016). Research shows how these options are greatly influenced by indirect but very efficient mechanisms that aim to keep children from disadvantaged backgrounds away from tertiary education (Ball & Vincent, 1998). Family choices concerning HE may rely on abstract ('cold') knowledge, consisting of official communications that describe university policies, examination results, occupational levels, and so on, as well as on informal ('hot') knowledge, based on direct experience from the circle of family and friends about the advantages of attending university. Whereas middle-class students can draw on both sources of information, children from working-class backgrounds are excluded from access to first-hand, 'hot' knowledge. Therefore, they can only rely on 'cold' information, which is difficult not only to acquire, but also to decode. Consequently, the cycle of exclusion from HE tends to repeat for these children, not due to a lack of information, but because they have very limited opportunities to experience participation in HE (Gale & Parker, 2015; Jerrim & Vignoles, 2015).

Furthermore, other, more direct, mechanisms prevent underrepresented students from accessing HE. Public financing of most European universities, for example, is currently directly related to rates of student retention and success achieved by each institution (Kaiser et al., 2015; Mountford-Zimdars & Harrison, 2016). Consequently, HE administrations show a growing tendency to enact procedures that favour access and retention of qualified learners who are 'guaranteed' to complete their studies on time. These procedures position most non-traditional learners – e.g. those with children or learning difficulties – as 'second-class' students who are considered a burden for the organisation. This matches the widespread elitist narrative of HE that describes the effort to widen participation as the opposite of the desirable aim of pursuing academic excellence (Reay et al., 2009). Underrepresented students are depicted in this narrative as 'problematic', and therefore as draining more resources than 'normal' learners. This description favours the spread of 'moral panic' among high- and middle-class families, which in turn contributes to strengthening a view of diversity as a negative factor that leads to lower standards of education (Leathwood & O'Connell, 2003). Several HE organisations concur in promoting the elitist narrative by considering diverse students a potential threat to their institutional reputation. According to this view, greater participation of disadvantaged learners would make academic courses less prestigious and consequently less attractive for regular students, who look at enrolment in HE as an investment based on the marketability of the university's name with a view to their future careers (Archer, 2007; Guri-Rosenblit, 2007).

On the whole, European universities are currently engaged in the difficult task of finding a balance between the formal claim for equity and the pressing demand for excellence (Brennan & Naidoo, 2008; Meyer et al., 2013). These two aspects are not intrinsically at odds, in theory. As some experiences described in this book show, a few HE institutions have been able to build their reputations precisely by developing systematic policies and practices that aim to support underrepresented students as a part of their quest for excellence.

However, this requires a broader definition of the common meaning attributed to high quality in HE. Otherwise, the valuable efforts made to achieve greater equity in tertiary education risk being silenced by the excellence mantra, which reduces academic prestige to a market good to be persuasively sold by branded HE institutions.

2   Widening Participation through Organisational Learning

The topic of developing a diversity culture in tertiary education by broadening participation and supporting the so-called social dimension of HE has been widely explored in the scientific literature (Brennan, 2018; Harwood, 2016; Hinton-Smith, 2012; Holford, 2014; Holmegaard et al., 2017; Rodríguez-Gómez et al., 2019; Thomas, 2012). Transnational reports, especially in the European Union, provide periodic accounts of the state of the art of inclusion in member countries of the European Higher Education Area (EHEA) regarding specific aspects, like enrolment and success rates for underrepresented students or comparisons of the policies and practices adopted in several universities (EHEA, 2015a, 2015b). However, investigations into the impact of the programmes designed to foster wider participation of disadvantaged students remain underdeveloped, especially concerning the way the inclusion of learners could be promoted through strategic changes implemented at the organisational level by HE institutions. For example, whereas universities are increasingly engaged in attracting prospective students through well-organised open days and advertising campaigns, initiatives to develop cooperation with secondary schools that would favour the transition of children from disadvantaged backgrounds to tertiary education, or improve staff competences in supporting those students throughout their educational path, are still undertaken in fits and starts. These actions are rarely underpinned by a clear conceptual framework that could help the institution to systematically advance the transformation required at the organisational level to support change (Banerjee, 2018).

The literature emphasises that universities are complex organisations based on a bureaucratic but decentralised structure that relies on the standardisation of skills (rather than work processes or outputs) to achieve coordination (Henkel, 2002; Mintzberg, 1993). This mix of standardised and decentralised functions reflects the nature of academic activities, which are both predictable and complex. As professional bureaucracies that depend on trained professionals to fulfil their operational tasks, HE institutions surrender a large share of their power to the teachers themselves and to the departmental structures within which they work. Consequently, authority over many decisions is delegated to the professional expertise of individuals and departments, leaving only limited power for institutional leadership. Compared to other kinds of organisations, which rely on a strong leadership model as the main leverage for implementing organisational change, universities have an inherently slower and more articulated approach to achieving transformation, often based on the buy-in of individuals who are in a position to influence the choices of those who belong to their professional network (Bryman, 2007; Tierney, 2008). In this environment, where decision-making activities are loosely coupled and highly distributed, setting a shared agenda with the aim of widening participation involves making a special effort, as dealing with promoting diversity has strong implications for the organisation's culture as a whole.

Investigations in the EHEA have highlighted how the results of programmes that aim to widen the participation of underrepresented students in HE are frequently limited or insufficient (Croll & Attwood, 2013; Crozier et al., 2008; ESU, 2019a). Reports often point to the lack of leadership in academic institutions as one of the main reasons for this recurring failure. However, the way academic structures are organised within the university organisation, with single departments acting like semi-autonomous and relatively independent bodies, clarifies why achieving coordinated change through action driven by the centre of the institution is so problematic (Gornitzka & Maassen, 2000). Promoting a diversity culture in a system characterised by high functional independence and distributed leadership implies developing a systematic approach to the way universities as organisations can learn to achieve a more inclusive culture concerning non-traditional learners.

Even though organisational learning has a long research tradition, starting with the work of Herbert Simon in the 1950s, indications from investigations in this field have not been adopted extensively by HE institutions with regard to the implementation of organisational change. By showing how organisations evolve, both through the learning activities developed by members and the contribution of knowledge provided by newcomers, Simon elucidated the processes through which organisational culture grows and changes over time (Newell & Simon, 1972). More recently, Chris Argyris provided an influential contribution to the area of organisational learning studies by differentiating between two theories of action: the espoused theory and theory-in-use (Argyris, 2004). According to Argyris, people's activities in specific situations are always carried out through mental maps, which orient the way actions are planned, implemented and reviewed. Those maps, or "theories-in-use", are normally different from the ideas people explicitly assert when they speak about the rationale for their actions, i.e. the espoused theories. However, individuals are rarely aware of the discrepancies between the alleged and actual frameworks they adopt as guidelines for their decisions in everyday life. The reason why the theories people use may be different from the theories they say they use is that this split allows them to avoid threatening and embarrassing situations. Individuals protect and defend the self against potentially disruptive changes by enacting defensive reasoning, which is based on four principles: be in unilateral control, win and do not lose, suppress negative feelings, and behave rationally. However, this reaction to situations that are perceived as threatening or embarrassing tends to inhibit learning. Consequently, reducing or removing the threat also hinders the ability to change the issues that caused the problem.

Argyris transposed these dynamics to organisational life: when organisations face situations that could expose them to embarrassment or threat, they perform defensive routines that avert possible risks, but also prevent discovery of the cause of embarrassment or threat. These routines include sending mixed messages about the issue, acting as if they are not mixed, making these features undiscussable, and finally 'making the undiscussability undiscussable' (Argyris, 1980). In parallel, Argyris introduced the pivotal notion of single- and double-loop learning (Argyris, 1982, 2002). Single-loop learning helps detect and correct errors that do not require changing the values that preside over the existing theory-in-use and organisational defensive routines. By contrast, double-loop learning enables the organisation to detect and correct mistakes whose correction requires changes, not only with regard to action strategies, but also the values that guide the theory-in-use. Consequently, double-loop learning questions the status quo and encourages rare events, which can lead to deep change by adopting the following principles: producing valid information, favouring informed choice, and promoting vigilant monitoring of the degree of effectiveness of the implemented actions.

Organisational learning is not the only theoretical framework for how change may be supported in organisations. However, one advantage of this perspective is that it does not privilege single- or double-loop learning as a vector for change, but simply suggests that the learning loop should be shaped appropriately for the problem at stake (Easterby-Smith et al., 2000). Organisational learning acknowledges that most of the issues that take place every day in an organisation do not require radical changes in order to be solved. Accordingly, it is the analysis of the needed level of solution that leads to complying with or, conversely, challenging the existing assumptions and values of the organisation. Moreover, unlike other approaches (e.g. sensemaking theory), the organisational learning perspective is based on a data-oriented and rational approach, which assumes that individuals are prone not only to making mistakes and relying on defensive reasoning, but also to identifying errors, correcting them and managing change. The collection and review of data play a crucial role in helping organisations undertake periodical analyses and amending malfunctions. This effort can be sustained through activities that facilitate the process of analysis, for example by encouraging the examination of unsurfaced assumptions and biases, stimulating self-reflection and creating room for new ideas to emerge. It can also be supported by systematically nurturing specific conditions and factors, such as a sense of mutual trust, inter-group collaboration, and a more circular organisation as an expression of a democratic hierarchy (Levitt & March, 1988; Lipshitz et al., 2002).

In addition to providing a coherent theoretical foundation for organisational change, Argyris' contribution has been crucial in developing the concept of organisational learning capability (Dibella et al., 1996). Capabilities are management initiatives and practices that help generate ideas and then generalise those ideas, so they have an impact across multiple organisational boundaries (Yeung, 1999). To achieve this, organisations should be actively engaged in identifying what have been defined as 'learning disabilities' of the structure (Snyder & Cummings, 1998). Learning disabilities that affect the generation of ideas are: blindness (inability to assess environmental opportunities and threats accurately); simplemindedness (deficiencies in analysis and solution generation); homogeneity (lack of variety in skills, information, ideas and values); and tight coupling (excessive coordination between different organisational units). However, other disabilities may hinder the generalisation of ideas as well: paralysis (inability to implement new actions or procedures); superstitious learning (inability to interpret accurately the meanings of experience); and diffusion deficiency (inability to share ideas with all relevant parts of the organisation). This focus on learning capabilities reflects the researchers' concern about providing a solid framework for the implementation of change as a viable process that produces a clear impact on the organisation. In this regard, this view is also germane to the organisation development approach, initiated by Kurt Lewin to connect research, training and action. Organisation development is a system-wide application and transfer of knowledge to the planned development of the strategies that lead to improving organisation effectiveness (Cummings & Worley, 2015). In Lewin's original formulation, this process is strictly linked to the action research perspective, which brings together "action and reflection, as well as theory and practice, in participation with others, in the pursuit of practical solutions to issues of pressing concern" (Bradbury, 2015, p. 1).

3 Doing Action Research to Foster Inclusive Change

Action research is traditionally built on three main steps ('unfreeze, change and refreeze') that enable participants to deconstruct the organisational status quo, introduce and explore the effects of change, and then help improvements become permanent and integrated into the organisational structure (Weick & Quinn, 1999). More precisely, the process involves: (1) building a picture of the issue by gathering information about the problem to be investigated and its context; (2) developing an understanding by analysing the situation, as well as reflecting on participants' experiences and critical incidents; (3) implementing sustainable solutions, by identifying priorities for action and constructing action plans (Stringer, 2014).

This model, based on a critical exploration of the assumptions embedded in the organisational culture and coupled with a search for changes that can be achieved through planned action, is especially suitable for the analysis of the exclusionary mechanisms at work in the academic environment and the design of effective programmes to promote positive change concerning inclusive policies and practices. In this regard, investigations have shown that organisational learning concerning the inclusion of disadvantaged students in tertiary education faces a number of typical barriers at the institutional level (Elliott et al., 2013; Chun & Evans, 2018):

– Lack of leadership commitment and/or support from the institutional infrastructure to execute that commitment. Due to the distributed (and sometimes fragmented) nature of leadership in HE institutions discussed above, programmes that aim to promote the inclusion of disadvantaged students are destined to fail or, at least, be confined to isolated initiatives, unless there is a clear commitment from the leadership connected with systematic backing from the university teaching and administrative structures;
– Programmes to foster inclusion working in silos. The ethos of widening participation can be better expressed through a holistic approach, which invests in the whole academic institution through cross-cutting programmes developed at different departmental and administrative levels. However, the question of inclusion is often framed as a sectoral business, which should be implemented only in specific areas or specialised services. Therefore, programmes that aim to advance the participation of underrepresented students tend to be brought about in silos within the academic structure. As a result, the lack of transversal coordination severely limits the dissemination and effectiveness of the programmes, which struggle to reach the audience that would most benefit from learning about this topic;
– One-off and discontinuous programmes versus constant, long-term efforts. Most programmes designed to promote better policies and practices concerning the participation of disadvantaged students in HE are managed in the form of single seminars or one-off short courses. As such, they usually have a very superficial effect on the organisational culture of HE institutions. Certainly, these kinds of activities play a positive role in informing

and sensitising HE teachers and staff to questions regarding students' participation. However, a deeper impact can only be achieved if initiatives to raise awareness are coupled with specific and systematic actions endorsed by the university's strategic plan, as well as being supported by long-term programmes that are periodically assessed and reviewed, with the aim of fostering student inclusion;
- Lack of collaboration between administrative departments, limited resources allocated. As we have noted, HE institutions are professional bureaucracies built on a highly decentralised system, in which each organisational unit is partially independent, and teachers enjoy considerable freedom. In this environment, organisational learning about improving student participation cannot be fulfilled through a top-down approach only. Even within the same academic institution, every structure tends to develop a micro-culture that influences the way difference is perceived and supported. Consequently, fostering cooperation on this matter between departments should be pursued actively, favouring periodic exchanges of knowledge and practices. This implies a stable investment of resources, which cannot be limited to extemporaneous or promotional activities;
- Failure to involve faculty in developing and facilitating student participation. Most of the core activities organised by universities – like teaching, examining or counselling students – are managed directly by teachers. Because of the high degree of teachers' autonomy, any institutional plan to promote the participation of disadvantaged students in HE cannot succeed unless it manages to get a genuine commitment of the faculty. Accordingly, initiatives concerning this topic need to be formulated in a language that can be easily understood and welcomed by teachers. This avoids programmes being openly rejected, or formally accepted by the staff but covertly dismissed in practice;
- Lack of long-term assessment of the effects of the transfer of learning on widening participation. Most programmes designed to foster inclusion in HE are not equipped with assessment tools that would allow the institution to evaluate the level of learning acquired through the actions undertaken. Even programmes that include an assessment module often limit this to a routine form that is administered only to meet the requirements of the quality assurance system. As a consequence, it is difficult to gauge the outcomes of learning activities that are directed at widening participation and, more generally, assessing the impact they will have on the university structure in the long run. To do so, longitudinal analyses that aim to identify causal relationships should be supported as an integral part of these programmes;

- Diversity resistance and backlash. Diversity resistance is "a range of practices and behaviours within and by organisations that interfere, intentionally or unintentionally, with the use of diversity as an opportunity for learning and effectiveness" (Thomas, 2008, p. 5). It is not uncommon for attempts to widen participation in HE to be met with resistance, both at the individual and organisational levels. In this regard, resistance to inclusive programmes can be overt or manifest more subtly. The former encompasses verbal or physical harassment and intentional forms of discrimination against individuals, which are countered through human resources policies and practices that are designed to expand participation; the latter builds on silence concerning inequities, exclusion or discrediting non-traditional students, as well as conveying mixed messages about participation (e.g. "it is utopian" or "too complex") and secondary victimisation. Resistance may also produce backlash to participation programmes in HE, as a negative response to initiatives that someone sees as providing undeserved benefits to some individuals or groups (Kidder et al., 2004).

Resistance to diversity is a deep reflection of the dichotomy between espoused theory and theory-in-use, as described by Argyris. Whereas the value of inclusion is ostensibly accepted and endorsed by HE institutions, programmes that would help put it into practice are often obstructed or rejected, mostly covertly. In this regard, Trowler (1997) identified a typology of four main strategies adopted by academics in the face of structural organisational change. Individuals who 'swim' are those who are happy with the change and willing to accept it, as they see it as a professional opportunity that does not require them to adopt coping or reconstructing strategies. 'Sinking' academics, in contrast, are critical of change and its consequences on their professional life. They think change will increase their workload or reduce resources but accept it, though reluctantly. A third group is formed by those who are mostly pleased with the change but prefer to 'reconstruct' the new policies by reinterpreting them through 'regressive' strategies. As a result, programmes fostering change are formally accepted but actually worked around or only partially implemented. Finally, 'coping' academics are unhappy with the change, as they perceive it as a threat to their well-established professional tasks. Consequently, this group actively engages in bypassing or disregarding all activities connected to the proposed change.

This typology helps understand how important it is to involve HE staff in plans to bring about changes related to widening participation. If a programme is seen as a danger to collective and individual identity, or as generating high levels of anxiety linked to the change required, the organisation will lack the motivation to learn. This is especially true for universities, as institutions that build their reputation on a sense of legitimacy based principally on structural stability and the reproduction of the organisational form (Rush & Wilbur, 2007; van Vught, 2008). Reputation – the core value in the HE sector – is developed by elaborating rules and institutional scripts that bolster the institution's status through a 'mimetic isomorphism' process. This process aims to gain legitimacy by imitating the forms and norms of already recognised organisations in the field (Ashworth et al., 2009; Morphew & Huisman, 2002). Consequently, HE institutions are not supposed to promote radical transformations, but rather pursue plans for gradual change, which are seen as being more compatible with the image of solidity that organisational structures want to convey (Boyce, 2003). Against this background, it would be advisable for universities to implement incremental programmes to widen participation by supporting targeted actions, which should be coordinated through cooperation between departments and the university administration. Past experience shows that it is also important to create specific guidelines and tools for translating policies into practices, as well as involving some university leaders who will work as 'change agents' to favour the implementation of the process (Trowler et al., 2012).

4   Individual, Group and Organisation as Change Units

Another important aspect that has been the subject of broad scientific debate is at what level – individual, group or the organisation as a whole – change intended to widen the participation of disadvantaged students should take place (Sullivan et al., 2001; Wang & Ahmed, 2003). Achieving change at all three levels is undoubtedly crucial, as transforming policies to improve student inclusion implies dealing with the social relations underlying the system of power and equity within HE institutions, but the variety of individual experiences these relations affect in everyday life must also be taken into account. Collective histories take shape at one end of the spectrum, whereas at the other we find individual biographies (Strauss, 1995). Accordingly, some studies emphasise that change that moves towards inclusion in HE should involve both the institutional and individual dimensions, as they cannot be managed in isolation (May & Bridger, 2010). In this regard, effective and sustainable change should focus simultaneously on both the procedures through which academic administrations develop institutional policies and on the way teachers carry out learning and teaching practices. This perspective underlines the need to involve academics in the desired improvements regarding inclusion. This would avoid imposing a top-down approach that (as noted above) could be rejected and would instead help form alliances with teachers through debates that would acknowledge academic autonomy and freedom.

However, taking the individual experience into account is not enough to guarantee change in this field. Programmes that have the aim of widening participation must also cultivate organisational and collective capabilities, which strengthen innovation and cooperation by promoting a shared mindset and accountability culture that encompasses the equity dimension. Moreover, the idea of fostering inclusion in HE by focusing on individuals or groups has been criticised by some scholars, especially when it is disconnected from parallel change at the organisational level (Chavez et al., 2003; Williams, 2013). For example, the objective of promoting the adoption of different attitudes and behaviours by staff at the individual level, usually pursued by the university administration through training courses on diversity, does not lead to organisational learning unless it is genuinely supported by other sectors in the system (administration, departments, leadership). Similar criticisms have been directed at other attempts to widen HE participation on an individual or group basis, according to a strategy known as 'structural diversity' (Hurtado et al., 1999). While in recent years European universities have been quite successful in favouring disadvantaged students' access to HE, this policy can actually be beneficial only if institutional regulations, practices and the culture are actively reshaped through the implementation of strategic plans that aim to support the retention and success of all learners. Otherwise, programmes that are intended to foster the integration of specific student categories tend to create an environment of negative competition between groups looking for greater recognition from the HE institution. Consequently, it is not uncommon today to find universities where the rights of some categories are respected and promoted while other minorities are ignored or dismissed. Moreover, strategies conceived to target specific groups of disadvantaged learners, which treat them as if they were a homogeneous entity, always risk strengthening negative stereotypes and intensifying a deficit view of diversity. This perspective implies that the minority subjects must take on the task of understanding 'normals', by integrating into an academic structure that basically remains unaltered (Sturm, 2011; Wilson, 2012).

Another side effect of this conception of minorities, which is especially widespread in colleges in the USA, is the adoption of strategies based on tokenism, through which HE institutions make only a symbolic effort to pursue equity by allowing a limited number of people from underrepresented sexual or racial minorities to enrol or be hired as university staff (King et al., 2010). Even though apparently well-intentioned, these policies actually make it more difficult to fulfil the goal of improving inclusion in HE, as they only cover up the structural reasons behind the inequality. In this respect, Tienda (2013) suggests that a genuine approach to the inclusion of non-traditional students should entail a systematic review of HE curricula in order to accommodate in advance the needs of students from different backgrounds. This would allow universities to expand their ability to welcome and systematically support underrepresented students, instead of 'patching up' critical situations that emerge on an ongoing basis through making repeated, ad hoc adaptations. In this regard, research highlights that programmes launched by HE institutions to promote participation can be classified into three main categories, built, respectively, on contingent, alternative or inclusive strategies (Waterfield & West, 2006). Contingent strategies put in place special arrangements (e.g. PPT presentations with fonts adapted to the needs of visually impaired students, or second language courses for foreign learners), with the aim of assimilating disadvantaged individuals into the existing structure. These strategies, which are essentially compensatory schemes managed by dedicated employees, require only limited involvement from the staff working in university departments. Alternative strategies offer a repertoire of activities that replace normal procedures, e.g., allowing students to do a viva voce instead of a written assignment, or enabling transsexual or transgender students to use a double identification card. They usually target specific objectives and groups but, again, tend to remain in the realm of special practices run by single branches of the administration, which periodically sensitises academics regarding the alternative procedures to be employed. Finally, inclusive strategies are those that are not confined to making students fit into the existing system, but also work on making the university organisation more permeable to diversity. They make available a flexible range of learning and teaching activities to all students by, for example, assessing the same learning outcomes in different ways, while preserving academic and professional standards. By promoting resource planning, curriculum change, and relevant staff development, inclusion programmes help overcome the limitations usually related to policies and practices aimed at minority students (Abes, 2005). Instead of activities based on assimilation or accommodation perspectives, which leave the HE organisation essentially unaltered, inclusive strategies deal with the structural barriers to change, as they aim to build a more sustainable and equitable environment for all learners.

5 Old and New Approaches to Inclusive Change

As we have noted, the adoption of inclusive strategies in HE usually works in tandem with a view of participation that goes beyond conventional policies directed at opening access to university. It emphasises the value of listening to students' voices, not just as a formal requirement of the quality system, but as a vital component of the learning process in which the HE organisation is involved. However, to date, most of the initiatives that aim to widen the participation of underrepresented students are based on the more traditional framework developed by Bolman and Deal (1991), which is composed of four main dimensions: structural, human resources, political and symbolic. Starting from this framework, investigation has mostly focused on some specific aspects of academic organisation, such as mission statements and strategic plans, advisory committees, resource allocation and evaluation (Kezar et al., 2008). Mission statements that explicitly mention broadening participation as a developmental objective for the institution are the customary way through which HE leadership can express support for policies in this area. Acting as a reminder of the organisation's values, statements help incorporate inclusion into institutional norms and assumptions. They also indicate priorities to be pursued by the organisation through strategic plans, which provide a clear roadmap for the implementation of activities that have the aim of promoting participation. In short, the combination of mission statements and strategic plans is crucial for creating a positive climate towards inclusion in HE organisations.

As part of the institutional efforts made in this direction, advisory committees are usually established to examine questions related to equity and inclusion and prepare recommendations about initiatives to foster inclusion in the academic structure. Usually composed of representatives from faculties, administrative staff and students, these committees play an important role in making the topics related to widening participation visible, as well as in urging the central administration and departments to address and eliminate possible barriers that affect the inclusion of disadvantaged students. Moreover, the structural framework points to resource allocation and evaluation as critical components of HE systems that genuinely aspire to build a culture of equity within the university. Mission statements, strategic plans and advisory committees are powerless without the appropriate investment of resources to support the implementation of inclusive programmes over time. Likewise, the evaluation of interventions should systematically analyse the real impact of the actions taken to keep track of progress and setbacks and ensure that the institution has an adequate level of accountability in this regard.

However, as we have mentioned, the structural framework also presents some limitations, especially in terms of supporting a bottom-up approach to inclusion. In the absence of significant involvement by all stakeholders, programmes that aim to widen participation fail or have very little effect because of a lack of commitment or emerging conflicts that often lead to cross vetoes regarding interventions (Chesler et al., 2005; Pendry et al., 2007). The effectiveness of mission statements and strategic plans is strictly linked to the ability to expand the conversation to all levels of the HE structure. Institutional committees or councils naturally tend to circumscribe the role of participants in formal consultation. Therefore, the actual agenda concerning the space and pace of the inclusion process is often set by a restricted number of people working at the highest levels of the organisation, instead of being the outcome of extended decision-making activity, which would bring in those who have a key role in implementing inclusive programmes. As a consequence, the structural framework tends to disregard essential aspects of the equity process, "such as the experiences of individuals affected, the interactions in the implementation process, and the importance of organisational culture, symbols and meaning making" (Kezar et al., 2007, p. 73). Effective policies and practices in the field of HE inclusion require plans to be designed and fulfilled based on consensus-building strategies, which can be developed through the leadership's commitment to providing open space for debate by listening to different voices, appreciating the diversity of contributions, and putting to work all of the resources that have been collected through this participative process. Consensus-building approaches help inclusive programmes have a deeper impact by encompassing and valuing multiple viewpoints, thereby supporting the university ethos and building momentum for positive action (Musil et al., 1999; Sevier, 2000).

6   Starting and Supporting Programmes to Widen Participation in Higher Education

The way changes that will widen participation should be started and sustained has also been analysed through research (Burke, 2012; Fuller, 2011; Greenbank, 2006; Moore, 2013). Usually, HE institutions tend to pursue first-order changes that do not alter the system, for example by launching single programmes or adding on targeted services to help specific groups of students. These options are preferred to second-order changes that imply deep reform of the structures and culture of the organisation. First- and second-order strategies to bring about change have been developed in HE through two competing approaches, with the aim of, respectively, achieving co-optative or transformative change (Aguirre & Martinez, 2006). The co-optative approach is based on incremental policies meant to achieve 'small successes' in the area of inclusion, with a special focus on protecting the core structure of the university's organisation.

By adopting a rational-bureaucratic style, it undertakes low-level changes in specific sectors, which work as buffers that help maintain the organisational culture unaltered. This approach is supported by scholars who argue that, considering the structural diversity of organisational entities and the wide degree of autonomy of individual academics within HE institutions, small-scale actions brought about at the departmental level or which focus on specific student categories have a higher success rate and sustainability than programmes that aim to generate a major change across the whole organisation (Knight & Trowler, 2000; O'Donnell, 2015).

Conversely, the transformative approach intends to produce deeper and more? widespread change in the HE structures by modifying institutional cultures over time (Eckel & Kezar, 2003). Its goal is to promote radical transformations by helping the institution to embed the values of equity and inclusion within the organisational culture, ensuring that change will have a strong and long-term impact on underrepresented students. However, transformative change is especially hard to bring about in HE, because of both the high independence level of departments and individuals, and the time required to support the effort made to achieve deep cultural change. Investigations have shown that programmes built on transformative strategies are quite rare, compared to initiatives focused on fostering the inclusion of specific student groups (Kezar, 2011). As we have noted, the way distributed leadership is developed and nourished throughout HE organisations is a pivotal factor in this regard. Good leadership implies envisaging and disseminating a shared vision of the role that the inclusion of disadvantaged students plays in the structure of HE, as well as acquiring extensive knowledge of the context in order to better understand the potential amplitude and pace of the desired transformation (Adserias, 2016; Eckel & Kezar, 2003). This activity should be connected with the objective of promoting the students' and staff's sense of belonging to the academic community. This relies on a clear recognition of diversity as adding value to HE, in terms of the contribution students from various backgrounds can make to achieving a richer understanding and experience of academic life (Locks et al., 2008).

Implementing second-order changes, such as those described above, involves a special kind of learning from the university organisation. Transformative learning is a method that has proved especially effective in this respect, as an approach that can bring about a deep shift in the subjects' perspective, through which established habits of mind become more open and permeable (Cranton & Taylor, 2012; Marrocco, 2009). Originally focused on facilitating critical reflection and self-reflection, transformative learning has gradually expanded to embrace other dimensions, like intuition, imagination and emotion, as triggers for change. Accordingly, transformative learning often includes experiential learning practices that enable participants to acquire a more sensitive and critical perspective towards questions related to equity and inclusion, and to build stronger bonds, starting from a deeper understanding of diversity as a shared value. Transformative learning activities promoted in HE usually help individuals and groups to analyse a perspective on exclusion and inclusion that is in contrast with the prevailing viewpoint, as a way of deepening previously held assumptions, beliefs and values. As a result, they contribute to fostering the potential for transformation by changing structures of habitual expectation and making possible more inclusive, discriminating, and integrative perspectives that, in turn, lead to the acquisition of emancipatory knowledge (Mezirow, 1991).

7 Factors Affecting Inclusive Change in Higher Education

The management of programmes to generate change that will widen the participation of disadvantaged students in HE through participative and transformative approaches is less predictable than traditional strategies that have the aim of implementing organisational change through a top-down model. The primary reason for this is that expanding participation is, first of all, a methodology in which processes and outcomes are strictly intertwined. In addition, the structure itself of HE organisations is naturally resistant to accepting change strategies built on a 'command and control' style. Initiatives that aim to foster student participation, in particular, need to consider the relevant features of the academic environment. They include previous efforts towards promoting inclusive policies and practices; identifying the most urgent, effectual and feasible questions to be addressed regarding inclusion in the institution; what progress has already been achieved, partially or permanently, what setbacks have been encountered; and what the positive and negative factors behind those outcomes are. Moreover, programmes designed to value and promote diversity in HE frequently face multiple issues (Chun & Evans, 2015). The long-term effectiveness of positive actions to promote inclusion is typically limited if they are conceived as an emergency response to patch up critical situations. In addition, high turnover rates for key roles in the administration can affect the strength and stability of policies for inclusion and related practices. Equity initiatives can also become scapegoats for power conflicts between departmental or interdepartmental cliques that want to prevent the expansion of opposing groups. Furthermore, questions related to the inclusion of underrepresented students are commonly perceived as troublesome or irritating and, consequently, often pinballed from the central administration to departments, and vice versa. Finally, as the assessment of activities concerning this subject is rarely supported in a systematic way, it is normally difficult to get an overall picture of the progress achieved in this area over time.

As we have emphasised above, of the elements that play an important role in fostering an inclusive agenda in HE, investigations have indicated that the adoption of an action research approach is especially beneficial. Action research was defined by Lewin as a method that "proceeds in a spiral of steps, each of which is composed of a circle of planning, action and fact finding about the results of the action" (1946/1948, p. 206). It is a values-oriented community process that relies on building collaborative relationships with stakeholders, so as to develop new solutions to practical and sometimes pressing issues that affect their lives within the organisations. As such, action research is based on a multi-method style of inquiry that involves different roles and groups at different levels of the HE institution (Reason & Bradbury, 2008). In this way, it contributes to creating a sense of ownership regarding the question of equity and inclusion, through fostering systematic dialogue and reflection that help to both deepen the understanding of the questions at stake and have a durable impact on policy and practice. To this end, action research should involve the systematic collection of evidence regarding institutional barriers to equity in the academic organisation, as well as an accurate description of policies and practices that facilitate the participation of underrepresented students. This analysis would encompass a careful reconsideration of language, including the terminology employed by the institution to define and manage minority groups, as the terms adopted in documents, statements and meetings can reflect and, in turn, reinforce negative stereotypes concerning diversity.

As we have mentioned, the examination of previous experiences of inclusive programmes in HE also emphasises the critical role that change agents can play when adequate power and visibility are assigned to them. According to Battilana and Casciaro (2012, p. 381), "changes that diverge from the status quo [...] are particularly challenging to implement. They require change agents to distance themselves from their existing institutions and persuade other organisation members to adopt practices that not only are new, but also break with the norms of their institutional environment". As we have noted, academic institutions are organisations based on great mutual independence and weak ties, in which departments and groups are only loosely connected. This low degree of structural closure favours the development of informal networks that fill organisational 'holes' and offer good potential for brokerage between departments and groups (Burt, 2005). By using their position as brokers within these networks, change agents can thus influence the initiation and implementation of change regarding inclusion, thereby helping to generate novel ideas, tools and guidelines for promoting inclusive practices.

Underlining the role of information in fostering change, Smith (2015) highlights that the actual impact of initiatives to widen the participation of minority students strictly depends on the ability of change agents, and those who support their actions, to build on a systemic perspective that will provide solid ground for change. To this end, she identifies six key elements that help HE institutions achieve viable results in this respect:

- Building a framework for change (and related indicators) that is embedded in the specific context of the institution;
- Adopting an approach to information based on an organisational learning viewpoint. This will ensure that information on progress, challenges, strategic decisions and successes will circulate widely and involve the entire organisation;
- Paying special attention to ensuring that initiatives undertaken to promote inclusion are actually manageable and sustainable in the long run:
- Avoiding the adoption of a generic approach to programmes and practices by developing monitoring procedures that help account for key elements and trends;
- Favouring an institutional change strategy instead of tackling issues one at a time. This helps shift the focus from a short-sighted view of inclusion as an outcome of single actions to the responsibility of the institutions in supporting the participation of all students;
- Ensuring that information and evidence that emerge from the inclusive process will be made available to all stakeholders and used as a starting point for reflection and further action.

8 Institutionalising Change towards Inclusion in Higher Education

The transformation of the HE environment to move towards equity and inclusion can be achieved only through interventions that fully acknowledge the importance of underlying organisational factors in favouring the inclusion of underrepresented students. These factors, which are the building blocks of inclusive change in HE, encompass the readiness of the context for initiatives related to inclusion; a deep understanding of the cultural norms and trends that typify the university site; the alignment of inclusive programmes with the institutional mission; and a clear endorsement and support from the leadership concerning the desired transformations.

As we have noted, programmes that are intended to have a lasting effect on the participation of underrepresented students in HE should start with a careful examination of the conditions and levels of inclusion within the academic context. The examination can be developed in the form of a gap analysis brought about through collaboration and reflective dialogue with stakeholders, so as to lay the foundations for the future design and implementation of programmes to reduce inequalities and discrimination (Temple & Ylitalo, 2009). A gap analysis helps assess the situation, identify indicators and benchmarks, define objectives, and gauge advances using quantitative and qualitative tools (Miller, 2016; Yooyen, 2011). Through the analysis, usually supported by the use of balanced scorecards, it is possible to acquire an overview of the state and pace of institutional change as it moves towards widening participation, including critical aspects such as access and equity, the organisational climate, how diversity is reflected in the curriculum, and progress made with regard to teaching and learning activities. Moreover, indicators provided by the gap analysis will enable the administration to carry out regular comparisons with other HE institutions to assess advances and set benchmarks for further progress in crucial sectors of the organisation.

Another relevant group of methods used to assess the inclusion of minority groups in HE is ecological mapping, which offers a detailed picture of the way organisational structures promote or hinder processes and practices for fostering participation. An interesting example of ecological mapping is the diversity mapping framework (Halualani et al., 2010), an evaluation tool that helps HE institutions take stock of the efforts made to promote a university culture grounded in inclusion, in terms of principles, values, objectives, outcomes and the allocation of resources. This approach, which has been applied to several universities, begins with data collection. Information is gathered through a survey (emailed to the university administration and departments at different staff levels), an analysis of the university webpages concerning diversity, and conversations held during visits paid to the main offices at the university site. Afterwards, a content analysis of the university curricula is performed, concerning the level to which they actually reflect and articulate an appreciation of diverse backgrounds and viewpoints. Data are subsequently analysed using the Diversity Engagement and Learning Taxonomy Assessment (DELTA). This classification system categorises the engagement of the HE institution with diversity practices? according to a six-level scale, which starts with knowledge and awareness and continues with skills, interaction, advanced analysis, evaluation-critique, social agency and action, and innovative problem-solving. The second phase of the process develops a visual map of the collected data, which helps visualise how diversity dimensions are managed in academic structures (administration and departments), courses and programmes. The thematic focus of initiatives targeting, for example, English language learners, low-income students, or first-generation freshmen, is examined to make relevant issues visible and support stakeholders' reflections. This way, through the aid of visual maps, reflection can focus on the general and specific goals the institution should intentionally pursue in the future to strengthen the participation of minority students. As a result, the mapping framework draws a path towards inclusion that is not limited to single, short-lived initiatives confined to academic silos, but encompasses a wider time-frame and helps overcome institutional boundaries by connecting and making sense of information that is usually scattered throughout the organisation.

Even though the process of carrying out an ecological mapping exercise can differ from one approach to another, overall, these methods share a focus on providing a comprehensive overview of inclusion in HE institutions by using both quantitative and qualitative tools. The resulting overview is not limited to delivering an analytical description of the actual state of the organisation with regard to participation, but also paves the way for developing organisational learning by fostering sustainable changes in the university culture concerning student inclusion. Research suggests that this change can be understood as following an evolutionary pattern divided into four main steps. The pattern starts, firstly, with a commitment from the institution to promoting diversity (mobilisation); secondly, the commitment is translated into specific actions and programmes (implementation); thirdly, the impact of these interventions is ascertained through systematic assessment (evaluation); and finally, progress is stabilised by ensuring that the effort to sustain a diversity culture is constantly incorporated into organisational policies and practices (institutionalisation).

Programmes that succeed in achieving the latter level – institutionalisation of change – are usually based on a combination of elements that promote a participative approach, build on existing resources and achieve sustainable outcomes by supporting in-depth organisational learning. More specifically, evidence from research indicates that the following measures are especially valuable in fulfilling the institutionalisation of programmes to include underrepresented students (Chun & Evans, 2018):

– Ensuring that initiatives promoting inclusion will align with the mission and goals identified by the HE institution;
– Guaranteeing that the change process will be carried out in a strategic and iterative way, and supported by the systematic assessment of milestones, weak points and opportunities for further advances;

- Connecting inclusive transformation to a coherent theory of change that considers the unique organisational features of the HE institutions;
- Identifying agents of change and ensuring they will have adequate competences, power and visibility within the university in order to fulfil their tasks;
- Adopting a participative approach that fosters inclusion by leveraging extensive and systematic collaboration of stakeholders;
- Running positive initiatives to foster inclusion in individual departments in the form of pilots, which can be aligned with the needs of the local structure and support the transfer of the acquired knowledge to other departments;
- Employing an approach based on experiential learning, as a more dynamic way of developing awareness of issues regarding equity and inclusion in the organisation instead of relying on traditional lectures or presentations to address the topic of diversity;
- Helping academic structures to identify positive precedents and good practices as a starting point for defining new objectives and promoting further actions to widen the participation of underrepresented students.

In closing, it is important to underline that the endeavour of widening participation in HE is fraught with many obstacles, as tackling inequality implies both overcoming organisational constraints and dealing with the political implications that are linked to this kind of programme. For this reason, the goal of fostering greater levels of equity and inclusion in HE can be achieved only if it is conceived as an enterprise that involves the entire academic community in an ongoing learning process that is open to democratic debate and reflection.

Acknowledgement

This document has been produced as a part of the project "ACCESS4ALL – Laboratory for Policies and Practices of Social Development in Higher Education" (Ref. 2015-1-ES01-KA203-015970) co-funded by the European Union (Erasmus+ Programme).

References

Abes, E. S. (2005). Identity development of diverse populations: Implications for teaching and administration in higher education. *The Journal of Higher Education, 76*(1), 117–119.

Adserias, R. P., Charleston, L. J., & Jackson, J. F. (2017). What style of leadership is best suited to direct organizational change to fuel institutional diversity in higher education? *Race Ethnicity and Education, 20*(3), 315–331.

Aguirre Jr., A., & Martinez, R. O. (2006). Diversity leadership in higher education. *ASHE Higher Education Report, 32*(3), 1–113.

Allen, W. R. (2005). A forward glance in a mirror: Diversity challenged – Access, equity, and success in higher education. *Educational Researcher, 34*(7), 18–23.

Archer, L. (2007). Diversity, equality and higher education: A critical reflection on the ab/uses of equity discourse within widening participation. *Teaching in Higher Education, 12*(5–6), 635–653.

Argyris, C. (1980). Making the undiscussable and its undiscussability discussable. *Public Administration Review, 40*(3), 205–213.

Argyris, C. (1982). The executive mind and double-loop learning. *Organizational Dynamics, 11*(2), 5–22.

Argyris, C. (2002). Double-loop learning, teaching, and research. *Academy of Management Learning & Education, 1*(2), 206–218.

Argyris, C. (2004). *Reasons and rationalizations: The limits to organizational knowledge.* Oxford University Press.

Ashworth, R., Boyne, G., & Delbridge, R. (2009). Escape from the iron cage? Organizational change and isomorphic pressures in the public sector. *Journal of Public Administration Research and Theory, 19*(1), 165–187.

Baez, B. (2003). Affirmative action, diversity, and the politics of representation in higher education. *The Journal of Higher Education, 74*(1), 96–107.

Ball, S. J., & Vincent, C. (1998). 'I heard it on the grapevine': 'Hot' knowledge and school choice. *British Journal of Sociology of Education, 19*(3), 377–400.

Banerjee, P. A. (2018). Widening participation in higher education with a view to implementing institutional change. *Perspectives: Policy and Practice in Higher Education, 22*(3), 75–81.

Battilana, J., & Casciaro, T. (2012). Change agents, networks, and institutions: A contingency theory of organizational change. *Academy of Management Journal, 55*(2), 381–398.

Becher, T., & Trowler, P. A. (2001). *Academic tribes and territories: Intellectual enquiry and the culture of disciplines.* SRHE and Open University Press.

Berrey, E. C. (2011). Why diversity became orthodox in higher education, and how it changed the meaning of race on campus. *Critical Sociology, 37*(5), 573–596.

Bolman, L. G., & Deal, T. E. (1991). Leadership and management effectiveness: A multi-frame, multi-sector analysis. *Human Resource Management, 30*(4), 509–534.

Boyce, M. E. (2003). Organizational learning is essential to achieving and sustaining change in higher education. *Innovative Higher Education, 28*(2), 119–136.

Bradbury, H. (Ed.). (2015). *The Sage handbook of action research.* Sage.

Brennan, J. (2018). The social dimension of higher education: Reproductive and transformative. In B. Cantwell, H. Coates, & R. King (Eds.), *Handbook on the politics of higher education.* Edward Elgar Publishing.

Brennan, J., & Naidoo, R. (2008). Higher education and the achievement (and/or prevention) of equity and social justice. *Higher Education, 56*(3), 287–302.

Bryman, A. (2007). Effective leadership in higher education: A literature review. *Studies in Higher Education, 32*(6), 693–710.

Burke, P. J. (2012). *The right to higher education: Beyond widening participation.* Routledge.

Burt, R. S. (2005). *Brokerage and closure: An introduction to social capital.* Oxford University Press.

Chavez, A. F., Guido-DiBrito, F., & Mallory, S. L. (2003). Learning to value the "other": A framework of individual diversity development. *Journal of College Student Development, 44*(4), 453–469.

Chesler, M., Lewis, A. E., & Crowfoot, J. E. (2005). *Challenging racism in higher education: Promoting justice.* Rowman & Littlefield Publishers.

Chun, E., & Evans, A. (2015). *The department chair as transformative diversity leader: Building inclusive learning environments in higher education.* Stylus Publishing, LLC.

Chun, E., & Evans, A. (2018). *Leading a diversity culture shift in higher education: Comprehensive organizational learning strategies.* Routledge.

Cranton, P., & Taylor, E. W. (2012). Transformative learning theory: Seeking a more unified theory. In E. W. Taylor & P. Cranton (Eds.), *Handbook of transformative learning theory: Research, theory, and practice* (pp. 3–20). Jossey-Bass.

Croll, P., & Attwood, G. (2013). Participation in higher education: Aspirations, attainment and social background. *British Journal of Educational Studies, 61*(2), 187–202.

Crosier, D., & Parveva, T. (2013). *The Bologna process: Its impact in Europe and beyond.* UNESCO.

Crozier, G., Reay, D., Clayton, J., Colliander, L., & Grinstead, J. (2008). Different strokes for different folks: Diverse students in diverse institutions–experiences of higher education. *Research Papers in Education, 23*(2), 167–177.

Cummings, T. G., & Worley, C. G. (2014). *Organization development and change.* Cengage Learning.

Dibella, A. J., Nevis, E. C., & Gould, J. M. (1996). Understanding organizational learning capability. *Journal of Management Studies, 33*(3), 361–379.

Easterby-Smith, M., Crossan, M., & Nicolini, D. (2000). Organizational learning: Debates past, present and future. *Journal of Management Studies, 37*(6), 783–796.

Eckel, P. D., & Kezar, A. J. (2003). *Taking the reins: Institutional transformation in higher education.* Greenwood Publishing Group.

EHEA. (2015a). *Widening participation for equity and growth. A strategy for the development of the social dimension and lifelong learning in the European Higher Education Area to 2020.* Author. http://www.ehea.info/media.ehea.info/file/2015_Yerevan/71/5/Widening_Participation_for_Equity_and_Growth_A_Strategy_for_the_Development_of_the_SD_and_LLL_in_the_EHEA_to_2020_613715.pdf

EHEA. (2015b). *Report of the 2012–2015 BFUG working group on the social dimension and lifelong learning.* Author. http://www.ehea.info/media.ehea.info/file/2015_Yerevan/71/3/Report_of_the_2012-2015_BFUG_WG_on_the_Social_Dimension_and_Lifelong_Learning_to_the_BFUG_613713.pdf

Elliott, C. M., Stransky, O., Negron, R., Bowlby, M., Lickiss, J., Dutt, D., Dasgupta, N., & Barbosa, P. (2013). Institutional barriers to diversity change work in higher education. *SAGE Open, 3*(2), 1–9.

ESU. (2019a). *Bologna with student eyes 2018: The final countdown.* Author.

ESU. (2019b). *Social dimension policy paper 2019.* Author.

EUA. (2019). *Diversity, equity and inclusion in European higher education institutions.* Author. https://eua.eu/downloads/publications/web_diversity%20equity%20and%20inclusion%20in%20european%20higher%20education%20institutions.pdf

European Commission/Eurydice. (2014). *Modernisation of higher education in Europe: Access, retention and employability 2014.* Publications Office of the European Union. http://commit.eucen.eu/sites/commit.eucen.eu/files/Eurydice_AccRetEmpl_May2014_165EN.pdf

Eurostudent. (2019). *The plurality of transitions into and within higher education.* Author. https://www.eurostudent.eu/download_files/documents/EUROSTUDENT_INTELLIGENCE_BRIEF_32019.pdf

Fuller, A., Heath, S., & Johnston, B. (Eds.). (2011). *Rethinking widening participation in higher education: The role of social networks.* Taylor & Francis.

Gale, T., & Parker, S. (2015). Calculating student aspiration: Bourdieu, spatiality and the politics of recognition. *Cambridge Journal of Education, 45*(1), 81–96.

Gorard, S., Smith, E., May, H., Thomas, L., Adnett, N., & Slack, K. (2006). *Review of widening participation research: Addressing the barriers to participation in higher education.* HEFCE.

Gornitzka, Å., & Maassen, P. (2000). Hybrid steering approaches with respect to European higher education. *Higher Education Policy, 13*(3), 267–285.

Greenbank, P. (2006). Widening participation in higher education: An examination of the factors influencing institutional policy. *Research in Post-Compulsory Education, 11*(2), 199–215.

Gurin, P., Dey, E., Hurtado, S., & Gurin, G. (2002). Diversity and higher education: Theory and impact on educational outcomes. *Harvard Educational Review, 72*(3), 330–367.

Guri-Rosenblit, S., Šebková, H., & Teichler, U. (2007). Massification and diversity of higher education systems: Interplay of complex dimensions. *Higher Education Policy, 20*(4), 373–389.

Halualani, R. T., Haiker, H., & Lancaster, C. (2010). Mapping diversity efforts as inquiry. *Journal of Higher Education Policy and Management, 32*(2), 127–136.

Harwood, V., Hickey-Moody, A., McMahon, S., & O'Shea, S. (2016). *The politics of widening participation and university access for young people: Making educational futures.* Taylor & Francis.

Henkel, M. (2002). Emerging concepts of academic leadership and their implications for intra-institutional roles and relationships in higher education. *European Journal of Education, 37*(1), 29–41.

Hinton-Smith, T. (Ed.). (2012). *Widening participation in higher education: Casting the net wide?* Palgrave Macmillan.

Holford, J. (2014). The lost honour of the social dimension: Bologna, exports and the idea of the university. *International Journal of Lifelong Education, 33*(1), 7–25.

Holmegaard, H. T., Madsen, L. M., & Ulriksen, L. (2017). Why should European higher education care about the retention of non-traditional students? *European Educational Research Journal, 16*(1), 3–11.

Huisman, J., Meek, L., & Wood, F. (2007). Institutional diversity in higher education: A cross-national and longitudinal analysis. *Higher Education Quarterly, 61*(4), 563–577.

Hurtado, S. (2007). Linking diversity with the educational and civic missions of higher education. *The Review of Higher Education, 30*(2), 185–196.

Hurtado, S., Milem, J., Clayton-Pedersen, A., & Allen, W. (1999). *Enacting diverse learning environments: Improving the climate for racial/ethnic diversity in higher education.* Jossey-Bass.

Jayakumar, U. (2008). Can higher education meet the needs of an increasingly diverse and global society? Campus diversity and cross-cultural workforce competencies. *Harvard Educational Review, 78*(4), 615–651.

Jerrim, J., & Vignoles, A. (2015). University access for disadvantaged children: A comparison across countries. *Higher Education, 70*, 903–921.

Kaiser, F., Maoláin, A. Ó., & Vikmane, L. (2015). No future for the social dimension? In A. Curaj, L. Matei, R. Pricopie, J. Salmi, & P. Scott (Eds.), *The European higher education area: Between critical reflections and future policies* (pp. 449–466). Springer.

Kezar, A. (2011). *Understanding and facilitating organizational change in the 21st century: Recent research and conceptualizations: ASHE-ERIC higher education report.* Jossey-Bass.

Kezar, A., Eckel, P., Contreras-McGavin, M., & Quaye, S. J. (2008). Creating a web of support: An important leadership strategy for advancing campus diversity. *Higher Education, 55*(1), 69–92.

Kidder, D. L., Lankau, M. J., Chrobot-Mason, D., Mollica, K. A., & Friedman, R. A. (2004). Backlash toward diversity initiatives: Examining the impact of diversity program justification, personal and group outcomes. *International Journal of Conflict Management, 15*(1), 77–102.

King, E. B., Hebl, M. R., George, J. M., & Matusik, S. F. (2010). Understanding tokenism: Antecedents and consequences of a psychological climate of gender inequity. *Journal of Management, 36*(2), 482–510.

Knight, P. T., & Trowler, P. R. (2000). Departmental-level cultures and the improvement of learning and teaching. *Studies in Higher Education, 25*(1), 70–83.

Leathwood, C., & O'Connell, P. (2003). 'It's a struggle': The construction of the 'new student' in higher education. *Journal of Education Policy, 18*(6), 597–615.

Levitt, B., & March, J. G. (1988). Organizational learning. *Annual Review of Sociology, 14*(1), 319–338.

Lewin, K. (1946/1948). Action research and minority problems. In G. W. Lewin (Ed.), *Resolving social conflict*. Harper & Row.

Lipshitz, R., Popper, M., & Friedman, V. J. (2002). A multifacet model of organizational learning. *The Journal of Applied Behavioral Science, 38*(1), 78–98.

Locke, W. (2014). The intensification of rankings logic in an increasingly marketised higher education environment. *European Journal of Education, 49*(1), 77–90.

Locks, A. M., Hurtado, S., Bowman, N. A., & Oseguera, L. (2008). Extending notions of campus climate and diversity to students' transition to college. *The Review of Higher Education, 31*(3), 257–285.

Marginson, S. (2017). The world-class multiversity: Global commonalities and national characteristics. *Frontiers of Education in China, 12*(2), 233–260.

Marrocco, M. M. (2009). Understanding and promoting transformative learning: A guide for educators of adults. *Canadian Journal of University Continuing Education, 35*(2), 67–69.

May, H., & Bridger, K. (2010). *Developing and embedding inclusive policy and practice in higher education*. Higher Education Academy.

Meyer, H. D., St John, E. P., Chankseliani, M., & Uribe, L. (Eds.). (2013). *Fairness in access to higher education in a global perspective: Reconciling excellence, efficiency, and justice*. Sense Publishers.

Mezirow, J. (1991). *Transformative dimensions of adult learning*. Jossey-Bass.

Miller, B. A. (2016). *Assessing organizational performance in higher education*. John Wiley & Sons.

Mintzberg, H. (1993). *Structure in fives: Designing effective organizations*. Prentice-Hall, Inc.

Moore, J., Sanders, J., & Higham, L. (2013). *Literature review of research into widening participation to higher education*. HEFCE.

Morphew, C. C., & Huisman, J. (2002). Using institutional theory to reframe research on academic drift. *Higher Education in Europe, 27*(4), 491–506.

Mountford-Zimdars, A., & Harrison, N. (Eds.). (2016). *Access to higher education: Theoretical perspectives and contemporary challenges*. Taylor & Francis.

Muijs, D., & Rumyantseva, N. (2014). Coopetition in education: Collaborating in a competitive environment. *Journal of Educational Change, 15*(1), 1–18.

Musil, C. M., Garcia, M., Hudgins, C. A., Nettles, M. T., Sedlacek, W. E., & Smith, D. G. (1999). *To form a more perfect union: Campus diversity initiatives*. Association of American Colleges and Universities.

Newell, A., & Simon, H. A. (1972). *Human problem solving*. Prentice-Hall.

O'Donnell, V. L. (2016). Organisational change and development towards inclusive higher education. *Journal of Applied Research in Higher Education, 8*(1), 101–118.

Olssen, M. (2016). Neoliberal competition in higher education today: Research, accountability and impact. *British Journal of Sociology of Education, 37*(1), 129–148.

Pendry, L. F., Driscoll, D. M., & Field, S. C. (2007). Diversity training: Putting theory into practice. *Journal of Occupational and Organizational Psychology, 80*(1), 27–50.

Reason, P., & Bradbury, H. (Eds.). (2001). *Handbook of action research: Participative inquiry and practice*. Sage.

Reay, D., Crozier, G., & Clayton, J. (2009). 'Strangers in paradise'? Working-class students in elite universities. *Sociology, 43*(6), 1103–1121.

Reay, D., David, M. E., & Ball, S. J. (2005). *Degrees of choice: Class, race, gender and higher education*. Trentham Books.

Reichert, S. (2009). *Institutional diversity in European higher education. Tensions and challenges for policy makers and institutional leaders*. European University Association.

Riddell, S., & Weedon, E. (2014). European higher education, the inclusion of students from under-represented groups and the Bologna Process. *International Journal of Lifelong Education, 33*(1), 26–44.

Rodríguez-Gómez, D., Gairín, J., Dovigo, F., Clements, K., Jerónimo, M., Lucas, L., Marin, E., Mehtala, S., Pinheiro, F. P., Timmis, S., & Stîngu, M. (2019). Access4All: Policies and practices of social development in higher education. In J. Hoffman, P. Blessinger, & M. Makhanya (Eds.), *Strategies for facilitating inclusive campuses in higher education: International perspectives on equity and inclusion* (pp. 55–69). Emerald Publishing Limited.

Rusch, E. A., & Wilbur, C. (2007). Shaping institutional environments: The process of becoming legitimate. *The Review of Higher Education, 30*(3), 301–318.

Sevier, R. A. (2000). *Strategic planning in higher education: Theory and practice*. CASE Books.

Shaw, J. (2009). The diversity paradox: Does student diversity enhance or challenge excellence? *Journal of Further and Higher Education, 33*(4), 321–331.

Smith, D. G. (2015). *Diversity's promise for higher education: Making it work*. JHU Press.

Snyder, W. M., & Cummings, T. G. (1998). Organization learning disorders: Conceptual model and intervention hypotheses. *Human Relations, 51*(7), 873–895.

Strauss, A. (1995). Identity, biography, history, and symbolic representations. *Social Psychology Quarterly, 58*(1), 4–12.

Stringer, E. T. (2013). *Action research*. Sage.

Sturm, S., Eatman, T., Saltmarsh, J., & Bush, A. (2011). *Full participation: Building the architecture for diversity and public engagement in higher education*. White Paper, Columbia University Law School, Center for Institutional and Social Change.

Sullivan, W., Sullivan, R., & Buffton, B. (2001). Aligning individual and organisational values to support change. *Journal of Change Management, 2*(3), 247–254.

Teichler, U. (2008). Diversification? Trends and explanations of the shape and size of higher education. *Higher Education, 56*(3), 349–379.

Temple, J. B., & Ylitalo, J. (2009). Promoting inclusive (and dialogic) leadership in higher education institutions. *Tertiary Education and Management, 15*(3), 277–289.

Thomas, K. M. (Ed.). (2008). *Diversity resistance in organizations*. Lawrence Erlbaum.

Thomas, L. (2012). Building student engagement and belonging in higher education at a time of change. *Paul Hamlyn Foundation, 100*, 1–99.

Tienda, M. (2013). Diversity≠inclusion: Promoting integration in higher education. *Educational Researcher, 42*(9), 467–475.

Tierney, W. G. (2008). *The impact of culture on organizational decision-making: Theory and practice in higher education*. Stylus Publishing, LLC.

Trowler, P. (1997). Beyond the Robbins trap: Reconceptualising academic responses to change in higher education (or ... quiet flows the don?). *Studies in Higher Education, 22*(3), 301–318.

Trowler, P., Saunders, M., & Bamber, V. (Eds.). (2012). *Tribes and territories in the 21st century: Rethinking the significance of disciplines in higher education*. Routledge.

Usher, A. (2015). Equity and the social dimension: An overview. In A. Curaj, L. Matei, R. Pricopie, J. Salmi, & P. Scott (Eds.), *The European higher education area: Between critical reflections and future policies* (pp. 433–447). Springer.

Van Vught, F. (2008). Mission diversity and reputation in higher education. *Higher Education Policy, 21*(2), 151–174.

Vignoles, A., & Murray, N. (2016). Widening participation in higher education. *Education Sciences, 6*(2), 13–16.

Wang, C. L., & Ahmed, P. K. (2003). Organisational learning: A critical review. *The Learning Organization, 10*(1), 8–17.

Waterfield, J., & West, B. (Eds.). (2006). *Inclusive assessment in higher education: A resource for change*. University of Plymouth.

Weick, K. E., & Quinn, R. E. (1999). Organizational change and development. *Annual Review of Psychology, 50*(1), 361–386.

Williams, D. A. (2013). *Strategic diversity leadership: Activating change and transformation in higher education*. Stylus Publishing, LLC.

Wilson, J. L., Meyer, K. A., & McNeal, L. (2012). Mission and diversity statements: What they do and do not say. *Innovative Higher Education, 37*(2), 125–139.

Yeung, A. K., Yeung, E. D. A. K., Ulrich, D. O., Nason, S. W., & Von Glinow, M. A. (1999). *Organizational learning capability*. Oxford University Press.

Yooyen, A., Pirani, M., & Mujtaba, B. G. (2011). Expectations versus realities of higher education: Gap analysis and university service examination. *Contemporary Issues in Education Research, 4*(10), 25–36.

CHAPTER 10

The ACCESS4ALL Toolkit for Promoting Inclusion in Higher Education

David Rodríguez-Gómez

Abstract

Inequalities in training for reasons of geographic, ethnic or social origin and in relation to job opportunities, salaries and incomes are critical dimensions of social exclusion. To combat the permanent nature of such exclusion, it is essential to develop educational policies and actions to extend access to opportunities. ACCESS4ALL[1] is an Erasmus+ project which main aim is to promote the educational and social inclusion of underrepresented groups as well as of non-traditional learners, thereby broadly satisfying one of the main priorities of the European Union (i.e., the improvement of the capacities of organisations active in the fields of education, training and youth, notably in the areas of strategic development, quality of learning provision, equity and inclusion, and qualitative and targeted activities for specific groups) and clearly addressing one of the important features of the Erasmus+ programme: promoting equity and inclusion by providing access to learners who are from disadvantaged backgrounds and have fewer opportunities compared to their peers. ACCESS4ALL addresses those needs by designing an operational framework that systematises, orders and promotes the effective development of actions to promote access and retention for underrepresented groups and non-traditional learners in Europe: the A4A Toolkit.

Keywords

A4A toolkit – social exclusion – educational policies – underrepresented groups – non-traditional learners – equity – inclusion – strategic planning

1   Introduction

Inequalities in training for reasons of geographic, ethnic or social origin and in relation to job opportunities, salaries and incomes are critical dimensions of social exclusion. To combat the permanent nature of such exclusion, it is essential to develop policies – especially educational ones – that extend access to opportunities. In this sense, within the framework of the Bologna Process, there has been a social dimension of higher education since the Prague Communiqué of 2001, which emphasised the need to work towards the inclusion of students and the need to promote the possibilities of mobility for all. Successive declarations and communiqués (from Berlin in 2003 to Paris in 2018) have continued to insist on the need to promote the social dimension in constructing and consolidating the European Higher Education Area (EHEA) and, specifically, the need to create more flexible learning pathways into and within higher education as well as the provision of suitable student services. Reports by the EACEA/Eurydice (2012) underline this when they indicate that, despite the major progress made in European educational systems, there are still some challenges that need to be tackled: the promotion of measurable set targets related to the social dimension; the establishment of systems to monitor the participation of underrepresented groups in higher education (HE); and the incorporation into HE of policies that include measures that are needed to assist vulnerable groups and that already exist in other areas of Europe.

ACCESS4ALL is an Erasmus+ project (Key Action 2 – Cooperation for innovation and the exchange of good practices) envisioned as a complement to prior projects such as those identifying vulnerable groups and promoting and monitoring more inclusive policies in higher education (e.g., the European Access Network, or EAN; EquNet; STAY-IN; GLAS; ExpandO; and the Bologna Follow-up Group, or BFUG on the social dimension). ACCESS4ALL also complements studies that demonstrate problems associated with the access and success of vulnerable groups (due to factors such as socioeconomic background, disability, ethnicity, migrant status, etc.), and non-traditional students (part-time students, those with demanding family responsibilities, adult learners, etc.) in HE.

ACCESS4ALL therefore aims to add to the many initiatives and efforts carried out to comply with one of the main priorities of the European Higher Education Area for the decade to come: greater overall participation and increased participation of underrepresented groups in higher education (Leuven/Louvain-la-Neuve Communiqué, April 2009). ACCESS4ALL takes as its starting point all the achievements of the projects mentioned previously and addresses those needs by designing an operational framework that systematises, orders and promotes the effective development of actions to promote access and retention for underrepresented groups and non-traditional learners in Europe: the A4A Toolkit.

In this framework, the main aim of ACCESS4ALL is to promote the educational and social inclusion of underrepresented groups as well as of non-traditional learners, thereby broadly satisfying one of the main priorities of the European Union (i.e., the improvement of the capacities of organisations active in the fields of education, training and youth, notably in the areas of strategic development, quality of learning provision, equity and inclusion, and qualitative and targeted activities for specific groups) and clearly addressing one of the important features of the Erasmus+ programme: promoting equity and inclusion by providing access to learners who are from disadvantaged backgrounds and have fewer opportunities compared to their peers.

2   Basic Elements of the A4A Toolkit

As we have said, the main aim of ACCESS4ALL is to promote the educational and social inclusion of underrepresented and non-traditional groups in the university context. This general goal was achieved through four specific objectives that have enabled the development of the various elements that make up the A4A Toolkit and which we will describe briefly in the following sections of this chapter:

- To establish a map with institutional policies to serve vulnerable people, as groups, in relation to academic access and success. This objective is linked to the systematisation and compilation of good practices in partnering and collaborating institutions[2] and is one of the key instruments in the A4A Toolkit.
- To establish guidelines to be developed by higher education organisations to promote initiatives aimed at promoting access and the successful development of students who are underrepresented in universities. This objective was covered by one of the most highly valued instruments of the project: the "A4A self-assessment tool".[3] This tool not only offers the possibility of diagnosing the state of higher education institutions in relation to their capacity for innovation and inclusion, but also suggests ideas and actions to improve this situation.
- To jointly create strategies and measures to promote access, retention and success among vulnerable students and non-traditional students at university. In order to guarantee the success of the processes of innovation and institutional improvement – in this case to foster more inclusive institu-

tions of higher education – it is essential for all collectives to be involved in these processes. In this case, and based on existing strategies and instruments (e.g., the Innovation Canvas), the "Pyramid Inclusion Model"[4] has been developed to systematise and offer guidance for the effective development of institutional proposals for improving inclusion. This model can be used in various contexts, since it is an interactive and dynamic model that allows the various institutional players to consider their current context and circumstances in relation to inclusion and provides useful suggestions for reflecting on key development objectives and positive actions that can be taken. The ideas arising from the application of the Pyramid Inclusion Model form the basis of a strategic plan to promote more innovative and inclusive higher education institutions.
- To create a laboratory for the creation of innovative and flexible strategies for furthering the social commitment of higher education institutions in relation to the most vulnerable groups of students. This last specific objective acts as a "synthesis objective", since it includes all the work carried out to achieve the previous goals. The achievement of this objective has led to the creation of a project website[5] where all the products generated in the actual project are provided in open format, as well as a collection of resources (e.g., publications, research and research groups directly linked to the main A4A topics, such as: inclusion, access, retention, vulnerable collectives and non-traditional students).

3   Bank of Good Practices

The Bank of Good Practices is based on a well-known strategy used in innovation processes such as benchmarking. As Parker (1996) reminds us, those who benchmark avoid continually reinventing the wheel. This is precisely the purpose of the Bank of Good Practices as part of the A4A Toolkit.

Benchmarking originated in the world of business but is currently used in all types of organisations, including higher education institutions (HEIS) (e.g., Paliulis & Labanauskis, 2015). The basic goal is to increase the competitive capacity of companies by optimising their processes. Lankford (2000) summarises the essence of benchmarking, differentiating it from less ethical actions: "benchmarking is basically learning from others. It is using the knowledge and the experience of others to improve the organisation. It is analysing the performance and noting the strengths and weaknesses of the organisation and assessing what must be done to improve" (p. 57).

There are two main types of benchmarking: external and internal. External benchmarking (competitive, cooperative or collaborative) consists of studying one or more organisations that have stood out because they have achieved good results in their field of expertise. Once these organisations have been identified and their "good practices" understood, the initial organisation itself is analysed, in order to learn from the comparison and apply any improvements that may be feasible. Internal benchmarking consists of detecting good practices in departments or groups within the organisation itself, assessing whether they can be applied to other areas in which the results are not so good and, if so, making any necessary changes accordingly. In this sense, as we will see, the A4A Bank of Good Practices can help us identify good practices in other institutions, including our own HEI.

Benchmarking helps give prominence to valuable experiences that might otherwise go unnoticed. In addition, it may function as an engine for generating ideas. It is well known that creative thinking draws on what already exists, associating it with the new or different. New creations do not come from nowhere, so although an experience detected as a good practice in one context is not always 100% replicable in another, the fact that it can be identified and analysed may lead to ideas that are indeed applicable, an unlikely occurrence if not for the "contagion" effect produced in the process.

The purpose of the Bank of Good Practices is to collect and share good practices for the improvement of the access, retention and successful completion of studies among vulnerable and non-traditional students in HEIs. The Bank of Good Practices is an essential tool for all HEIs interested in improving their accessibility following a review of practices developed by other HEIs.

The creation of the A4A Toolkit Bank of Good Practices involved categorising the type of practices to be indexed and the definition of selection criteria for these good practices.

In the context of this project, "practice" refers to the habitual implementation of a specific technique, method, process, activity, policy or strategy. We accept the proposal of the 2003 UNESCO Management of Social Transformations (MOST) Programme and consider as good practice any strategy that is innovative (leading to new and creative solutions for common problems); effective (having a positive and measurable impact on people or groups or on the organisation); sustainable (being consistent over time for as long as the participation of those involved allows it); replicable (being general enough to be useful in various contexts); and assessable (having a measurable impact on its field of application).

The criteria for the evaluation and selection of good practices are divided into formal and content criteria (see Table 10.1). Furthermore, the selected good practices include information on the success factors necessary for the successful and sustainable implementation of the good practices, as well as the challenges that may limit their implementation.

TABLE 10.1   Criteria for selecting good practices

Formal criteria	Content criteria
A1. ACCESS TO INFORMATION: Is the information about the practice publicly available? YES/NO A2. TIME FRAME: Since when has it been in use (time frame)? What is its maturity level (initial, intermediate, advanced)? Is there evidence of its duration in the long run? A3. NUMBER OF STUDENTS: How many students are involved? Is the number representative, considering the target group? A4. SCALABILITY: Has it been or can it potentially be scaled up and practised on a wider scale? Or has it been or can it potentially be scaled down (e.g., from larger to smaller institutions)? A5. TRANSFERABILITY: Has it been or can it potentially be transferred and applied to different (a) target groups, (b) institutions, and (c) societies? Can you name some practices that this initiative was developed from or has inspired? A6. ASSESSMENT: How has it been evaluated? How has it proved its relevance as the most effective way to achieve the objective? How was it successfully adopted? How has it had a positive impact on people? How has the impact been measured? A6.1. User evaluation (all stakeholders involved): YES/NO A6.2. Self-evaluation: YES/NO A6.3. Peer evaluation: YES/NO A6.4. External expert evaluation: YES/NO A7. CONTACT: Who can be contacted to seek support and networks for implementing the practice?	B1. SOCIAL JUSTICE PRINCIPLES (see Nelson & Creagh, 2013): B1.1. Self-determination: Have students participated in its (a) design, (b) enactment and (c) evaluation? Is it possible to make informed decisions about the participation? B1.2. Rights: Are all participants treated with dignity and respect? How have their individual cultural, social and knowledge systems been recognised and valued? B1.3. Access: Is there active and impartial access to the resources (e.g., curriculum, learning, academic, social, cultural, support and financial resources)? B1.4. Equity: Does it openly demystify and decode dominant university cultures, processes, expectations and language for differently prepared cohorts? B1.5. Participation: Has it led to socially inclusive practices? Does it increase students' sense of belonging and connectedness? B2. COLLABORATION: Is there collaboration between various stakeholders? Does the practice increase this collaboration? B3. STUDENT SATISFACTION: What is the student perception of this initiative? Is there evidence of their satisfaction? (See also A4.) B.4. STUDENT WELLBEING: How does it influence students' (a) psychological, (b) social, (c) academic, and (d) physical wellbeing? What kind of evidence is there for improved student wellbeing?

The established criteria were transferred to a template for collecting and sharing good practices.[6] Although the established criteria serve as a self-assessment tool for identifying good practices, before joining the Bank of Good Practices each proposal is subject to expert evaluation (e.g., by university staff members, policymakers and student union representatives).

Finally, a search engine was created (see Figure 10.1) that helps locate the good practice in which each user is interested, as well as a peer-assessment system that enables the debugging of the practices in the A4A Bank of Good Practices.

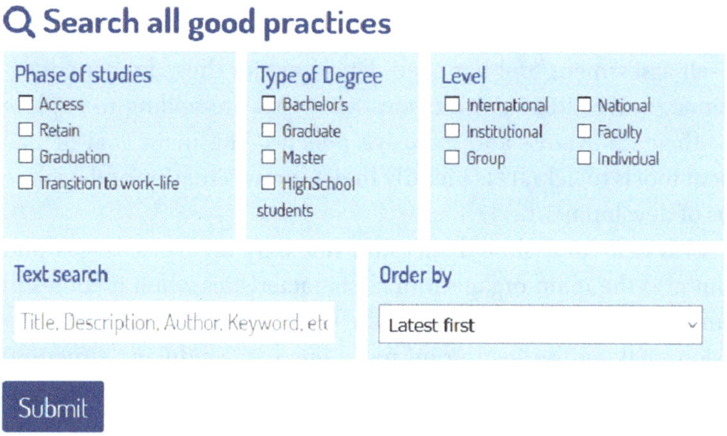

FIGURE 10.1   A4A Bank of Good Practices (Source: https://access4allproject.eu/bestpractices)

4   A4A Self-Assessment Tool

The design and implementation of interventions in any type of organisation, in our case higher education institutions, always and necessarily stem from a previous diagnosis of the current state of the organisation (Brown & Osborne, 2012; Waddell, Cummings, & Worley, 2011). Not surprisingly, the planned action should serve to strengthen key areas of the organisation, solve identified problems or respond to needs detected during the diagnostic evaluation. This type of evidence-based intervention is, in essence, one of the first practices specific to organisational development as a discipline and to what we know today as evidence-based management (Pfeffer & Sutton, 2006; Reay, Berta, & Kohn, 2009).

In the case of HEIs, as with other types of educational organisations, the processes of continuous improvement have traditionally been linked to self-assessment proposals (e.g., Bolívar, 1994; Gairín, 1993). For Santos Guerra (1993), self-assessment processes are important because they: allow us to reflect on what is being done; facilitate vertical and horizontal coordination; help understand what happens; promote dialogue and participation; allow rational decisions to be made; prevent overlapping; help influence what is considered to be substantial; allow for error correction; help intensify efforts on what is essential; allow us to learn new things; make the teaching team more consistent; become an example for students; and help improve teachers.

Among the many tools that may facilitate these self-assessment processes, rubrics have turned out – in recent years – to be among the most effective, since they not only confirm the current situation of the organisation, but also provide guidance for improving it.

The A4A self-assessment tool has been developed for those higher education institutions (universities, polytechnics, etc.) that are willing to explore and improve their innovative and inclusive policies. The main goal of this self-assessment tool is to help HEIs identify their current situation and explore feasible areas of development.

The self-assessment tool should measure not only an HEI's values and principles, but also the main organisational characteristics when it comes to promoting any kind of innovation, especially those aimed at improving students' inclusion, making the institution more open and reducing structural discrimination. An A4A HEI is not only an institution committed to students' inclusion, but also a dynamic institution continually involved in the process of innovation.

The A4A self-assessment tool covers six broad factors, organised into two main dimensions (see Table 10.2): (A) institution-related factors, since any

TABLE 10.2   A4A self-assessment tool: dimensions and factors

(A) Institution-related factors	(B) Inclusion-related factors
HEI organisational maturity: What is your HEI like? Institutional innovation management culture: Is your HEI flexible enough to deal with a volatile, uncertain, complex and ambiguous environment? Knowledge sharing: How does your HEI share its knowledge, both inside and outside the organisation?	Shared understanding of inclusion: Is there a clear and shared idea of inclusion in HEIs? Policies for inclusion: Do your HEI policies clearly encourage inclusion? Actions for inclusion: What kind of inclusion-related action is your HEI developing?

proposal for intervention in an organisation requires knowledge of the situation or the predisposition of the organisation to implement improvement processes; and (B) inclusion-related factors, focused directly on the basic elements that will guide the subsequent intervention.

Each factor included in this self-assessment tool comprises five indicators and each indicator have four possible scenarios. Users must choose only one scenario (that which best represents their HEI) from each indicator. If any dimension is not relevant to your own institution or you do not have enough information to answer, you can leave it blank.

The A4A self-assessment tool can be used by individuals (i.e., managers, faculty, staff and students), groups or any kind of formal institutional structure (e.g., departments, institutes, schools, etc.). The group and formal institutional structure aspect allow for discussions to be opened up within HEIs. The A4A self-assessment tool can be also used to compare different visions about the same HEI or observe how an institution's perceptions about innovation and inclusion change over time.

4.1   HEI *Organisational Maturity*

This first general and comprehensive dimension is constructed according to organisational development theories that focus on both individual and organisational-level change, development and transformation through planned interventions and are aimed at improving organisational effectiveness (Waddell, Cummings, & Worley, 2011). The factors included in these dimensions are related to both the internal context of the higher education institution as well as its relationships with the local environment in which it is located (Anderson, 2013).

So, with the aim of drawing a general institutional profile, the organisation's members should seek to reach an agreement on some general but important organisational practices related to how the HEI is working, its leadership style, organisational structure, task design and assignment and, finally, the relationships with its environment.

4.2   *Institutional Innovation Management Culture*

Change management culture refers to the nature and type of institutional values, processes, rules, manifestations and trends in relation to changing and adapting to the challenge of new external and internal demands.

In the university context, there is a tradition of identifying an institutional innovation culture. Clark (1998) points out that an institutional innovation culture is organised under five main components: a powerful management corpus, a periphery that is developed and promoted, diversified funding, motivated academics, and entrepreneurship orientation.

Considering not only the innovation management culture but also the challenge of equity in higher education, our proposal is oriented to the analysis of five components: the innovation role, governing board commitment, innovation communication, curricular development, and risk management.

4.3   Knowledge Sharing

Knowledge sharing is a knowledge management process, consisting of a mutual exchange of knowledge and the joint creation of new knowledge. Therefore, it is necessary to articulate knowledge acquisition, its organisation, distribution, reuse and transfer in accordance with collective and organisational benefit.

In higher education institutions, knowledge can be explicit or tacit, and it may come from both internal and external sources. When knowledge is identified, it can be shared and place itself at the service of people and promote processes of design, development and evaluation. Moreover, to the extent that knowledge is shared, it favours conservation by being accessible – through the support that technological tools can provide – to whoever will require those tools in order to improve performance, service delivery and decision-making.

4.4   Shared Understanding of Inclusion

To achieve a shared understanding of inclusion, it is necessary to consider the involvement of the many factors that make up these higher educational contexts. Therefore, it is necessary to clarify what these main factors are and whether they are institutional, organisational, personal or individual, cultural, social, curricular, political, ethical, and so on.

Likewise, in this process of managing to comprehend what this shared understanding of inclusion is, it is essential to bear in mind that this shared understanding and the practice of inclusion must guarantee the social justice principles understood as inclusion-related factors. That is, they must guarantee the self-determination of students (their ability to take their own decisions), their rights (dignity and respect for their individual cultural and social values and knowledge), and their access, equity and social participation in higher educational contexts.

4.5   Policies for Inclusion

Educational inclusion is real if the people with power and a high level of responsibility adopt policies that affect all agents in the education system. Policies for inclusion are only the first steps in looking after vulnerable students. There are also conditions for organisational development and improvement. These represent the basis for any future strategies to deal with vulnerable groups.

This dimension includes aspects related to university governance and management that are directly related to inclusion. These aspects involve: budget management, staff training (and especially the training that staff receive for dealing with vulnerable students), institutional structures supporting inclusion, and strategic actions to enhance the capacity of HE institutions to respond the needs of groups of vulnerable students. These dimensions are consistent with the *Index for Inclusion* guidelines (Booth & Ainscow, 2002).

4.6 Actions for Inclusion

Educational inclusion is understood as a process that must enable the right to education at all levels and for all subjects. To that end, educational inclusion requires the involvement of the individuals affected as well as the collaboration of institutional actors, civil society and public and private sectors.

In the field of higher education, we understand inclusion to be a process that reduces inequality and is linked to the creation of conditions of equity in access, participation, achievement, progress and academic completion. This can be achieved through the design, implementation and evaluation of measures aimed at ensuring opportunities for all and at different periods of a student's time at university.

Actions for inclusion must take into account the diversity of students, encourage their active involvement, identify human and material resources needed to support their academic life, and encourage their success on their educational trajectories.

The result of the questionnaire is an organisational profile that will guide the subsequent proposal for improvement. Based on the results of one's self-assessment, some guidance notes for improvement are suggested.

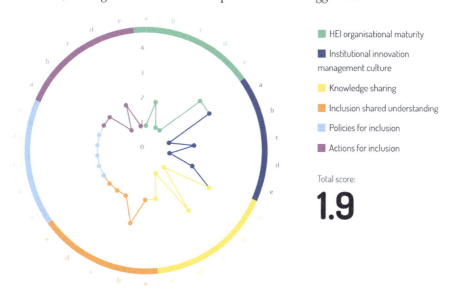

FIGURE 10.2   Example of the organisational profile output

The A4A Toolkit[7] also provides a broad Bank of Good Practices, a strategic plan for improving inclusion in HEIs and other materials that provide ideas and guidance for real institutional change.

5 Pyramid Inclusion Model

Once the organisation's current situation has been diagnosed, using the A4A self-assessment tool, and once the practices for the improvement of inclusion developed by other HEIs – available in the A4A Bank of Good Practices – have been reviewed, it is time to define the broad outlines of the intervention to be carried out in our own HEI. This planning will be carried out using the Pyramid Inclusion Model included in the A4A Toolkit and based on three basic elements: strategic planning, the use of planning schemes, and design thinking.

Planning forms the basis of innovation and quality. In the current context, it is unusual for us to be able to sufficiently and accurately anticipate all the variables of the final desirable scenario of an innovation or change process, as well as all the factors that may intervene during that process. It is therefore best to make proposals that are as flexible and organic as possible so that they can evolve throughout the process. This is where strategic planning makes sense: in response to a changing environment. Strategic planning must set the medium- and long-term goals of our HEI in a systematic and reasoned manner, as well as the strategies and follow-up and evaluation systems required to achieve them.

The process of ideation and planning any innovation is highly complex and involves mastering and fitting multiple variables. That is why several tools or schemes are available to facilitate the realisation and interrelation of the key elements to be considered in any innovation proposal. Some of the best-known tools are the Business Model Canvas and the Innovation Canvas. Both tools are schemes that guide the team responsible for the innovation through the process of the ideation and delimitation of the main elements to be considered in the subsequent planning and development phase.

The Innovation Canvas, in particular, is no more than a template printed on a poster onto which members of the organisation or the team responsible for innovation may continually add ideas or comments about the various dimensions or sections under consideration (Ahmed et al., 2014): value (value proposition), explore (opportunity identification, stories, learning), ideate (external systems, key functions, key features), market (revenue streams, cost structure, customer segments, channels, customer relationships, key partners, key activities, key resources), and design (critical to success, key components or modules, critical risks).

Strategies for the design and development of innovations have varied substantially in recent years and, although more traditional top-down approaches are still common, there is a clear trend towards much more collaborative strategies (e.g., Hayes, 2018). Similar arguments are made by Frølich et al. (2013) in their concept of "strategising", which was influential in the development of the A4A Pyramid Inclusion Model. They stress "the complex and multi-level processes with strong intra-organisational bottom-up and horizontal processes, involving a broad group of intra-organisational members" (p. 85) and see strategising as a process rather than a way of focusing on the content of strategy documents and plans.

Design thinking seems to be the proposal that best fits these new trends, which seek more holistic, collaborative and human-centred processes (Hassi & Laakso, 2011; Willness & Bruni-Bossio, 2017). Brenner, Uebernickel, & Abrell (2016) define design thinking as mind-set, process, and toolbox:

- As a mind-set, design thinking is characterised by three key principles: a combination of divergent and convergent thinking, a clear orientation towards needs that are declared as well as those that are not so obvious and, finally, the development of prototypes.
- As an innovation process, it combines phases of micro-processes (i.e., definition of the problem, analysis of needs, ideation, prototype development and testing) and basic elements of a macro-process to include all the structures of any design thinking project (i.e., design space exploration, critical function prototype, dark-horse prototype, funky prototype, functional prototype, X-is-finished prototype, and final prototype).
- Finally, as a toolbox, a design thinking process contemplates the use of multiple tools, strategies and techniques from various disciplines (e.g., engineering, information technology and psychology).

These ideas were influential in informing the A4A Pyramid Inclusion Model, which aimed to depart from the idea of laying out a fixed set of strategies and instead encourage reflection and planning through a dynamic interaction of stakeholders located within specific environmental and cultural organisations.

The A4A Pyramid Inclusion Model has been built to help key stakeholders within higher education institutions develop strategies and plans for widening access to higher education for students from underrepresented groups, increasing inclusive practices and ensuring success for all students. It is an interactive and dynamic model that allows institutional stakeholders to consider their current context and circumstances in relation to inclusion and provides helpful prompts for reflection on key development goals and positive action that can be taken. The model encourages diverse groups of individuals from across the university to meet and discuss key questions and strategic ideas in relation to a number of questions. The model is intended to be dynamic and a cutout

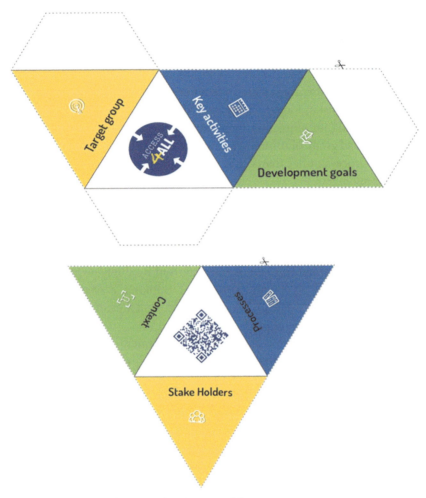

FIGURE 10.3   Building the Pyramid Inclusion Model

version is shown in Figure 10.3. Each institutional group is encouraged to use the model to explore the questions and how they relate to their own university and to use it to develop new strategic ideas and plans.

The key questions guiding the model for all HEIs to consider are as follows (see also Table 10.3):
- Environment: What do we have (including context, policies, practices, stakeholders and resources)?
- Aspirations: What do we want? (What are our aspirations as an HEI for inclusion?)
- Evaluation: How will our activities and practices be evaluated?

TABLE 10.3 A4A Pyramid for Inclusion Model: key questions guiding the process

Environment: What do we have?

Context	What is the context of European policy for informing the development goals?
	Is there any legislation relating to equality for all?
	What is the context of national policy relating to widening access?
	How can these enable or constrain the development goals?
	How do these development goals align with any European and national policies and legislation?
	What social justice principles inform practices and strategies?
	What relevant institutional and organisational aspects are there?
	What relevant institutional cultural dimensions are there?
	What institutional resources, infrastructure and funding are available?
Stakeholders	Who are the key stakeholders that might inform the development goals?
	Who are these stakeholders and how can they be involved?
	For example, students, academic staff, university leaders, and policy makers.
	Internal and external stakeholders (within and outside the university): for example, health services and counselling.
	There are potentially lots of stakeholders, depending on the development goals.
Processes	Institutional strategies for widening access to higher education for underrepresented groups.
	Institutional inclusion practices.
	Use of technology to improve access and inclusion within the institution.
	Evaluation of institutional practices for inclusion and widening access.
	Examples of good practices to inform change.

Aspirations: What do we want?

Development goals	What are the development goals?
	What issues or problems need to be considered?
	What challenges might be involved in achieving these goals?

(cont.)

TABLE 10.3 A4A Pyramid for Inclusion Model: key questions guiding the process (*cont.*)

Aspirations: What do we want?

Target group	What is the main target group or groups?
	How will the activities change things for the target group or wider group?
	Are we considering the needs of all students (or university actors or agents) regardless of whether they are classified as being at a disadvantage currently?
Key activities	What key activities are required for your development goals?
	How can these activities be put into operation?
	How can they be aligned and embedded within current activities?
	What resources are needed for these activities?

Evaluation

Measures of success	What information needs to be collected? What do you need to know? What is required by the HEI and stakeholders? For example, participants, diversity among participants, variety of services and activities, satisfaction, meeting the stated objectives.
	How will you know what has been achieved (criteria, indicators, standards)?
	Who is going to take part in the evaluation plan?
	How will relevant information and data be collected? For example, institutional records or indicators, surveys, and interviews.
	When will the evaluation be developed? When do feedback and reports need to be provided? How are the evaluation results going to be shared with stakeholders?

6   Conclusion

As we have seen, the three tools included in the A4A Toolkit not only facilitate some of the key tasks in any innovation or planned change process (i.e., institutional diagnosis, benchmarking, ideation and planning) but also, and much more importantly, motivate and serve as a driving force behind collective and institutional reflection on the values, policies and organisational strategies that promote the educational and social inclusion of underrepresented and non-traditional students in our universities.

Acknowledgement

This document has been produced as a part of the project "ACCESS4ALL – Laboratory for Policies and Practices of Social Development in Higher Education" (Ref. 2015-1-ES01-KA203-015970) co-funded by the European Union (Erasmus+ Programme).

Notes

1 See https://access4allproject.eu/
2 See https://access4allproject.eu/bestpractices
3 See https://access4allproject.eu/institutions
4 See https://access4allproject.eu/pyramid-inclusion-model
5 See https://access4allproject.eu/
6 Available under a Creative Commons (CC) licence at: http://www.access4allproject.eu/reports
7 Available on our website: http://www.access4allproject.eu/

References

Ahmed, J., Rogge, R., Kline, W., Bunch, R., Mason, T., Wollowski, M., & Livesay, G. (2014). The innovation canvas: An instructor's guide. In *121st ASEE annual conference and exposition* (pp. 1–12).

Anderson, D. L. (2013). *Organization development: The process of leading organizational change*. Sage Publications.

Bolívar, A. (1994). Institutional self-assessment for internal improvement. In M. A. Zabalza (Ed.), *Reform educational and school organization* (pp. 915–944). Tórculo.

Booth, T., & Ainscow, M. (2002). *Index for inclusion: Developing learning and participation in schools*. CSIE. http://www.eenet.org.uk/resources/docs/Index%20English.pdf

Brenner, W., Uebernickel, F., & Abrell, T. (2016). Design thinking as mindset, process, and toolbox. In W. Brenner & F. Uebernickel (Eds.), *Design thinking for innovation* (pp. 3–21). Springer.

Brown, K., & Osborne, S. P. (2012). *Managing change and innovation in public service organizations*. Routledge.

Clark, B. (1998). The entrepreneurial university: Demand and response. *Tertiary Education and Management, 4*(1), 5–16.

EACEA/Eurydice. (2012). *The European Higher Education Area in 2012: Bologna process implantation report*. EACEA.

Frølich, N., & Huisman, J. (2013). A re-interpretation of institutional transformations in European higher education: Strategizing pluralistic organizations in multiplex environments. *Higher Education, 65*, 79–93.

Gairín, J. (1993). Institutional self-evaluation as a way to improve educational centers. *Bordón – Pedagogy Magazine, 45*(3), 331–350.

Hassi, L., & Laakso, M. (2011). Conceptions of design thinking in the design and management discourses. In *Proceedings of IASDR2011, the 4th world conference on design research* (pp. 1–10).

Hayes, J. (2018). *The theory and practice of change management*. Palgrave.

Lankford, W. M. (2000). Benchmarking: Understanding the basics. *The Coastal Business Journal, 1*(1), 57–62.

Nelson, K. J., & Creagh, T. A. (2013). *A good practice guide: Safeguarding student learning engagement*. http://safeguardingstudentlearning.net/wp-content/uploads/2012/04/LTU_Good-practice-guide_eBook_20130320.pdf

Paliulis, N. K., & Labanauskis, R. (2015). Benchmarking as an Instrument for improvement of quality management in higher education. *Business, Management and Education, 13*(1), 140.

Parker, S. (1996). Measuring up: Size is no obstacle to benchmarking for competitive advantage. *Rochester Business Journal, 8*.

Pfeffer, J., & Sutton, R. I. (2006). Evidence-based management. *Harvard Business Review, 84*(1), 62.

Reay, T., Berta, W., & Kohn, M. K. (2009). What's the evidence on evidence-based management? *Academy of Management Perspectives, 23*(4), 5–18.

Santos Guerra, M. Á. (1993). The evaluation: A process of dialogue, understanding and improvement. *Research Magazine in the School, 20*, 23–35.

UNESCO. (2003). *MOST clearing house. Best practices*. http://www.unesco.org/most/bphome.htm

Waddell, D., Cummings, T., & Worley, C. (2011). *Organisational change: Development and transformation* (4th ed.). Cengage Learning.

Willness, C., & Bruni-Bossio, V. (2017). The curriculum innovation canvas: A design thinking framework for the engaged educational entrepreneur. *Journal of Higher Education Outreach and Engagement (TEST), 21*(1), 134–164.

Index

access   2–4, 9–12, 14, 15, 17, 19–21, 25, 29–33, 35, 37, 39–41, 43, 44, 46, 48–52, 66, 71, 75, 78, 82, 86, 88, 89, 93, 95, 97, 98, 105, 106, 109, 114, 125, 126, 146, 150, 154, 157. 160–168, 170, 171, 177, 186, 214–218, 222, 223, 225, 227
ACCESS4ALL   6, 21, 41, 75, 98, 104, 109, 161, 213–215

barriers   14, 16, 22, 37, 39, 44, 51, 67, 77, 86, 95, 107, 114, 148, 154, 167, 171, 175, 191, 196, 197, 201
Bologna process   3, 30–32, 39, 41, 44, 46, 48, 50, 85, 86, 105, 117, 214

challenges   2–5, 10, 13–17, 20, 23, 24, 46, 64, 68, 71, 73, 74, 79, 82, 94, 98, 107, 112, 114, 119, 131, 156, 161, 163, 164, 167, 202, 214, 217, 221, 227
change   5, 15–17, 51, 69, 73, 74, 76, 77, 110, 111, 118, 129, 148, 161, 165, 170, 176, 177, 183, 184, 187–191, 193–196, 198–205, 221, 224, 227, 228

disability 13–16, 17, 20–23, 34, 37, 49, 74, 93, 94, 96, 126, 138, 140, 142–144, 148–150, 163, 166, 169, 172, 173, 190, 214
diversity   4–6, 13, 15–18, 23, 24, 29–33, 43, 47–50, 67, 81, 82, 94, 106–108, 112, 112, 120, 122, 126, 127, 130, 131, 140–144, 152, 154–156, 162, 165, 167, 168, 184–188, 193, 195, 196, 198–201, 203–205, 223, 228

equal opportunities   11, 17, 18, 30, 31, 97, 107, 120, 122, 126, 142, 145, 149
equality   9, 10, 18, 19, 25, 30, 65, 67, 109, 143–148, 155, 163, 175, 227
equity   1, 4–6, 9–13, 15, 17–19, 21, 24, 25, 31, 32, 34, 46, 48, 50–52, 66–68, 77, 82, 87, 98, 106, 107, 122, 123, 131, 134, 140–142, 145, 161, 184–186, 194, 195, 197–203, 205, 215, 218, 222, 223
European Higher Education Area (EHEA)   3, 30, 31, 35, 46, 49, 51, 87, 88, 91, 93, 131, 140, 187, 188, 214

exclusion   1, 2, 4, 13–18, 21, 24, 25, 34, 49, 64, 94, 106, 186, 193, 200, 214

gender equality   25, 65, 143, 145–148, 155
good practices   5, 41, 51, 63, 64, 72, 78, 81, 87, 94–96, 98, 104, 107, 116, 123, 139, 141, 143–145, 148, 150, 153, 154, 156, 161, 165, 167, 170, 177, 184, 205, 215–219, 224, 227

inclusion   3–6, 10, 13, 15–17, 21, 23–25, 31–33, 37, 39, 43, 44, 46–48, 50, 51, 63–65, 69, 75–79, 85, 87, 88, 95, 96, 99, 105–114, 116, 119–123, 126, 128, 130, 132, 133, 136, 137, 139–145, 148, 152, 155, 156, 161, 164, 171, 175, 176, 183, 185, 187, 191–205, 213–216, 220–228
inequalities   1, 2, 5, 15–18, 30, 32, 77, 86, 95, 97, 106, 140, 141, 143, 144, 164, 177, 195, 203, 205, 214, 223
innovation   5, 76, 77, 106, 109, 110, 114, 123, 126, 128, 129, 133, 141, 165, 170, 195, 214, 215, 216, 220–225, 228

leadership   77, 82, 127, 164, 170, 177, 188, 191, 195, 197–199, 202, 221

migration   34, 86, 87

non-traditional students   34, 46, 47, 109, 193, 196, 214, 215, 217, 229

organisation   2, 11, 13, 33, 40, 51, 69, 76, 77, 79, 83–85, 89, 95, 98, 111, 129, 146, 165, 184, 186, 188, 189, 190, 193, 194, 196–199, 201–205, 216, 217, 219–222, 224

policies   2–4, 6, 10, 14, 21, 24, 33, 43, 44–47, 49, 51, 52, 76, 78, 79, 82, 83, 85, 86, 93, 95, 96, 109–112, 117, 119, 122, 128, 130, 131, 134, 135, 146, 156, 160, 161, 165, 177, 185–187, 191, 193–198, 200, 201, 205, 214, 215, 220, 222, 226, 227, 229
Pyramid for Inclusion Model   128, 216, 227, 228

quality   1, 4–6, 9–13, 17–19, 22, 32–34, 41, 43, 45, 46, 48, 49, 51, 74, 85, 114, 120, 121, 126, 133, 140, 184, 185, 187, 192, 197, 215, 224

retention   4, 9, 15, 16, 19–21, 30, 33, 41–47, 52, 66, 82, 86, 92, 94, 95, 98, 156, 166, 172, 186, 195, 215–217

self-assessment tool   76–78, 109, 110, 112, 113, 128–130, 215, 219–221, 224
sexual diversity   144, 155
social dimension   3, 30–33, 36, 39, 41, 42, 44, 46–52, 119, 121, 122, 140, 141, 156, 184, 187, 214
social justice   1, 4, 5, 13, 17, 18, 25, 30, 95, 218, 222, 227

special educational needs   40, 108, 113, 114, 115, 148
strategic plan   52, 78, 95, 96, 106, 110, 121–123, 126, 128, 129, 131–137, 144, 155, 161, 163, 185, 192, 195, 197, 198, 216, 224
success   18, 29, 32, 41–49, 51, 52, 73, 74, 94, 106, 107, 109, 111, 125, 126, 140, 141, 156, 161–173, 175–177, 184, 186, 187, 195, 198, 199, 202, 214, 215, 217, 223–225, 228

vulnerable groups   3, 4, 13, 15, 24, 49, 76, 77, 94, 96, 111, 122, 124, 125, 129, 214, 216, 222

widening participation   30–34, 88, 131, 162, 164, 166, 171, 173, 185, 187, 188, 191–193, 195, 197, 203, 205